A History of American City Government:
The Formation of Traditions, 1775-1870

A HISTORY
OF AMERICAN
CITY GOVERNMENT

Ernest S. Griffith

The Colonial Period

The Formation of Traditions, 1775–1870
 with Charles R. Adrian

The Conspicuous Failure, 1870–1900

The Progressive Years and Their Aftermath, 1900–1920

A HISTORY OF AMERICAN CITY GOVERNMENT

THE FORMATION OF TRADITIONS, 1775-1870

Charles R. Adrian and
Ernest S. Griffith

Published for the
National Municipal League by

PRAEGER PUBLISHERS
New York

A *History of American City Government: The Colonial Period*, by Ernest S. Griffith,
originally published in 1938, was reissued by the Da Capo Press, New York, in 1972.

Published in the United States of America in 1976
by Praeger Publishers, Inc.
111 Fourth Avenue, New York, N.Y. 10003

Library of Congress Cataloging in Publication Data
Griffith, Ernest Stacey, 1896–
    History of American city government.

    Vol 2 by C. R. Adrian and E. S. Griffith.
    Vols.   published for the National Municipal League by Praeger, New York,
have title: A history of American city government.
    Includes bibliographies.
    CONTENTS: [1] The colonial period.—[2] The formation of traditions, 1775–
1870.—[3] The conspicuous failure, 1870–1900.—[4] The progressive years and their
aftermath, 1900–1920.
    1. Municipal government—United States—History—Collected works. 2. Cities and
towns—United States—History—Collected works. I. Adrian, Charles R. II. Title.
JS309.G7   320.4'73   38-20925
ISBN 0-275-51230-4

Printed in the United States of America

CONTENTS

Preface   1

1 Cities in Preindustrial America   3

2 The Legal Status of Cities   29

3 Intergovernmental Relations   50

4 Municipal Functions and Political Issues:
   Health, Education, and Welfare   65

5 Municipal Functions and Political Issues:
   Public Safety, Utilities, and Other Activities   85

6 The Suffrage, Candidates, and Campaigns   107

7 Political Organizations and the Referendum   128

8 Interest Group Activity   141

9 Governing Bodies   156

10 Executive Officers   177

11 Municipal Finance   198

12 Conclusion: Trends and Changes   218

Appendix: Examples of Civil Disturbances in Cities, 1800–1870   227

Index   229

PREFACE

The period from the War of Independence until just after the Civil War was the age of the preindustrial city in the United States—a time of excitement, rapid change, massive urban growth, the creation of hundreds of new towns, dozens of which are now large cities, and a time for laying the foundation for ideas and institutions that would shape the later industrial-metropolitan America.

This book is the product of many years of collaboration in data collection, planning, and writing. Ernest Griffith collected material for the project for more than forty years; Charles Adrian, for somewhat more than twenty years. The material in this volume chronologically immediately follows that in Ernest S. Griffith's *A History of American City Government: The Colonial Period*, published by the Oxford University Press, New York, in 1938 and reprinted in 1972 by the Da Capo Press, New York.

The Civil War, like all major wars, tended to accelerate urbanization and bring about important technological changes. The story of the city during this period is told in Ernest S. Griffith's volume subtitled *The Conspicuous Failure, 1870–1900*. He then recounts the tale of urban developments during the Progressive era in a volume subtitled *The Progressive Years and Their Aftermath, 1900–1920*.

It is the intention of Charles Adrian to continue this series with a volume covering the period from 1920 to, probably, 1940. Richard S. Childs, still in lively correspondence with us in his ninety-third year of an eventful life in the cause of improved municipal government, has graciously made available his large library of material covering this period. If energy and mind are sustained long enough, an additional volume is needed on the city during World War II and the bursting forth of metropolitan suburbia in the years since.

The present volume is organized somewhat differently from the two that follow. It is arranged by topics rather than chronologically, reflecting Charles Adrian's personal preference and possibly showing the bias of a political scientist rather than a historian. This should present no difficulties, as each volume can stand by itself. The intention is to permit the reader to find material about an urban-government institution or function

1

in a single place. Within each topic, material is organized basically in chronological order.

Our policy has been to use few footnotes, primarily because so much of the original material from the pre-1870 period is not readily available. We have given credit for the longer quotations and in cases of substantial reliance on secondary sources. We used a great variety of sources: newspapers, official city records, diaries, official and other histories (which vary from poor to excellent), biographies, as well as secondary works by professional historians. On some cities there is a good deal of material; on others, very little. Some early historians paid serious attention to urban government; others tended to ignore it, concentrating on social and economic history. Among present-day historians, we especially admire the work of Nelson Blake, A. Theodore Brown, Alexander B. Callow, Jr., Wayne Gard, Charles N. Glaab, Constance McL. Green, Blake McKelvey, Nathan Miller, George R. Stewart, Richard C. Wade, and Sam Bass Warner, Jr. But there are too many whose works have been important to mention all. We particularly appreciate the fact that the various historical journals have in recent years paid increasing attention to urban history.

We have attempted to include events in the many cities that were small before 1870, including some that never grew large. We have deliberately tried to avoid making this merely a history of the governments of the dozen or so largest American cities.

Our work was assisted greatly by the librarians of the Library of Congress and of the University of California campuses at Berkeley, Los Angeles, and Riverside. Mary Kaufmann typed the final manuscript for us.

CHARLES R. ADRIAN
ERNEST S. GRIFFITH

Chapter 1

CITIES IN PREINDUSTRIAL AMERICA

IN THIS BOOK, we will examine the governments and the politics of American cities during the formative years, 1775 to 1870, the period leading up to the cities of an urban, industrial America. The time span is roughly that from shortly before the drafting of the Declaration of Independence to the beginning of the rapid industrialization following the Civil War. This was a period of vigorous urban growth, with villages and then cities following the movement of the pioneers westward or, along the Pacific Coast, northward.

This was an age, not of maturation, but of the childhood of cities and city governments in the United States. It was an age when the character of cities and regions was shaped and when institutions and processes were formed that were later to characterize the American city of early adulthood, during the years between about 1870 and 1920. Institutions, governmental structures, personnel and budget practices, and political patterns during this period were all of enormous importance in influencing the period that was to follow.

From the nation's earliest days, Americans have been ambivalent about cities. Despite awareness that cities might be an inevitable and essential part of the American landscape, eighteenth- and nineteenth-century observers viewed them with suspicion.

The best-known views on the subject in the Revolutionary era were those of Thomas Jefferson, who believed that the ideal form of American democracy was to be found in the New England town and its town meeting. The only hope for our form of government, in Jefferson's eyes, was to be found in the educated yeoman farmer and the small-town merchant who served him. He thought that local government had to "emerge as the paramount center of power" in the American political system. Jefferson's most famous comment on the subject was written in his *Notes on Virginia* (1782): "The mobs of great cities add just so much to the support of pure government, as sores do to the strength of the human body." At that time, this aristocratic Virginia planter had had little experience with cities and none at all with large cities, but he had a thorough knowledge of history, and what he had read about cities did not please him. Two years after publishing the *Notes*, Jefferson was sent to France as minister, replacing Benjamin Franklin. In Paris, he was able to observe one of the world's great cities, but this was during the tense times just preceding the Revolution in France, and what he saw did not cause him to change his mind. This was so even though he was somewhat sympathetic to the revolutionary sentiment that was emerging in France. From Paris he wrote to James Madison in 1787: "I think our governments will remain virtuous for many centuries, as long as they are chiefly agricultural; and this will be as long as there shall be vacant lands in any part of America. When they get piled upon one another in large cities, as in Europe, they will become corrupt as in Europe." And in none of the years that followed did he change his mind.

Two generations later, that optimistic believer in American progress, the Yankee Ralph Waldo Emerson, tended toward the same view of the city as did Jefferson, even though his views on the human condition were otherwise very much different. Although the city provided the locus for various "cultural" institutions, it was an artificial contrivance and one that tended to stultify man's creative abilities. Creativity, Emerson believed, was a rural trait, a belief that has been shown to be erroneous by more recent historical research.[1] As he noted: "I wish to have rural strength and religion for my children, and I wish city facility and polish. I find with chagrin that I cannot have both." (He was, in effect, anticipating the middle-class suburb of the twentieth century.) He noted too: "Cities force growth and make men talkative and entertaining, but they make them artificial." It was a prejudice against the city that was still very much alive in the 1970s, when urban institutions were seen to be "dehumanizing." But Emerson was somewhat ambivalent in his views and was honest enough to recognize, well before the Civil War, that many Americans saw the city as a symbol of opportunity. Thus, in *The Conduct of Life* (1860) he commented: "The boy grown up on a farm, which he has never left, is said in the country to have had *no chance*, and boys and men of that condition look upon work on a railroad, or drudgery in a city, as opportunity." Fundamentally, however, Emerson, like nearly all pre–Civil War American thinkers, did not make a clear distinction between urban and rural life as a fundamental cleavage. In what was perhaps his most famous essay, *Politics* (1844), Emerson did not touch on city politics. And his essay *American Civilization*, written during the Civil War, was not concerned with urbanization but showed a preoccupation with the problems of slavery. (Richard Wade has pointed out that the rural-urban cleavage can be traced from the period 1790–1830.)

Another Yankee, Henry David Thoreau, a romantic and an anarchist, was an opponent of the complex life. The city would be the last form of social organization that he would advocate. He was only one of a large number of nineteenth-century writers who were anti-urban and were applauded for their sentimental attitude toward the bucolic life, even by some of the same persons who were simultaneously and enthusiastically endorsing policies that would lead to a more rapid urbanization of the nation.[2]

Nathaniel Hawthorne, Herman Melville, Edgar Allan Poe, and a host of other American writers were hostile to urban life. For the most part, they claimed to be concerned about the effects created by the growth of European cities and expressed fear that urbanization in this country would have the same general results. The hostility toward urban areas was probably reinforced by the fact that they housed large concentrations of immigrants, always the object of suspicion.

Even toward the end of the 1775–1870 period, some such skepticism remained. In 1867, Samuel L. Clemens, just beginning to become known as a writer and on his first visit to New York, complained that the city was "too big" and made the usual comments about isolation and anonymity in the big city. Yet, on a subsequent visit to his home town of Hannibal, Missouri, he felt dissatisfied, and he lived the remainder of his life in cities.

Much has been written about the contrast between the aristocrat Jefferson with his empathy for the common man and democratic government and the elitist Alexander Hamilton, who was of more modest birth (although not of totally undistinguished lineage, as is sometimes suggested). The brilliant Hamilton undoubtedly understood the need for urban industrial development and, indeed, consulted with the planning engineer, Pierre L'Enfant, in the 1790s concerning a plan he had for the development of an industrial area at Paterson, New Jersey.

As Secretary of the Treasury, Hamilton was asked by Congress to draw up plans for a sound economy or, as the congressional request put it, for the "adequate support of the public credit." The most cited of these was the *Report on Manufactures*, which was submitted on December 5, 1791. In it, he proposed tariff protection of infant industries and federal support to encourage manufacturing. Industrial cities were undoubtedly a part of Hamilton's plan for America. But he was ahead of his time, and no congressional action stemmed from his recommendations; they were not forgotten, however.

In the 1820s Hamilton's ideas were revived. They emerged as part of the "American system" advocated in the House of Representatives by Henry Clay. Clay's proposals, which were never more than partially accepted, called for a protective tariff to guard the nation's infant industries, a national bank to provide a basis for a stable currency and encouragement of business and industry, and federal support for internal improvements that would provide for a nationwide transportation network. His "system" would have the effect of not simply an increase in national government powers, which has typically received the most attention, but also would encourage the rapid urbanization of the nation. In the Senate, Daniel Webster supported similar policies. Clay was on the frontier, in Kentucky, while Webster was a New England Yankee, but they both saw the same approach to "progress" for America. And from Hamilton's day onward, it was the industry-oriented who saw urbanization as the process by which America could develop wealth and power.

The politicians were probably more prompt than were the writers and intellectuals to recognize the importance of the cities as a part of America. Almost from the time of independence, politicians sought to find additional sources of voting support, and the propertyless working man of the city, disfranchised in most states at independence, certainly represented a potential category that deserved investigation. Although the populist movements from the beginning of the Republic until well into the twentieth century tended to concentrate upon rural causes, the urban working man and his vote were not neglected. Thus, Andrew Jackson accepted the urban worker as a producer of goods on a par with the yeoman farmer. And even when Americans were not thinking in terms of the city, they were almost always concerned about the need for the "growth" of the nation—population and economic increase that would result in a greater amount of net wealth.[3] But the means by which the burgeoning new cities should be governed was typically not a matter of immediate concern. In an optimist society, such problems could be left to take care of themselves. As a starting point, there was the traditional British approach to local government,[4] with its emphasis on local autonomy. If further changes would need to be made as the nation grew, no doubt they could be worked out. But there was no philosophizing or even concern about the proper governance of cities in the early days of the Republic, or even much as the period under study came to an end after the Civil War, just as the nation was about to experience a tremendous burst of urbanization and the difficulties that would accompany it.

The Cities Move Along with National Developments

During the colonial period, changes in the few small cities were largely a function of growth. In the first century after independence, the cities tended to march along with national developments. Great growth in the size and number of cities took place, but basic changes also took place in the cities as reflections of national trends and of the emerging American Dream. The Industrial Revolution and the beginnings of a national economic policy, coupled with the emergence of modern science and nascent populism, would shape the city.

The Industrial Revolution, which had had relatively little effect upon American cities during colonial times because of the British mercantilist policies, came to have great influence upon the cities after independence. It affected their patterns of growth and the ways in which people earned their living. Gradually a change in life style occurred that reflected a greater orientation toward the amenities of life made possible by greater prosperity, with less concern for mere subsistence.

Adam Smith's *The Wealth of Nations*, published in the same year as the Declaration of Independence, impressed upon those concerned about the need for the growth of America the need to develop industry and commerce independently of other nations. This implied the necessity of the growth of cities; but it was not often expressed in those terms, nor were the problems that cities would create given much thought in an optimistic frontier nation that seemed to have endless millions of acres of raw land asking to be developed. Problems and prospects were thought of in terms of the need for immigration, problems with the Indians, and the need for a more independent economy. Perhaps in one or two cases a wise thinker said that none of this could be done without a conscious plan for the developing of cities and their deliberate encouragement, but the problems were not usually thought of in those terms.

Finally, national trade policy had a major impact upon the cities of the era. That policy, in general, sought to protect infant industries—urban-centered, of course—to grow and thus to provide both employment and independence from European economies. At the same time, it called for the exportation of American agricultural products. To the extent that it succeeded, this second goal would promote the rapid growth of port cities particularly, but also of all cities marking a break in transportation as food and fiber were moved from farm and plantation to the ship.

As the United States began to work toward its twin goals in the arena of international trade of independence from the European manufacturing centers and establishment of the United States as a "breadbasket" of the world, the cities were bound to flourish. They were to recruit an expanding working class, drawn largely from Europe. Given the Jacksonian goal of universal manhood suffrage, they were also certain to experience higher levels of political conflict. Furthermore, as material goods and wealth in general came to be concentrated increasingly in the cities, the incidence of crime was also bound to increase. This is so because over-all crime rates are generally correlated with prosperity levels. This was compounded by the diversity of ethnic groups and their lack of agreed upon morality. As the cities became increasingly centers of local, national, and world trade, as well as manufacturing centers, they also became part of modern industrial society. That is, they were forced to confront the difficulties related to great extremes between wealth and poverty, and the related problems of crime, health, welfare, and a host of others that represent the costs in a society where opportunities are great but are not equally available to all and where success and status are measured primarily on the basis of personal achievement.

The Industrial Revolution was accompanied by the emergence of the age of science. Although science did not become king—the proprietor of basic ideas for technological change which resulted in changing life styles and standards of living—until after the Civil War, scientific attitudes or at least the attempt to find scientific answers already influenced daily life during the period. In particular, it had a strong influence upon attitudes toward public health and the closely related matter of water supply as the cities grew in size.

The new approach to the problems of public health was especially important. The growing size of the cities increased the risk of the spread of germs and of serious communicable diseases at a time when the rudimentary health sciences of the day were groping toward the germ theory. It was recognized that some diseases were communicable and that some of these entered the United States from time to time through the major ports. It was believed that putrid substances were somehow related to illnesses, but the association could not be precisely pinpointed. The filth theory emerged and continued to dominate throughout the period. However, the "contagionists" won out in their dispute with the "anticontagionists," and elaborate policies, centering upon quarantine procedures, were developed in an effort to eliminate the periodic epidemics. Municipal public health programs were developed, especially in port cities, where the city government usually was required by state law to establish a program, but characteristically the cost of administering the program was left to the local government, even though it was generally recognized that the purpose of the state law was to protect all persons within the state. The serious pollution of lakes and streams, together with concern for the need for fire protection, encouraged the engineering of elaborate water supply systems, some of them private (particularly in the East) but most of them municipally owned and administered.

By mid-century, the concern about sewage, offal, and dead animals in the streets and alleys had set the stage in larger cities for municipal responsibility for street cleaning, garbage collection, and pure water supplies. Prior to this, ordinances requiring householders to take steps toward cleanups often resulted in private firms accepting contracts from individuals. When the germ theory finally emerged toward the end of the century to provide the basis for a modern public health program, the cities were already at least basically prepared to administer and finance the necessary programs.

Perhaps the most important nineteenth-century social movement to develop nationally and to have its impact upon city government was populism. What the anthropologist Clyde Kluckhohn was later to call the "cult of the common man" came to dominate municipal and national politics alike during this period. Its central theme was not that the ordinary citizen should have the right to help choose his rulers, as was the idea of democracy in Europe, but that he should himself have a right to rule. The Revolution was itself part of a social movement that brought out the first expressions of populism.[5] Since then, a wave of populism has swept over the United States approximately every other generation. The first was reflected in the Declaration of Independence and in the attitudes of the early state legislatures. It was brought to a close by the adoption of the Constitution and the establishment of a new government under it in 1789. The next era of populism, the first under the new Constitution, not only put Andrew Jackson in the White House and brought people with new kinds of backgrounds into Congress but also had a profound effect upon the city, its structure, political style, and the items on the agenda of city councils.

Populism as a social movement had enormous impact upon government at all levels. Its most important effect was, of course, the granting of the suffrage to all men, or at least all white men. This made possible the use of political machinery for the advancement of the recently arrived poor immigrants. It also laid the groundwork for a vastly escalated level of political conflict in urban politics. Status conflicts, such as those between the recently urbanized rural-to-urban migrants of earlier immigrations and the newer immigrants, particularly the Irish beginning in the late 1840s, also became political conflicts. Similarly, religious differences between Protestants and Catholics as well as the beginnings of sharp racial conflicts appeared during this era and were exacerbated by the fact that most of those involved could vote and could seek to use government to further their own political goals. The summer ghetto riot appeared as early as the 1830s and reflected the difference between the American Dream that had been established by the hopes and aspirations of earlier immigrants—the white Anglo-Saxon Protestants—and the realities of poverty in the slums as experienced by the recent immigrants. (See the Appendix for a list of riots and their causes.) The frustration of rising expectations and the resulting reactions in the form of rioting became a fixed pattern of behavior that was to recur periodically throughout American history. It was an unfortunate side effect of a society organized primarily on the basis of status being determined by achievement.

Populism, with its emphasis upon the right of the common man to share in making public policy and of anyone to have a chance to move upward in terms of status and wealth, had an enormous effect upon the educational policies of the United States during its first century. In colonial America and in the years immediately following independence, the emphasis was upon private education. Formal education was considered a luxury available only to those who could afford it. Populism changed this outlook and gradually converted the concept of formal education from one of a rare privilege to a right and then to a compulsory requirement. During the first century of independence the foundations for free, universal public education were established. It was then only a matter of time before it would become a reality for all of those who wished to benefit from it, and the number of years provided would increase from a paltry few to beyond high school in the late twentieth century.

The outlines of the pattern for behavior in urban industrial America were established during the first century after American independence. The American Dream, with its opportunities, promises, and frustrations, took root during this period and was reflected in the growth of American cities and in the political patterns that developed. The values of colonial America, with its emphasis upon the blessings of rural and especially frontier America, changed during a single century to a culture that emphasized "progress" and expanding wealth based upon national policies that could be brought to fruition only through dependence upon the cities. In 1870 America was still primarily a rural nation, but the blueprint for the future had already been established and American cities had begun to show the basic outlines that they were to follow in their great growth pattern of the coming era.

The Founding of New Cities

The century of our concern was one both of the settling of new communities for the first time and of the incorporation as cities of urban places that had earlier been established. (See Table 1–1.) Of the fifty largest cities in the United States by the Census of 1970, only Baltimore (1797), New York (1686), and Philadelphia (1701) had been incorporated as cities before the nineteenth century. This list, however, would ordinarily include Boston, which had developed as a major port and government center but, because of the convenience of the traditional New England town structure, was not incorporated until 1822, and perhaps Norfolk, Virginia, which was incorporated as a town in 1705 and as a borough in 1736. (It became a city in 1845.)* All of the remainder of the fifty were incorporated as cities within the first seventy years of the

---

* Thomas Reed, *Municipal Government in the United States* (New York, 1926), p. 53, includes in his list Pittsburgh, which became a borough in 1764, a title that was equivalent to village in New York.

nineteenth century, with ten exceptions, all in the South, the Southwest, California, and Hawaii.

Of the *thirty* largest American cities in 1970, five were founded before 1700 and four more between 1700 and 1750. In the half-century that followed, Americans laid the groundwork for the largest number of communities that were to grow the most, nine being founded during that period. In the first half of the nineteenth century, seven additional cities were first settled. Only three of the thirty largest were begun between 1851 and 1870, and none since that time. These three cities were Denver (1858), Phoenix (1868), both interior cities, and Seattle (1852), at the northern end of the Pacific migration.

The relatively early founding of the cities that were to grow large is a testimonial to the importance of transportation not only as a factor in access, which helps determine when a suitable area is to be settled as an urban place, but also as a factor in the growth rate of the community. While a number of factors contributed to the continuing growth of our largest cities, all of them were major points requiring a break in transportation. That is, they were located where land travel ended and water travel began, or where one type of land travel was substituted for another, or one type of water travel for another.

The years 1835–60 were the years in which the "fall line" of the rivers was especially influential in determining the location of textile mill towns in New England. On the Merrimac, for example, Manchester, Nashua, Lawrence, Haverhill, and Lowell saw dams built and mills opened up. Lawrence was a model city in its planning and its initial paternalism. Self-government and the Irish immigrants brought political conflict.

Later, Dallas was a cotton marketing center where goods brought to town by horse and wagon were transferred to railroads, and Buffalo grew as the western terminus of the Erie Canal, where goods were taken off of barges and loaded onto Great Lakes ships, or the reverse. All of the major port cities were, of course, break-in-transportation centers, but so were many inland cities. In the 1840s and 1850s, Kansas City grew as a major staging area for westward migration. Pioneers would move up the Missouri River to that point, then land, be outfitted, and join a wagon train headed westward. Cities could not grow much, of course, unless they were needed for transportation or trade purposes, or were near the raw materials needed for manufacturing, or were centers of government. Columbus, Nashville, and the arbitrarily located Indianapolis are examples of cities that grew partly because they were state capitals. But in all cases the transportation factor was one of early central importance. Later, the shift from waterways and highways to the railroads affected the growth rate of many cities as well as the patterns of trade.

The founding of American cities took place chronologically in the

TABLE 1-1

Selected American Cities

City	Date First Settled	Date First Incorporated	Incorporated as a City	Basis of Early Growth	Origin of Name	Ranking in 1970
Atlanta	*1836	1843	#1847	Transportation, distribution	From Atlantic	27
Baltimore	1661	1729	#1797	Shipping, trade	George Calvert, Lord Baltimore	7
Birmingham	1871	1871	1871	Iron and steel production	Birmingham, England	48
Boston	1630	1822	#1822	Port	Boston, England	16
Buffalo	1758	1816	#1832	Port at western terminus of Erie Canal	Buffalo Creek	28
Chicago	1779	1833	#1837	Break in transportation	Indian: (The meaning is uncertain)	2
Cincinnati	1788	1802	#1819	Meat packing	Society of the Cincinnati	29
Cleveland	*1796	1814	#1836	Break in transportation, iron manufacturing	Moses Cleaveland (original spelling), a surveyor	10
Columbus	*1797	1816	#1834	Trade, state capital	Christopher Columbus	21
Dallas	*1841	1856	1871	Cotton market	George M. Dallas, Vice President of the United States	8
Denver	*1858	1861	#1861	Outfitting gold prospectors	James W. Denver, Territorial Governor of Kansas	25
Detroit	1701	1802	#1815	Shipping, trade	French: de troit, "strait" (now called Detroit River)	5
Fort Worth	*1843	1873	1873	Cattle trade	Major General William J. Worth	33
Honolulu	Unknown	1907	1907	Sugar, shipping	Hawaiian: "sheltered haven"	44
Houston	*1836	1837	#1837	Temporary capital of republic	Samuel Houston, President of the Texas Republic	6
Indianapolis	*1820	1836	#1847	State capital	Greek: polis, "city"; hence, "Indiana City"	11
Kansas City	*1839	1850	#1853	Staging area for the West	Kansa Indians	26
Los Angeles	1781	1821	#1850	Trade, cattle market	Spanish: El Pueblo de Nuestra Senora la Reina de Los Angeles	3

City	First settled	Incorporated	Incorporated as city	Reason for growth	Origin of name	No.
Memphis	*1798	1819	#1826	Break in transportation, trade	Memphis, Egypt	17
Miami	*1835	1896	1896	Railroad from Eastern cities, tourism	Miami River, from Miami Indians	42
Milwaukee	*1818	1833	#1846	Break in transportation, elevators	Algonquin: "good land"	12
Minneapolis	*1819	1856	#1867	Lumbering	Indian: *minne*, "water"; Greek; *polis*, "city"	32
Mobile	1702	1814	#1819	Port	Adaptation of local Indian tribal name	58
New Orleans	1718	1722	#1805	Port	Philipe, Duke of Orleans	19
New York	1613	1653	1686	Port	James, Duke of York	1
Newark	1666	1836	#1836	Break in transportation, tanneries	Newark-on-Trent, England	36
Norfolk	1682	1705	#1845	Port	Thomas Howard, Duke of Norfolk	47
Oakland	*1852	1852	#1852	Break in transportation	Groves of oak trees in area	38
Omaha	*1854	1857	#1857	Break in transportation	Omaha Indians	41
Philadelphia	1682	1701	1701	Port	Greek: "brotherly love"	4
Phoenix	*1867	1881	1881	Trade	Phoenix, the Grecian sun bird	20
Pittsburgh	1754	1794	#1816	Embarkation to the West	William Pitt, English politician	24
Portland, Oregon	*1845	1851	#1851	Trade	Portland, Maine	35
St. Louis	1764	1808	#1822	Fur trade	Saint Louis IX, King of France	18
San Antonio	1718	1809	#1837	Trade	Saint Anthony of Padua	15
San Diego	1769	1834	#1850	Port	San Diego de Alcalá	14
San Francisco	1776	1776	#1850	Port	Saint Francis of Assisi	13
San Jose	1777	1850	#1850	Trade	San Jose de Guadalupe	31
Seattle	*1851	1869	#1869	Port	Seathl, Indian chief	22
Tulsa	*1880	1898	1898	Cattle shipping	Creek: *Tulwa*, "town"	43
Washington	*1791	1802	#1802	Seat of government	George Washington	9

* First settled between 1790 and 1870.
# Incorporated as city between 1790 and 1870.

same general order as did the major migration flows. The earliest settlements were along the East Coast, roughly following a north to south pattern for the English and other North Europeans. The Spanish, on the other hand, had made their early settlements on the Caribbean islands, in Mexico, and in Central and South America. They, therefore, followed a south to north pattern on both the East and West Coasts of what is now the United States. Because the Spanish began settlement first and on the Atlantic side, the oldest urban areas in the United States are in Florida. St. Augustine, which was founded in 1565, is generally regarded as the oldest city in the United States. But it was not properly located for growth and, in 1970, had a population of less than 15,000. The early Spanish cities of Florida were not destined to grow, and the largest city in that state in 1970 was Jacksonville, laid out on the King's Road (which connected Florida and Georgia), where it crossed the St. John's river, in 1822. It became a city in 1832. The second largest city, Miami, was not even founded until 1835 and did not experience any rapid growth until the 1890s, when a railroad connected it with the large Eastern cities.

To the north of the Spanish settlements, the first permanent settlement is commonly regarded as having been Jamestown, Virginia, which was founded in 1607. But the settlers there suffered a series of disasters, and the town was finally abandoned at the end of that century and was never rebuilt. The communities that were destined to grow into major cities were located in the northeast. Salem, Massachusetts, was founded in 1628; Boston, the oldest of our larger cities, two years later. After the East Coast was settled, there were four principal migration routes inland. One of these was from New York City up the Hudson, and across the mountains to Buffalo. That city was founded in 1758. At first the Mohawk River was the important means of transportation, but Buffalo did not begin its rapid growth until the Erie Canal was opened in 1825. The city then became a major gateway to the West.

A second pattern was through the valleys of Pennsylvania from Philadelphia to Pittsburgh at the point where the Allegheny and Monongahela Rivers joined to form the Ohio. Pittsburgh represented a break-in-transportation center to a great natural waterway and was easier to reach than was Buffalo, so it developed earlier and faster. Although Pittsburgh was founded in 1754, only four years earlier than Buffalo, it became an incorporated place (a borough) in 1794, some twenty-two years before Buffalo and was incorporated as a city in 1816, one-half a generation earlier. Between 1803 and 1815, the value of manufacturing in Pittsburgh grew from $350,000 to $2,600,000—especially glass and iron. Allegheny County, for which Pittsburgh has always been the seat, was founded in 1788 and became a springboard for the founding of other cities farther down the Ohio. Marietta was the first settled community in what was to become the state of Ohio. It was established that same year, and so was Cincinnati only a few months later. The shift after about 1845 from water to railroad transit had a powerful effect upon the growth of cities. Rivers flowed southward, or angled in that direction, but the railroads moved more directly in a westerly direction, thus encouraging the development of Midwestern cities ahead of those in the South.

A third migration path ran from Virginia and the Carolinas across the Appalachians following the Wilderness Road into Kentucky and Tennessee. The South and near South, of course, remained essentially an agricultural and rural area until well into the twentieth century. The largest city in this area, Louisville, was settled largely as a result of the Ohio River route, rather than by way of the Wilderness Road.

The final overland route westward was from the Carolinas and Georgia around the foot of the Appalachians, where Atlanta was established (but not until 1836), and then on into Alabama, Mississippi, and Tennessee, all essentially rural states. By 1970 Atlanta had become the twenty-seventh largest city in the nation and was the metropolis of the Southeast, but the only other city of considerable size that could be said to be located along this route is Birmingham, which was not founded until 1871. It grew into an important iron and steel city because of its close proximity to iron ore, coal, and limestone. The largest city in the area, Memphis, was founded in 1798 and became a city twenty-eight years later, but its path of migration was not overland. Rather it became an important trading center and a break-in-transportation serving settlers who moved up the Mississippi from the port of New Orleans.

Lands along the Gulf of Mexico were settled by both French and Spaniards. The prospects for growth here, with one notable exception, were relatively poor. Ships from Europe could more easily and quickly reach the East Coast ports and, with plenty of land available nearby for farming, these were the logical terminal points. The great exception was New Orleans, which was, of course, located at the critically important break-in-transportation point between Atlantic shipping and the enormous Mississippi River basin. New Orleans was founded in 1718 and became a city in 1805. Forty years later, the tonnage shipped by boat in the Mississippi system exceeded that of all the East Coast ports combined. New Orleans was handling twice as much freight, by weight, as was the port of New York, and it had grown to become the fourth largest city in the United States. With the coming of railroad transportation, New Orleans's location became less salient, and through the next century its population dropped relatively, sinking from fourth to fifteenth place.

There were other important, or at least potentially important, Gulf ports. Mobile got started before New Orleans, in 1702, but its growth rate has always been much slower because of its inferior natural advantages. Galveston was founded by Spaniards in 1785 and named for the viceroy of Mexico. It became a city in 1839 but did not begin its growth spurt until after World War II. Houston was founded not by the Spanish but by two American real estate promoters, and not until 1837. The city remained relatively small and unimportant until it was reached by railroad in 1858. Combined with its port facilities, this made it an important transportation center for food and fiber. It was not until oil was discovered in Texas in the early twentieth century and a ship canal was completed, however, that Houston became a major city. It has since become the metropolis of the Southwest and the sixth largest city in the nation.

San Antonio was founded as a *presidio*, that is, a Spanish military base, in 1718. Nearby, five missions were founded along the San Antonio River. In 1730, a *pueblo* (village) was founded within the area that is now San Antonio. Other Texas cities were founded by American *empresarios* (colony founders) in the 1820s and 1830s, and others were located along the Abilene Trail, which connected Texas cattle ranches with Kansas railroads between 1867 and 1890. But for the most part urbanization in the Southwest is a twentieth-century phenomenon.

In the West, the oldest city is Santa Fe, more specifically *La Villa Real de la Santa Fe de San Francisco* (The Royal City of the Holy Faith of Saint Francis). It was founded in 1609 and has been under Spanish, Mexican, and American control continuously since that time except for the 1680s and 1690s, when the Spaniards were routed by Indians.

On the West Coast exploration had begun as early as 1542, but no attempts were made at permanent settlement until the eighteenth century. When the settlements were first begun on a permanent basis, they were established on a south-to-north basis; a series of missions was established, the first at San Diego in 1769, each calculated to be one day's travel north of the preceding. These were located as far up the coast as Sonoma, well beyond San Francisco Bay. They were designed to provide a civilian settlement with a principal purpose of converting the local Indians to Christianity, but each was the potential location of a community that could in the future become a city.

Four presidios were also established—at San Diego (1769), Monterey (1770), San Francisco (1776), and Santa Barbara (1782). The one at San Francisco was still a military base in the 1970s.

In 1775 the king sent Philip De Neve to become the governor of Alta California. He established his capital at the presidio of Monterey and immediately embarked upon a plan for colonizing the province. He decided that this required the establishment of a number of pueblos. The first was that of San Jose, near San Francisco, founded in 1777, and the second was Los Angeles, four years later. *El Pueblo de Nuestra Señora la Reina de Los Angeles* (The Village of Our Lady, Queen of Angels) served as a marketing town, especially for cattle but also for other agricultural products, which were supplied to the missions and the presidios.

The Pacific Northwest was settled first from the sea, but later also by way of the Oregon Trail. John Jacob Astor, the greatest of the frontier fur traders, established a trading post at Astoria, Oregon, in 1811. Portland, actually on the Willamette River, serves as the port city at the mouth of the Columbia. It was founded in 1845 and named after the city in Maine on the toss of a coin between two settlers ("Boston" lost). The great Columbia Valley was the western terminus of the Oregon Trail which led from Independence, Missouri, near Kansas City, along the North Platte, through the South Pass in Wyoming, along the Snake River in what is now Idaho, into the valley of the Columbia. Along this route in the 1840s, thousands of pioneers moved into the Oregon country, settling on farms and founding towns. After the boundary dispute between the United States and Britain was ended by negotiated agreement in 1846, settlement proceeded rapidly, yet Seattle, on Puget Sound and now the twenty-second largest city in the United States, was not settled until 1852. It became a city in 1869.

The interior, the area between the Missouri and the inland valleys of the West Coast states, was generally settled later than the regions previously described. The great Mississippi-Missouri complex of rivers provided for a vast transportation and communications network, of course, and these areas developed rapidly after river steamboats were developed in the second decade of the nineteenth century. By about 1820, river steamboats were moving more freight than all other forms of transportation combined in the port of New Orleans. But beyond the navigable headwaters of the Missouri, it was necessary to travel by land. Many of the western rivers were too shallow and too filled with sandbars to permit efficient transportation. Few cities grew up along the Platte, the Snake, or other streams along the Oregon Trail. Pocatello, Idaho, for example, was not founded until 1822, and even in the 1970s it had a population of only about 40,000 people. Like many other interior cities, it grew after the railroad reached it and it became a division point, offering important employment and opportunities for merchants. No cities ever did grow up along the rugged terrain of the Old Spanish Trail, which ran from Santa Fe to Los Angeles.

The cities of Utah were founded under special circumstances. As a result of persecution, the Mormons (members of the Church of Jesus Christ of Latter-Day Saints) made their great trek from Illinois to the Oregon trail and then southwestward from South Pass into what is now Utah. Irrigation was begun immediately, and the valley of the Great Salt Lake was quickly populated. Salt Lake City was founded in 1848 and grew rapidly, not only as a governmental and religious center, but also as a rest and reprovisioning station for the Forty-niners, who rushed to the California gold fields the following year.

Alaska, in the 1970s, is in many ways still a frontier state. Its largest city, Anchorage, has a population of less than 50,000. The city was not founded until 1914. It was a break-in-transportation center, connecting sea traffic with the Alaska Railroad, of which it became the headquarters. The first settlement by white pioneers was founded in 1784 by Russians at Three Saints Bay, on Kodiak Island. This did not become a permanent settlement, but some colonization of Alaska was undertaken by the Russians, with the fur trade as an incentive. The oldest continuously occupied urban place in Alaska is Sitka, which was founded in 1799 as New Archangel. It was founded by Alexander Baranof, the manager of the Russian-American Company, which was organized that year by the Czar and which provided the only Western government in Alaska until the American purchase in 1867. The headquarters for the company, and hence the capital city, was at Three Saints Bay until 1807, when it was moved to Sitka. Although Sitka in the 1970s had a population of only a little more than 3,000 persons, it was the commercial and governmental center of Alaska until the capital was moved to Juneau in 1906. Some Alaskan towns were founded as a result of the gold rush at the end of the nineteenth century. Nome (1899) is an example. It boomed to a population of about 40,000, then quickly declined. It was incorporated as a city in 1901, but its population in the 1970s was only about 2,500. Gold mining remains its most important economic base, however. Fairbanks is the northernmost city of any size in the United States, being located at 65° north. This places it only 130 miles south of the Arctic Circle. Its 1970 population was 14,771, making it the second largest city in Alaska. It was founded in 1902, when gold was discovered in the area. It remains to this day a center of gold mining and the trading center for the interior.

Unlike Alaska, Hawaii has a city of considerable size. Honolulu was the forty-fourth largest city in the United States in 1970. The time of its founding is not known precisely. Polynesians were using it as a port, and a village existed on the site, when the harbor was first discovered by Europeans in 1794. Its name, significantly, means "sheltered haven" in Hawaiian. It is likely that a village or villages have existed in the area of Honolulu for 2,000 years. The United States annexed Hawaii in 1898, and Honolulu was incorporated as a city in 1907. Since the early nineteenth century, it has been a major port and transshipment point for the Pacific, and since American annexation it and the nearby port of Pearl Harbor have had major military installations. Although Honolulu is the only city of any size in Hawaii, there are a number of other urban places. None of them is incorporated, for local government consists of five county governments. Because the counties perform the usual urban functions, they can be regarded as a type of municipal government, however.

The period we have under consideration in this book was one during which American cities were formed and urban political styles began to develop. This was still essentially a period of preindustrial America. To be sure, an urban working class was developing, factories did exist, and industrial activities were a basis both for economic opportunity and for political unrest, as Arthur Schlesinger and others have shown.[6] Still, the cities were founded and grew for the most part because they were essential for purposes of trade, transportation, and communication.

Urban Population

By today's standards, early America had only a few small towns and no large cities. Even so, Philadelphia at the time of the American revolution was perhaps the second largest city in the English-speaking world, and rapid change was just over the historical horizon. In the twenty years following 1820, persons engaged in manufacturing increased by 127 per cent. Immigration was accelerating, and immigrants were no longer moving directly to rural and small-town areas but were increasingly remaining in the cities of the Eastern Seaboard. In the decade preceding the Census of 1850, the nation's urban population increased by 92.1 per cent, an all-time high. Between 1820 and the outbreak of the Civil War, the urban population increased ninefold. The fastest rate of growth was in the metropolitan areas. As early as the 1840s, the suburbs of large cities had the highest growth rate of all:

City	Core City (percentage of growth) 1840–50	Suburbs (percentage of growth) 1840–50
Boston	61.0%	84.7%
New York	64.9	130.3*
Philadelphia	29.6	74.8

* Includes Brooklyn, then a separate city.

In the Census of 1790, Philadelphia was still the largest city with a population of 42,520. New York, the nation's major port, was still a small town just on the edge of the spurt in growth which was to last for decades and make it one of the world's largest cities. Of the ten largest cities and towns in the United States in that first census, only those two cities plus Baltimore would be found in the top ten in 1970. Indeed, the urban concentrations of 1790 could hardly be expected, on the basis of population alone, to presage their future development, for only six cities and towns in the entire United States had a population of 10,000 or more. (See Table 1–2.)

TABLE 1–2

U.S. CITIES WITH LARGEST POPULATION, 1790–1890

City or Town	Population	City or Town	Population
1790		*1830*	
1. Philadelphia, Pennsylvania	42,520	1. New York, New York	202,589
2. New York, New York	33,131	2. Philadelphia, Pennsylvania	161,410
3. Litchfield, Connecticut	20,342	3. Baltimore, Maryland	80,625
4. Boston, Massachusetts	18,038	4. Boston, Massachusetts	61,392
5. Charleston, South Carolina	16,359	5. New Orleans, Louisiana	46,310
6. Baltimore, Maryland	13,503	6. Charleston, South Carolina	30,289
7. Ransselaerwick, New York	8,318	7. Cincinnati, Ohio	24,831
8. Salem, Massachusetts	7,921	8. Albany, New York	24,238
9. Balls Town, New York	7,333	9. Washington, D.C.	18,827
10. Newport, Rhode Island	6,716	10. Providence, Rhode Island	16,832
1800		*1840*	
1. Philadelphia, Pennsylvania	69,403	1. New York, New York	312,710
2. New York, New York	60,489	2. Philadelphia, Pennsylvania	220,423
3. Baltimore, Maryland	26,114	3. Baltimore, Maryland	102,364
4. Boston, Massachusetts	24,937	4. New Orleans, Louisiana	102,193*
5. Charleston, South Carolina	20,473	5. Boston, Massachusetts	93,383*
6. Salem, Massachusetts	9,457	6. Cincinnati, Ohio	46,338
7. Providence, Rhode Island	7,614	7. Brooklyn, New York	36,233
8. Richmond, Virginia	5,737	8. Albany, New York	33,721
9. Portsmouth, New Hampshire	5,339	9. Charleston, South Carolina	29,261
10. Albany, New York	5,289	10. Washington, D.C.	23,364
1810		*1850*	
1. New York, New York	96,373	1. New York, New York	515,547
2. Philadelphia, Pennsylvania	91,874	2. Philadelphia, Pennsylvania	340,045
3. Baltimore, Maryland	35,583	3. Baltimore, Maryland	169,054
4. Boston, Massachusetts	33,250	4. Boston, Massachusetts	136,881
5. Charleston, South Carolina	24,711	5. New Orleans, Louisiana	116,375
6. New Orleans, Louisiana	17,242	6. Cincinnati, Ohio	115,435
7. Salem, Massachusetts	12,613	7. Brooklyn, New York	96,838
8. Providence, Rhode Island	10,071	8. St. Louis, Missouri	77,860
9. Richmond, Virginia	9,735	9. Washington, D.C.	51,687
10. Albany, New York	9,356	10. Albany, New York	50,763
1820		*1860*	
1. New York, New York	123,706	1. New York, New York	805,658
2. Philadelphia, Pennsylvania	112,772	2. Philadelphia, Pennsylvania	565,529
3. Baltimore, Maryland	62,738	3. Brooklyn, New York	266,661
4. Boston, Massachusetts	43,298	4. Baltimore, Maryland	212,418
5. New Orleans, Louisiana	27,176	5. Boston, Massachusetts	171,840
6. Charleston, South Carolina	24,780	6. New Orleans, Louisiana	168,675
7. Washington, D.C.	13,247	7. Cincinnati, Ohio	161,044
8. Salem, Massachusetts	12,731	8. St. Louis, Missouri	160,773
9. Albany, New York	12,630	9. Chicago, Illinois	109,260
10. Richmond, Virginia	12,067	10. Buffalo, New York	81,129

TABLE 1–2 (*continued*):

City or Town	Population	City or Town	Population
1870		7. Baltimore, Maryland	332,313
1. New York, New York	942,292	8. Cincinnati, Ohio	255,139
2. Philadelphia, Pennsylvania	674,022	9. San Francisco, California	233,959
3. Brooklyn, New York	396,099	10. New Orleans, Louisiana	216,090
4. St. Louis, Missouri	310,864		
5. Chicago, Illinois	298,977	*1890*	
6. Baltimore, Maryland	267,354	1. New York, New York	1,515,301
7. Boston, Massachusetts	250,526	2. Chicago, Illinois	1,099,850
8. Cincinnati, Ohio	216,239	3. Philadelphia,	
9. New Orleans, Louisiana	191,418	Pennsylvania	1,046,964
10. San Francisco, California	149,473	4. Brooklyn, New York	806,343
11. Buffalo, New York	117,714	5. Boston, Massachusetts	448,447
12. Washington, D.C.	109,199	6. St. Louis, Missouri	451,770
		7. Baltimore, Maryland	434,439
1880		8. San Francisco, California	298,997
1. New York, New York	1,206,299	9. Cincinnati, Ohio	296,908
2. Philadelphia, Pennsylvania	847,170	10. Cleveland, Ohio	261,353
3. Brooklyn, New York	556,663	11. Buffalo, New York	255,664
4. Chicago, Illinois	503,185	12. New Orleans, Louisiana	242,039
5. Boston, Massachusetts	362,839	13. Pittsburgh, Pennsylvania	238,619
6. St. Louis, Missouri	350,518	14. Washington, D.C.	230,392

* Errors were made in Boston and New Orleans in the 1840 Census. Boston was underestimated by about 8,000. New Orleans overestimated by at least 10,000 to 15,000.

By 1820 both New York and Philadelphia had passed the 100,000 population mark, and in 1850 the former became the first American city to exceed one-half million. By 1870 New York was the most important port for immigrants and hence the place where large numbers of the most destitute and of those who did not intend to take up farming settled down. It had nearly reached the one-million mark. In that year, almost one-third of the urban population lived in cities of over 250,000. And in the half-century following 1820, the American urban percentage increased from 7.2 to 25.7.

Even by 1870, however, American cities were still vastly different in proportionate size and in ethnic and racial makeup from those of the 1970s. Only four of the ten largest in 1970 were included in a similar list for 1870. These were New York-Brooklyn, Philadelphia, Chicago, and Baltimore. The other six in the 1870 list are, however, also large cities today, just outside the top ten. (See Table 1–1 for a list of the ten largest cities in 1970 and for their patterns of growth.) Of the largest ten in 1970, New York, Philadelphia, and Baltimore had been included in the Census of 1790. Washington did not make its appearance in the list until 1820, and then with only 13,000 people. It was later to drop out as industry grew more rapidly than government. It did not reappear until the great growth in government employment in the twentieth century. St. Louis became one of the largest cities in 1850 and Chicago a decade later, both reflecting the importance of transportation centers during the period of rapid Midwestern growth.

Of the other ten largest in the United States, Los Angeles was still a small community in 1870, waiting for the arrival of the railroads, which would bring increasing numbers of migrants from the Midwest and the South. Detroit did not begin its rapid spurt of growth until the coming of the automobile industry and its rising importance after 1910. Houston was still an unimportant community in those days, was not to emerge as a major city until after the discovery of oil in Texas near the beginning of the twentieth century, and would not enter the list of really large cities until after World War II. Cleveland entered the top ten in 1890 as a result of Midwestern growth and of the increasing importance of the iron industry. Dallas, a great commercial city, made the top ten in 1970.

All cities, during the period of our concern, had large percentages of foreign-born, reflecting the large rate of immigration during the nineteenth century. Many of the foreign-born were not citizens, a fact that was exploited by urban political leaders in the period just after our study ends, when one of the major activities of urban political machines was to expedite citizenship for immigrants, in return for which they expected their support at the polls. In 1870, 44.4 per cent of the population of New York was listed as "foreign." The figure for Chicago was 43.3 per cent and for Boston 35.1 per cent. (See Table 1–3.)

Throughout the period of this study, the black American was primarily a rural resident. Of the cities outside the deep South and the Border states, San Francisco had the largest nonwhite population in 1870, about 9 per cent of its total, and this was the result of the fact that more than

TABLE 1–3

FOREIGN POPULATION IN TEN LARGEST CITIES, 1870

Rank	City	Total Population	Foreign	Percentage Foreign
1	New York	942,292	419,094	44.4
2	Philadelphia	674,022	183,624	27.2
3	Brooklyn	396,099	—*	—
4	St. Louis	310,864	124,378†	
5	Chicago	298,977	144,557	43.3
6	Baltimore	265,354	56,484	21.3
7	Boston	250,526	87,986	35.1
8	Cincinnati	216,239	79,612	36.8
9	New Orleans	191,148	48,475	25.3
10	San Francisco	149,473	73,719	49.4

* No census data on foreign population for Brooklyn.
† No census data on foreign population for the city of St. Louis; figure on foreign population is for St. Louis County.

12,000 Chinese immigrants resided in the city, nearly ten times as many as there were blacks. New York's population was only 1.5 per cent black, and Chicago's was about the same. The Border city of Baltimore was about 15 per cent black and, in the Deep South, New Orleans 23 per cent. The last had the largest black population of all American cities, more than 50,000 persons, but proportionately Washington was highest. There, one resident in three was black; many were recently freed slaves who had migrated to the capital city, which, to their later disillusionment, they believed would offer freedom, protection, and opportunity. (In 1850 Washington was 27 per cent black.)

The Colonial Inheritance

The government of American cities in the formative years was borrowed principally from English precedent. Where the English took over from settlers of the other nationalities, such as the Dutch in New York and the Swedes in Delaware, they generally and rather quickly substituted their own practices for those in existence. Terminology and structure differed somewhat from one town to another, but the fundamental organization was the same. In general, municipal charters came from the colonial governor or proprietor rather than from the legislature, just as in England the Charter had come directly from the Crown. The legislative bodies did have some authority over the cities, particularly in granting or withholding powers of taxation, but also in connection with substantive powers and some matters of organization. Cities were given powers and privileges, but the charters did not stress their responsibilities as agents of the central government, as happened in charters granted as the nineteenth century progressed.

The frequent practice at the beginning of the period under discussion was for a city to have a governing body consisting of mayor, aldermen, and councillors. Usually this did not indicate at the outset a bicameral legislative branch, except that the mayor and aldermen tended to have judicial powers. For legislative and administrative purposes, the two usually met as a single body. In fact, at the outset the aldermen were often chosen by the council as a whole from its own number, all of whom had been popularly elected. The size of the council was generally from twelve to twenty-five members, counting both categories.

The Philadelphia charter of 1701 provided for twelve councilmen and eight aldermen. The common council of New York and Albany was established in a somewhat different manner, with aldermen plus assistants, both elected, and both having a vote in the common council. Under provisions in New York beginning in 1731, there were seven aldermen and seven assistant aldermen. The number in Albany was six of each. The voters also selected assessors, constables, and tax collectors. In the larger municipalities, these were often elected by wards. The chief executive officer and presiding officer over the council was called the mayor or, sometimes, burgess. He was not popularly elected, however, usually being appointed by the governor or proprietor in the colonial period and in the early days under the Constitution. The recorder, or city attorney, was also usually appointed by the governor.

The municipality was viewed legally as a public corporation with an existence separate from that of either its citizens or its officers. The officers generally had both legislative and executive powers. Thus, the mayor and recorder could commonly vote on the council, and committees of the council frequently were involved in participating in the administration of municipal functions and services. The mayor, recorder, and aldermen also commonly performed judicial functions. Terms of office were usually for one year, but there were some exceptions. Officers generally served without pay, although fees were collected for the performance of some services, and a few full-time officials did receive salaries. There was no civil service of a professional character, and most of the functions of city government in the period at the end of the eighteenth century were carried out by volunteers or by citizens who were co-opted into serving as firemen, street repairers, watchmen, or whatever, and were fined if they failed to perform the assigned responsibilities. These responsibilities fell upon the individual citizen, however, ordinarily from one to five days a year.

While, in general, the pattern of municipal government at the time the United States gained its independence remained in effect throughout the 1789–1870 period, there was an increase in genuine bicameralism, and the mayor's functions became more and more differentiated.

Urban services during the formative years did not differ much in kind from those of contemporary urban society, although they did differ in degree and scope. Discontent was common in the urban ghetto, as we learn from a famous quotation from Alexis de Tocqueville, a Frenchman writing about America in the 1830s:[7]

The lower orders which inhabit these [larger American] cities constitute a rabble even more formidable than the population of European towns. They consist of free Blacks in the first place, who are condemned by the laws and by public opinion, to a hereditary state of misery and degradation. They also contain a multitude of Europeans who have been driven to the shores of the New World by their misfortunes or their misconducts; and these men inoculate the United States with all their vices, without bringing with them any of those interests which counteract their baneful influence. As inhabitants of a country where they have no civil rights, they are ready to turn all the passions which agitate the community to their own advantage; thus, within the last few months serious riots have broken out in Philadelphia and in New York. Disturbances of this kind are unknown in the rest of the country [that is, in rural and small-town areas], which is no wise alarmed by them, because the population of the cities has hitherto exercised neither power nor influence over the rural districts.

Tocqueville, like Jefferson a generation earlier, viewed the urban proletariat as a real threat to democracy. He feared that a democratic republic, like the United States, would not be able to survive unless an armed force could be created which would be independent of the urban population and hence "able to repress its excesses." He argued that such a guard should be subject to majority control, which, of course, in the period about which he was writing meant the residents of rural and small-town areas. (In fact, the state militia was not infrequently called upon to suppress riots, for the city police often could not or would not do so.)

In later chapters we shall develop in some detail the issues in the clash of interests that were involved in the development of American cities. Not only were there tensions between persons of different classes and between competing interests, but urban development was accompanied by a good deal of debate over the functions that city government should perform and the manner in which they ought to be performed. In general, cities had responsibility for police and fire protection, providing or regulating the water supply and, later on, the sources of lighting, the surfacing and maintenance of streets, the regulation of markets, the regulation and sometimes removal of nuisances, including dead animals and garbage, the policing of fair weights and measures, the regulation of traffic, the regulation of tradesmen and peddlers, the construction and maintenance of wharves and levees and their control, the operation of slaughterhouses, the protection of the public health, and sewage and other waste disposal. Although the means were often primitive and the administration was amateurish, the issues and problems have a modern sound to them. Some of them seem very modern indeed, such as the efforts of frontier cities to prevent the sale of adulterated food or the skyrocketing of prices in the market as a result of monopolistic or conspiratorial efforts to raise prices on goods brought long distances from the Eastern cities. On the other hand, some activities of the towns sound like something out of the past—or future—such as the practice of setting prices on certain commodities in some cities.

Although the era of independence began with cities that had derived their powers for the most part from colonial governors and proprietors, as time went on the legal status of the cities changed very considerably, as we shall see in Chapter 2. Their legislatures, already in the British pattern, were aided by the post-Revolution reaction against executive officers and by the commitment of Jacksonian democracy to support of the legislative branch. They thus came to control the taxing and substantive powers in the largest and many of the middle-sized cities and to dominate their decisions about organizational structure. City-state relations grew more complex and more tense. Meanwhile, the national government continued to carry on its paternalistic (or perhaps "rich uncle") approach to the encouragement of westward expansion in both rural and urban areas.

Meanwhile, the problems of the emerging cities and the costs of dealing with them became ever more complex:

> By 1815 Western towns had witnessed the appearance of all the urban problems which confronted Eastern cities and already these questions exerted a growing pressure on local government. In nearly every field of municipal authority—police, fire, streets, water, and health—conditions deteriorated so rapidly that a series of emergencies appeared requiring decisive action. Any one of these was great enough to tax the ingenuity of local authorities, yet the crisis came on many fronts. Indeed, the multiplicity of issues was the real danger. Communities could handle some of the challenges, but not all. Yet their interrelatedness made success in any single one difficult.
>
> This was the ironic situation, for in the first years of the nineteenth century the expansion of municipal power to cope with these problems constituted the central tendency of local government in the West. Having begun with extremely limited jurisdiction, towns managed to broaden their authority continually until it covered wide areas of town life. Some of this increased control was embodied in amendments to early charters, and the rest resulted from the city's inching into the twilight zone which separated state and local power, pleading "necessity and immemorial usage" as their authority. By the end of the first generation of city life on the frontier, communities were largely self-governing, having appropriated either by a grant or allocation nearly all the necessary weapons to deal with problems arising from urban conditions.[8]

In this book we shall see the cities grow from the wilderness to the edge of industrial America: their populations change from predominantly Anglo-Saxon to a polyglot waiting for the melting pot to warm up; and their politics from a low-keyed, cooperative effort to provide basic urban services to the beginnings of the great bossed machines of the early industrial era, with control slipping from the middle-class, Main Street merchant to the leaders of the working-class immigrant groups. The formative years established a pattern of practices that have become the traditions of American city government and still affect them in dozens of ways today. It was also a period in which cities began to fight the battles that are still facing us, those of slum living conditions, school segregation, sewage and waste disposal, water resources, the maintenance of healthful sanitary conditions under high-density circumstances, the care of the poor, the education of all, traffic hazards and congestion, the containment of exploiters, the maintenance of order despite racial and class tensions. These and other major issues appeared and from time to time reappeared to challenge the decision-makers of our urban communities.

Appendix to Chapter 1

PERCENTAGE OF POPULATION INCREASE, 1790–1880

New York
1790–1800	118.04%
1800–1810	59.32%
1810–1820	27.78%
1820–1830	63.76%
1830–1840	54.35%
1840–1850	65.18%
1850–1860	17.82%
1860–1870	16.96%
1870–1880	28.01%

Philadelphia
1790–1800	63.22%
1800–1810	32.37%
1810–1820	22.74%
1820–1830	43.13%
1830–1840	36.56%
1840–1850	54.37%
1850–1860	66.32%
1860–1870	19.18%
1870–1880	25.69%

Boston
1790–1800	36.05%
1800–1810	33.33%
1810–1820	30.22%
1820–1830	41.79%
1830–1840	52.10%
1840–1850	46.58%
1850–1860	29.92%
1860–1870	40.87%
1870–1880	44.83%

Baltimore
1790–1800	93.39%
1800–1810	36.26%
1810–1820	76.31%
1820–1830	28.51%
1830–1840	26.96%
1840–1850	65.15%
1850–1860	25.65%
1860–1870	25.86%
1870–1880	24.29%

Charleston
1790–1800	25.15%
1800–1810	21.14%
1810–1820	.28%
1820–1830	22.23%
1830–1840	—3.39%

Salem
1790–1800	19.39%
1800–1810	16.24%
1810–1820	.93%

Providence
1800–1810	32.27%
1810–1830	67.13%
(2 decades)	
1830–1840	37.66%

Richmond
1800–1810	69.68%
1810–1820	23.95%
1820–1830	33.09%

Albany
1800–1810	76.89%
1810–1820	34.99%
1820–1830	91.90%
1830–1840	39.12%
1840–1850	50.53%

New Orleans
1810–1820	0 %
1820–1830	168.58%
1830–1840	120.67%
1840–1850	13.87%
1850–1860	44.94%
1860–1870	13.48%
1870–1880	12.89%

Washington, D.C.
1820–1830	42.12%
1830–1840	24.04%
1840–1850	121.22%
1850–1870	111.27%
(2 decades)	
1870–1890	110.98%
(2 decades)	

Cincinnati
1850–1860	39.51%
1860–1870	34.27%
1870–1880	17.99%

Brooklyn
1840–1850	167.26%
1850–1860	175.36%
1860–1870	48.54%
1870–1880	40.53%

St. Louis
1850–1860	106.49%
1860–1870	93.35%
1870–1880	12.75%

Chicago
1860–1870	173.63%
1870–1880	63.69%

NOTE: The reader should be aware that some of the greatest percentage increases were accounted for by annexations.

POPULATED CITIES IN TERRITORIES

1850	
Santa Fe, New Mexico	4,846
1860	
Salt Lake City, Utah	8,236
South Clear Creek, Colorado	5,966
Denver, Colorado	4,749
Santa Fe, New Mexico	4,635
Pembina, Dakota	3,554

Notes

1. Various editions of the works of Ralph Waldo Emerson are available. For an extensive bibliography covering the entire period of this book, see Oscar Handlin and others (eds.), *Harvard Guide to American History* (Cambridge, Mass., 1954). For a more recent view of innovation, see Lewis Mumford, *The City in History* (New York, 1961) and Jane Jacobs, *The Economy of Cities* (New York, 1970).
2. Henry D. Thoreau, *A Week*, originally published 1849 and *Walden*, originally published 1854. Many editions available.
3. See Arthur M. Schlesinger, Jr., *The Age of Jackson* (Boston, 1945), and Walter Hugins, *Jacksonian Democracy and the Working Class* (Stanford, Calif., 1960).
4. See Ernest S. Griffith, *History of American City Government: The Colonial Period* (New York, 1938).
5. See J. Franklin Jameson, *The American Revolution Considered as a Social Movement* (New York, 1926). The social movement described by Jameson actually began somewhat earlier than he indicates.
6. Schlesinger, *op. cit.*, and Hugins, *op. cit.*
7. Alexis de Tocqueville, *Democracy in America*. Originally published in two volumes, 1835 and 1840.
8. Richard C. Wade, *The Urban Frontier* (Cambridge, Mass., 1959), p. 99.

Chapter 2

THE LEGAL STATUS
OF CITIES

During the 1789–1870 period the legal status of municipalities in the new American nation was clarified and firmly established on a different basis from that which had existed prior to the War for Independence. Two major developments were involved. One was the concept of the municipality as a child of the state. The other, called "Dillon's Rule," clarified the relationship between the parental states and their legal children.

The War for Independence and its successful conclusion on the side of the revolutionaries created many problems for the new nation. Among these was the need to find a new legal basis for the municipality; the British model, although a sound foundation, had to be modified somewhat. The cities themselves, at least those of over 7,500 population (Philadelphia was the largest and, in 1775, it had fewer than 30,000 persons) held less than 3 per cent of the nation's population, yet they had contributed far more than their share to revolutionary leadership and financing and endured more physical suffering during the war. They also suffered disproportionately from structural damage, expropriation, and the difficulties caused by bivouacked troops. Large fires also took their toll: New York had disastrous fires in 1776 and 1778.

In April, 1775, the city of New York fell into Tory hands. The following February, as the city moved onto a wartime footing, an extra-legal Committee of Fifty was established and ran the city until it was occupied by the British in September. The occupation lasted until November 25, 1783, and during most of that time the city was under virtually complete martial law, subject to policies imposed by the British commander. All municipal offices ceased to function, but an important event occurred a few months after the occupation when the New York Constitution of 1777 declared the city charter of 1732 and all Colonial borough charters still in force. When civilian government was re-established on February 10, 1784, the prewar charter and pattern of government were continued as before. In the new constitution, the legislature managed to settle an important question of law—who was to replace the King in controlling city charters—by providing for the maintenance of the *status quo* "until otherwise directed by the legislature" (Article 36).

The town of Boston was placed under British martial law from April 19, 1775, until March 5, 1776. After that the town meeting and its officers resumed responsibility and continued to govern exactly as before the war. The town form was so satisfactory and so widely accepted as the proper New England form of government that the state constitution of 1780 made no provision for the establishment of cities. Later, the state constitution prohibited the legislature from imposing city charters upon towns without their consent.

In other states the legislatures quickly moved to establish legal supremacy over their cities and villages. In 1777, the Pennsylvania legislature re-established the "ancient corporation of the Burgesses" of Lancaster as it had existed before the war. The same was done for Chester (1795) and Bristol (1785). The New Jersey legislature reissued the original charters of Perth Amboy and Burlington in 1784 and that for Elizabeth in 1789.

The Philadelphia charter of 1701, which had established a close corporation, was dissolved in 1776. The state Council of Safety controlled the local officers after that. The next year, the legislature passed "An Act to impower the Justices of the Peace for the city of Philadelphia to do and perform certain matters and things formerly directed to be done and performed by the Mayor, Recorder, and Aldermen of the said city." During the six-month British occupation beginning in November, 1777, the city was run principally by civilians under appointment by the British commander. Afterward the state legislature controlled the city until a new charter was granted in 1789.

The most immediate goal after independence was not reform; even in Philadelphia that was delayed for many years. The first target was, in most of the new states, to establish the legislatures as the successors to the Crown in relation to the cities. The state body seemed most assertive of its power in Pennsylvania and least so in already tradition-bound Massachusetts. But in all of the states, the outlines of the legal theory of the position of municipalities appeared early.

The City in Legal History

In most of the United States, the practice was to incorporate a municipality first as village, borough, town (in the East and Midwest, a term often used instead of village), or a pueblo, and not to seek city status until the community had grown to at least a few thousand inhabitants. This cautious procedure probably stemmed from a desire to provide a few basic urban services, such as police protection and control over weights and measures, but also to keep the government as simple and hence as inexpensive as possible. Some of these mid-stations on the way to cityhood retained for a while the institution of the town meeting. This was held at least once annually to elect officers, to pass on taxation and expenditures, and occasionally for other matters. Even some cities, such as New Haven, retained the "city" meeting for many years. Frontiersmen were, however, characteristically persons of modest means, chronically short of cash, and extremely anxious to keep down governmental costs so as to divert all accumulated funds into working capital.

If we look, then, at the original incorporation of municipalities, and not at the date of their becoming cities, we find quite a different pattern from what we might expect if we assumed that municipalities were literally created by their state governments. (Indeed, it is not always possible to determine just when a municipal corporation was first formed. In 1805, when the territorial legislature granted a charter for the city of New Orleans, the Louisiana courts held, on slight evidence, that New Orleans had already been a city under both the French and the Spanish, even though it had never had a charter.)[1] A large number of American cities were originally created by representatives of European kingdoms or by territorial governments acting on behalf of and representing the government of the United States directly. Thus of the twelve largest cities in the United States by the Census of 1970, only Chicago, Cleveland, Dallas, and Indianapolis were initially chartered by state governments. (See Table 2–1.) To this might perhaps be added Baltimore as a town

TABLE 2–1

LEGAL SOURCE OF FIRST INCORPORATION, TWELVE LARGEST CITIES, 1970

Rank in 1970	City	First Incorporated	Source of Authority
1	New York	1653	Dutch colonial government
2	Chicago	1833	State of Illinois
3	Los Angeles	1821	Spanish colonial government
4	Philadelphia	1701	Proprietary government
5	Detroit	1802	Indiana Territory
6	Houston	1837	Texas Republic
7	Baltimore	1729	Act of Assembly
8	Dallas	1846	State of Texas
9	Washington	1802	United States Government
10	Cleveland	1814	State of Ohio
11	Indianapolis	1836	State of Indiana
12	Milwaukee	1833	Northwest Territory

and the city of Washington, with its always anomalous position as an American city. Washington was created by the United States Government and was never considered to be in quite the same legal position as other cities. The Constitution had given Congress exclusive control over the Federal District, and congressmen have always jealously guarded this control, especially after the Civil War, even though there was no legal reason why power over *municipal* matters could not have been delegated to those residing within the city. Washington was incorporated as a city in 1802, and Georgetown, which had been incorporated by Maryland in 1789, was reincorporated by Congress in 1805. But both charters were revoked in 1871 after a radical Republican had built much of his political power on the increasingly large number of blacks in the District, something that alarmed many members of Congress.

The doctrine of state supremacy developed as follows. In medieval and Renaissance England, as well as generally in the rest of Europe, a city was created by a grant from the King, or sometimes from some other major nobleman. This was done by the granting of a *charter*, which spelled out the rights and privileges of the city and its residents. What the King granted, the King could also take away, although the burghers were always jealous of their special status, and it was usually not politically feasible for the King to seek to infringe upon these special rights and privileges once they were bestowed (even William the Conqueror was circumspect in his handling of cities). Hence, a certain tension has existed between the cities and their creators at least since medieval times and probably stretching back into the ancient past.

Gradually the chartered cities were recognized by the King's courts as *corporations*. That is, they were accepted as having a permanent existence, independent from either the officials or the residents of the city. At law they were considered to be artificial persons and had their own rights, privileges, and duties, including the right to sue and be sued and to exist in perpetuity. (The King could, of course, deprive an artificial person of its life just as he could a human person.) By the fourteenth century, this concept of a city as a corporation was well established in English law. At that time, municipal (or public) corporations were not clearly distinguished from other such corporations that might be established by the King, for example, the Hudson's Bay Company or the East India Company. Later, however, both British and American courts began increasingly to distinguish between public and private corporations. Today in England, municipal corporations still receive their charters from the sovereign, although decisions in this respect, as in virtually all others that are formally those of the sovereign, are made by Parliament, or more precisely, by the cabinet rather than by the sovereign himself.

The early charters were not in any specific form, did not necessarily include the same kinds of provisions, and were essentially grants of privileges, but later charters began to assume a more definite form. By the start of the post-Revolution period charters were written documents that established the municipality (village, borough, or city) as a corporation (often called a "body corporate and politic"), described its powers, and provided for at least some of the basic organizational structure.

In what was to become the United States, municipalities were not actually created by European kings but rather were established by colonial governors or even their subordinates, acting in the name of the sovereign. Thus, the Viceroy of New Spain, or persons acting in his name, established municipalities in Florida, Texas, New Mexico, and California. In the English colonies, charters were granted by the royal governors or the proprietors, except in the royal colonies of New England, where no permanent municipal incorporations took place until after the War for Independence. In New England and New York, the town, and in some other parts of the nation the township or county, occupied a position different from that of the incorporated municipalities. These were called quasi-corporations and had no separate charters. Instead, they were merely considered as carrying out policies established by the central government. This was true even though in New England the town became famous as a policy-making institution of local government. Although different in a number of respects from municipalities, the town served effectively to govern smaller urban as well as rural communities, and so no need was felt to create municipal corporations until sometime after the War for Independence.

Loyalty to the town and belief in its economical nature were deep-seated in New·England. Persons who were dissatisfied with the system, for one reason or another, did sometimes agitate for adoption of a city charter. This was especially true in the area's largest city, Boston. Demands for change were heard often, until the area was incorporated in 1822. During one such period of pressure, in 1784, a plan was submitted that called for the establishment of a small electoral college (thirty-eight electors) to choose a mayor. It would have increased the duties of the selectmen (to be renamed aldermen) but would have left considerable power with the town meeting. This and other proposals were duly investigated, but Samuel Adams reported "no defects" in the existing system.

As cities grew, relative (and sometimes absolute) attendance fell off at town meetings. The sense of identity declined and people saw less and less meaning in attending the annual sessions. As that happened, those who had an immediate stake in making decisions naturally took advantage of the situation. In 1821, the year before Boston finally became a city, the lamplighters dutifully attended the annual meeting, found themselves in a majority, and voted themselves a pay increase.

With the coming of the War for Independence, the legal parentage of American municipalities underwent a considerable change. The concept of confederation and then federation automatically gave the states rather than the national government residual powers over local government. The national government was said to have only specified powers (by the Tenth Amendment), and these did not include authority relative to local governments.

The colonial governors had been generally viewed as agents for the King, and hence with suspicion and hostility. The American executive went into a deep eclipse from which it did not emerge for many decades. At the same time, however, the legislative branch emerged as a heroic institution. Having been locally elected, its members were viewed as representative of popular opinion and hence compatible with the spirit of the Revolution. From the time when the royal or proprietary governors fell into disfavor until the newly created states began to select their own, the legislative bodies assumed control over executive functions, including control over municipal corporations. A power that had always rested in the executive, that of creating municipalities and determining their powers, had passed to the legislatures for the first time. Just as medieval townsmen had jealously guarded their special privileges, so did the legislatures now guard their right to control the structure and powers of municipalities.

The Form of the Charter

A new form of municipal charter emerged and was to dominate the pattern of charter-making between the War for Independence and the mid-nineteenth century. This was the *special-act charter*. It was granted specifically by a legislature to a particular community. Being special in character even within a given state, the powers and structure granted to one municipality might be quite different from those granted to another. The new pattern by which charters were granted quickly became accepted throughout the land. Although Congress retained control of the District of Columbia for itself, for the territories beyond the admitted states, it authorized the legislatures, and not the territorial governors, to grant charters of incorporation.

Because each city charter, or village or borough charter, was a unique instrument granted by the legislative body, it followed that any changes in municipal powers or structure, that is, any amendments to the charter, would have to be made by the legislatures. The result was that throughout the nineteenth century there was an ever expanding amount of *special legislation* granting or withholding powers from municipalities or overruling decisions made by local legislative and administrative officials. The transfer of control over charters from the executive to the legislature, which had been seen as a movement toward greater democracy during the revolutionary period, now came to be viewed with increasing skepticism by officials and residents of the expanding American municipality. Urbanites still sought, as they had in the Middle Ages, to guard their special privileges and position in society, but they now found that they were often in a weak position to do so. The legislatures had assumed control over this governmental power, and they were in no mood to surrender it. Legislative control created a very different political situation from executive control. While the King, or his governors or proprietors, usually found it wise to have the cities on his side and supporting him in political conflict, and while all urban residents were members of his constituency, this was not so in respect to legislators. Few members of any given legislature were residents of or property owners in any given municipality whose charter might be under consideration for change by special legislation. The opportunities for logrolling and for selling favors, particularly franchises over public utilities as they developed, were obvious and were seized upon by legislators in many states.

Special acts were not used simply as a device for illegal profit-making by legislators or for substituting state for local policy making. Particularly in the states away from the East Coast, such exploitation does not appear to have been the common practice. In Iowa, for example, "the people of the local community not only had in many instances a considerable share in formulating their charters in accordance with local needs, but they also had in effect authority to amend their charters. Special-charter cities had little difficulty in securing amendments from the legislature. . . . While such charters and their amendments were subject to legislative control, the records do not show the existence of a meddlesome attitude on the part of the General Assembly."[2] Furthermore, most of the time the legally asserted power of the state was not involved except when a community so requested. In the 1815 case *Mayor of New York and others* v. *Ordrenan*, 12 John 122, the judge said this was "almost the invariable course of proceedings."

Resistance to the use of the special act increased throughout the first half of the nineteenth century. Increasingly, there was talk of using the *general-act charter*, a plan that had been adopted in France at the time of its Revolution, which prevented legislative control over given municipalities by requiring that the law apply generally to municipal corporations. In 1851 Indiana and Ohio adopted constitutional provisions prohibiting special legislation. But the practice continued in many states, and the formal prohibition was often circumvented. Cities grew rapidly in the nineteenth century and thus often became places where quick profits could be made. Where a kickback or inside knowledge could lead to personal profit, many legislators could not resist participating in what they must have seen as a part of the great American pattern of economic growth. Thus members of the Pennsylvania legislature in 1870 authorized their political and business friends to construct elaborate municipal buildings for Philadelphia. They did not hesitate to impose the obligation for paying for these unrequested structures upon the residents and other taxpayers of that city.

The 'use of special legislation became the basis for the major family quarrels in the first half of the nineteenth century. The states insisted upon their parental authority, while their children were adamant in their view that they were capable of running their own affairs. Although the special-act charters themselves were not always a basis for conflict— they certainly were sometimes—various legislative acts concerning local affairs were a matter of continuing and expanding conflict. On only a few occasions was the question legally one of whether the states had supremacy over local governments. In the great bulk of cases, debate centered on the wisdom or fairness of state pre-emption in decision making.

Local citizens objected that state obligatory legislation was forcing their taxes to be higher than they would need to be, and they especially objected because they suspected—quite rightly in many cases—that state legislators were receiving bribes or kickbacks in return for favors granted. Local protests resulted from such state decisions imposed upon municipalities as the following: the granting of exclusive franchises to private companies for the sale of water and gas or the operation of street railways; the sale of privately owned land, unrequested, to the city for parks and recreation purposes; the location or vacation of streets for the financial advantage of selected land developers; the development of streets and sewers for the advantage of privileged land developers, with the cost charged to the municipal general fund; enforced municipal contributions to canal and railroad companies by the municipalities; and the increasing or decreasing of municipal officeholder salaries, according to whether or not they were in current favor with the state legislative majority. All of these offenses also could have been, and were, committed by city councils where the legislature did not take advantage of a profitable situation. Such behavior was objected to locally, but it seemed even more outrageous when the offense was committed by the state legislature. Some substantive local powers were also removed from the authority of municipal government and control of them turned over to state officers or boards. In 1861, for example, the Missouri legislature took control of the police away from the city of St. Louis and turned it over to a special Board of Police under state control, but the annual budget for operation remained an obligatory charge against the city. Since the board, rather than the city, determined how many men should be on the force and what they should be paid, the city was in effect forced to sign a legal blank check. St. Louis was only one example. Several other cities, including New York, also found their police under state control. Under such circumstances, the reformers of the era, in typical American fashion, sought remedies through the legal process.

The earliest approach to a remedy was to write into state constitutions prohibitions against certain actions by the state legislatures that would tend to interfere with what was interpreted as being a local right or function. Hence, the New York and Wisconsin constitutions of 1848 guaranteed each municipality the right to elect its own officers or have them locally appointed. Others guaranteed local control over police, streets, or the granting of local public utilities franchises. Some were changed to prohibit the appointment of special state boards designed to administer matters strictly of municipal concern. The first such specific guarantee was written into a state constitution in 1812, and they continue to be written in the present day.

About a decade after this first type of attack, a second one appeared. Massachusetts began to imitate the English practice by which special legislation affecting only a specific municipality could not be adopted except after a public hearing, preceded by public notice in the community concerned. The goal of such a provision was to allow legislation to be tailor-made for a particular community while guaranteeing a local opportunity to be heard concerning the decision. This approach was not immediately adopted in other states, but its popularity became quite widespread after the Civil War. Provisions incorporating this approach were especially popular in the new state constitutions that were adopted during the decade of the 1870s.

The next step was to outlaw special legislation on matters of municipal concern. The New Jersey constitution of 1844 was the first to enumerate in detail matters upon which special legislation was forbidden. The first blanket constitutional prohibitions appeared in the Midwest which, as throughout its history, was suspicious of governmental "abuses" in the East. In 1851 the Ohio constitution was amended to provide that "the general assembly shall pass no special act conferring corporate powers." Indiana followed this precedent a few months later. In Iowa special legislation increased in amount with virtually every legislative session after 1838.[3] As a consequence, that state's constitution of 1857 (its second) prohibited all special legislation dealing with municipal concerns in specific communities. It provided that "where a general law can be made applicable, all laws shall be general, and of uniform operation throughout the state." Kansas adopted this rule two years later. In the Midwest during the following decade this language was widely adopted in making similar prohibitions.

The trend was then picked up in other parts of the nation, although it was never accepted in much of the South, perhaps in part because general legislation had been favored by some of the carpetbagger governments immediately following the Civil War and hence may not have been viewed kindly by the Southern aristocracy when it resumed control. In any case, the action in Arkansas in 1868 to outlaw special legislation and that in Florida in 1865 did not become the pattern of the South. In the rest of the country, however, special legislation generally was outlawed, and the result was a need to find substitute ways of dealing with the unique problems of particular cities when it was discovered that legislation that applied to all municipalities alike was not feasible. In general, during the period immediately following 1870 various approaches to a solution, including constitutional provisions for municipal home rule, the classification of cities, and optional charters to be selected by local choice, were developed.

As it turned out, however, under judicial interpretation, the term "the general law" proved to be quite vague in meaning, as did the term "uniform operation." The result was that these prohibitions lent themselves to numerous types of evasions. They did, however, make it more difficult for the legislature to use this device, and even where methods of evasion were easily accepted by the courts, they indicated something of the public mood and what was expected of legislatures by constitution writers.

The rules against special legislation had an inhibiting effect but certainly did not put an end to efforts to impose specific legislation on communities of a particular size or type or even upon specific communities. Thus, the Iowa legislature in the 1856–57 session enacted fifty-six laws in anticipation of the new constitutional provision against special legislation, but only three laws in the following session. Two of these were declared null and void by the state supreme court.[4] By 1862 the legislature was beginning to regain its upper hand. It passed four special laws in that year, three of which survived in the courts. In fact, the state high court rather quickly lent its assistance to the legislature in its effort to find a way around this barrier. It interpreted special legislation as being that in which the language of an act was such as to prevent it from *ever* being applied to more than one city.[5] This gaping loophole in the idea of general legislation was quickly picked up by attorneys for other states. Minnesota, for example, began to adopt legislation that applied to "all cities" above a certain size. But since Minneapolis, St. Paul, and Duluth, the largest cities in the state, differed widely in population, it was easy to write special legislation for those three cities. Whenever any one of the cities began to approach the population boundaries, the legislature simply amended the existing act by raising the applicable population figure. All of this deliberate effort at circumvention was sustained by the state courts.[6] In Ohio, for many years the state Supreme Court permitted the legislature to classify each of the eleven largest cities of the state separately.[7]

The Iowa legislature wasted no time in using the classification dodge. The first legislature to meet under the new constitution (in 1858) provided for a general municipal incorporation act. It provided for such general charters on the basis of three population categories, but in later years, in effect, it extended these to six by the separate classification of cities under the old special charters (which were preserved by the "save harmless" clause of the constitution), and to those operating under the commission and council-manager plans.[8] Furthermore, some acts of the legislature were subsequently made to apply only to cities of a certain size and the populations named were not necessarily the same as those of the three classes of charters.

Dillon's Rule

In addition to the legal rule of the municipality as a child of the state, a second rule was developed in the middle years of the nineteenth century. This was "Dillon's Rule." It was a logical outgrowth of the doctrine of state supremacy and held, in essence, that if there was any basis for doubt, a municipality did not possess a particular right, privilege, or power.

Throughout the nineteenth century, judges in all states gave a narrow interpretation of municipal and other local government powers and resolved all questions of doubt in favor of state government institutions. In 1872 John F. Dillon, a scholarly Iowa judge, published the first edition of his classic legal study on *Municipal Corporations*.[9] He was able to summarize existing processes as follows:

> It is a general and undisputed proposition of the law that a municipal corporation possesses and can exercise, the following powers, and no others: First, those granted in express words; second, those necessarily or fairly implied in, or incident to, the powers expressly granted; third, those essential to the accomplishment of the declared objects and purposes of the corporation—not simply convenient, but indispensable. Any fair, reasonable, substantial doubt concerning the existence of a power is resolved by the courts against the corporation, and the power is denied.

Dillon's work was carried on through five editions, the last published in 1911. It became the standard reference work on municipal corporation law and he found that throughout this period there was no need to make any significant change in the rule. Indeed, it became so standard that it was the basis for a discussion of municipal power in the successor authority by Judge Eugene McQuillin.[10]

Obviously, Dillon's Rule was one of strict construction, using such terms as "necessarily" and "essential." Dozens of cases are cited in municipal corporation law textbooks to show the extremely narrow interpretation of grants of authority by the courts in virtually all states.

The development of the law of municipalities was somewhat uneven in the early years, with a good deal of trial and error but with the focus gradually becoming sharper until it was possible for Judge Dillon to put together a standard work and show a remarkable degree of commonality, although not complete uniformity, among the various states.

In New England, as the town governments sometimes proved inadequate to meet the demands of increasing urbanization, the state legislatures engaged in some experimentation. Connecticut, for example, introduced the borough (the standard English term for a municipality) as an intermediate stage between the town and the city. Bridgeport received the first of the borough charters in 1800. In general, the borough organization proved to be very popular among the municipalities; but the legislature was reluctant to create new municipal corporations, and the great political power of the towns, we can assume, was aimed against such moves. (The characteristics of the borough will be outlined in Chapter 7.) Still, boroughs were created at Stonington (1801), Guilford (1815), Essex (1820), and Killingsworth (1820), all special charters, but all based upon the Bridgeport model. In 1818 Litchfield was incorporated as a village, but this bit of experimentation apparently did not find much favor and appears to have been the only village organization ever to exist in Connecticut.

The community of Batesville in Arkansas gives something of an illustration of trial and error development. The community had given enough for an academy, that is, a semiprivate high school, to be founded there in 1829. By 1841 the community leaders wanted the growing area to be incorporated. The county court (the county's legislative body) then took this action. Four years later the incorporation was dissolved, although whether this was for financial reasons or because of a doubt of legal right of the county to act is uncertain. In 1848 the state legislature incorporated Batesville on a basis that was undoubtedly constitutional.

Fort Smith, Arkansas, was granted a charter by the legislature in 1853, but this was set aside by the courts the following year on the grounds that it delegated powers to the corporation in too drastic a fashion. The legislature then granted another charter.

Municipal Home Rule

Characteristically, reformers sought legal remedies to overcome what they considered excessive and expanding state domination over local affairs as the nineteenth century progressed. Two legal concepts were developed. One was the short-lived doctrine of the inherent right of local self-government, the other was the more important idea of municipal home rule. The former was given its classic statement by Thomas M. Cooley, a Michigan judge, in 1871. He defended local self-government as a matter of "absolute right," arguing that it stemmed from a legal tradition running back to the time of the Angles and Saxons and to their ancestors who were members of the ancient German tribes. He argued that this tradition had been transferred to the American states through the common law, though this was in fact not possible, since statute law has always superseded the common law and no doctrine of inherent right had been even faintly visible in Britain at least since the time of William the Conqueror. He bolstered his argument by citing some of the natural-rights philosophers of the eighteenth century. Judge Cooley's argument was not only legally weak, as later commentaries indicated,[11] but it was not even controlling in the case before his court and hence was merely a statement of opinion by him. That is, the statement was an *obiter dictum*, a view expressed that was not essential to the decision because the actual legal finding was made on some other ground. Nevertheless, his ruling attracted a great deal of attention and struck a responsive chord. His dictum was later cited by judges in California, Iowa, Kentucky, Nebraska, Texas, and especially Indiana. It never became a ruling principle, however, and had no permanent effect upon American city government, except perhaps to reflect the eternal desire of local citizens to be free of controls by their central governments.

A different approach, also one of ancient lineage, was that of home rule. In earlier times, a sort of *de facto* home rule existed in municipalities. In England, the King generally did not interfere with the action of local legislatures unless they threatened a commitment he had made or they proposed to do something that was obviously a threat to the carrying out of national policy. Similarly, the towns of early New England had a great deal of discretionary latitude. They "organized and managed their own local affairs and services. Each town retained its own individuality and functioned to a great degree without reference to any higher authority, except for those few laws which were commonly accepted by all communities."[12]

The New England town system was challenged by the strong assertion of legal rights by the state legislatures in the early nineteenth century. The vision of municipalities ruling themselves on matters of local concern never disappeared, however.

Municipal home rule represented in part an effort by the middle-class businessmen of cities to recapture control from the emerging working-class-oriented political machines. In its first manifestations, however, it was merely an effort to accommodate to the changing legal situation in which the use of the special charter was falling from favor and the general act charter was beginning to appear. The problem was how to deal with the existing special-act cities and the amendment of their charters. Should they continue to be amended by special acts? Or should all special-act charters be made null and void and the communities required to adopt new general-act charters? Either approach was a possibility, but something else was proposed in Iowa, which, like other states, had historically used only special-act charters. In 1851 the legislature enacted a law establishing a single method by which charters could be adopted and new communities incorporated. It provided that when the residents of a community voted to have the area become a city, they would also choose persons to serve as members of a charter commission. Within general limits established by the state law this commission could draw up a charter that would then be submitted to the voters for their approval or disapproval.[13]

The new state constitution of 1857 prohibited all special legislation and required that general acts be made to apply to all communities where they could be made applicable. The next year, when the legislature met under the new constitution, these restrictions were interpreted as outlawing this unique form of home rule as authorized by the state legislature, and the act was repealed, never having been used, except for the provision allowing existing special-act charters to be amended by this procedure. This practice has continued among the special cities of Iowa up to the present time.

In 1875 Missouri held a constitutional convention. One of the practical political problems of the time was to gain enough support within the city of St. Louis to secure the adoption of a new constitution. Political leaders and many citizens of St. Louis had long been dissatisfied with legislative supervision and, from their point of view, domination of local policy-making processes. The St. Louis delegation, therefore, came to the convention with a set of proposals that served as their price for supporting a new constitution. What they proposed was what has since come to be known as constitutional home rule. This was a proposal to permit municipalities of over 100,000 population (as yet, only St. Louis) to have their city charters framed, adopted, and amended by local procedures. This right, furthermore, was to be protected by a constitutional provision placed beyond the reach of the legislature. In the St. Louis plan, and in most of those that followed, the approach was essentially that provided in the Iowa act of 1851, but with the difference that the provision now enjoyed constitutional guarantees.

Municipal home rule was uniquely an American institution. It reflected the frontier emphasis upon local self-government and the desire to be protected from the often exploitative activities of strangers in distant decision-making centers. The plan developed to maturity in the last quarter of the nineteenth century and the first quarter of the twentieth century, a period of rapid American urbanization. Efforts to secure municipal home rule centered in the nation's rapidly growing large cities.[14]

Cities and the Civil War

The effect of the Civil War was traumatic to the legal status and activities of the Southern cities and of Washington, D.C. Richmond was the capital and quintessence of the Confederacy during the war. Most other Southern cities had a checkered career, interrupted by Union occupation or commercial blockade. A port city such as Norfolk was hard hit. So also was New Orleans, with much of its profitable Mississippi River trade cut off. Memphis was captured early in the war, yet its public schools continued to operate.

At the beginning of the war Richmond's aristocratic city council reflected the prevailing mixture of hope and determination. When the city seemed threatened, it appropriated for its defenses. Its governance was a mixture of civil and military rule. Vice greatly increased, and venereal disease was rampant among the soldiers. In 1863 the council bought salt and retailed it at 5¢ a pound, when black market prices had reached 70–90 cents. In the winter of 1862–63, refugees swarmed into the city. Some rioting and looting for clothing and other necessities followed. In 1864 the council appropriated more than $150,000 for relief of the poor. It increased salaries of municipal employees and appointed a Board of Supplies to secure food from the countryside—without much success. The Confederacy finally abandoned the city, and fires destroyed portions of it.

Little Rock, Arkansas, was made the capital of the Arkansas Territory in 1820, when it stood in the heart of the wilderness with only a few log huts. It was incorporated as a town by the territorial legislature in 1831 and as a city in 1835, the year before Arkansas was admitted to the Union as a state.

During the Civil War, Little Rock was occupied by Federal troops and subjected to martial law. A shadow municipal government was permitted by the occupying forces. A central market was established and regulated by the military authority. Prices were fixed and all trading was subject to heavy licenses designed to help pay part of the cost of occupation. After the war ended, a public meeting was held in which it was decided that the city government should be turned over to those who had held office under the Confederacy. The military commander refused to permit this but said he would accept any elected officials chosen according to state law. An informal citizens' group then met and selected election commissioners and the election day.

When election day came, it was discovered that the commissioners were not insisting upon the loyalty oath required by state law. The commanding general stopped the voting. In December, 1865, however, the state supreme court ruled that the oath requirement was unconstitutional. The former Confederate leaders then took the initiative, acting as a local party called the "conservatives," in holding an election and establishing a municipal government. The conservatives also came to power in state government and amended the Little Rock and other municipal charters to suit the conservative political aims of the group. In 1867, after some civil disturbances, the conservative mayor of Little Rock cooperated with the military in seeking to preserve order. Tension between the local authorities and the occupying Federal troops continued, however, and as late as 1868 the commanding general ordered the mayor and members of the council to vacate their positions and a new election to be held. The existing government accepted these orders.

Washington, D.C., has always had difficulties in determining how much municipal service is provided primarily for local residents and how much primarily for the nation as a whole as its national capital. Not surprisingly, long-time residents of the District have often felt that Congress has failed to afford equitable treatment. During the Civil War, the city and the District were subjected to particular pressures. Washington became a staging area for troops, a military campaign headquarters, the seat of all kinds of adventure-seekers and opportunists, and a provisioning station for the army, with a resulting huge increase in the number of slaughterhouses and their potential for befouling the environment.

The war brought vast changes to Washington and placed a severe strain on the municipal budget both during and immediately after the fighting. The civilian population doubled within a two-year period, and a city that had had a population of 61,000 in 1860 became one of nearly 200,000 within four years. During the war years, there were increasing problems with gambling, prostitution, drunken brawls, and "confidence" men. Juvenile delinquency, which had been an increasingly difficult problem in all cities during the turbulent 1850s, soared even higher during the war. The jail became badly overcrowded with a mixture of juveniles and professional criminals, the latter teaching their skills to the former. The city police were early made a Federal force, controlled by the national government and partly paid for by it. The provost marshal of the army was also given considerable powers.

Sanitation, in the face of a huge population increase and the large number of slaughterhouses, was a serious problem that tended to become worse. The young wife of a soldier wrote to her mother that ". . . there are no sewers, no cess pools or vaults for any purpose in the yards. . . . I was never in such a place for *smells*." A new water supply source was brought into the city by the army, but it was not in working order until July, 1864, and its effectiveness was limited by the inadequate sewerage system. Municipal garbage carts did not go to work until 1863, after which they were of considerable help in the collection not only of garbage but also of offal, dead animals, and other sources of odor and disease.

Fire losses were high in the city during the war. Many of the firemen had gone off to war. Fire hydrants were few and often ineffective. But there was a payoff to the city in that circumstances made it possible to unify eight fire companies in 1864 and to establish a paid department. The city entered the postwar era with a modernized department.

Heavy military and slaughterhouse wagons greatly damaged the streets of the city. Although Congress was urged to lend financial assistance for their repair and surfacing, it failed to do so.

After the war, the difficulties of the capital city continued. A rapid in-migration of freed slaves, now enfranchised, caused many whites to fear the loss of control over Washington government to blacks. The great increase in welfare and capital improvements expenditures added to the debt of the city, as did irresponsible spending. As 1870 approached, Congress was considering major changes in the form of government for the troubled city government. In 1871 it was to try establishing the District as a territory; three years later it was to end that experiment and end all local voting participation in the government of the District.

The reorganization of government in the South after the Civil War caused many of the Southern states and municipalities to adopt currently popular reform structures, although the counter-reform that took place after the removal of Federal troops encouraged many of the states to go back to their prewar practices. Thus, the Southern states were among the earliest to attempt to abolish special legislation and to establish general-act charters, but the South is today the principal area of the nation to use special legislation. Immediately after the Civil War most moves then regarded as progressive took place. For example, special legislation was outlawed in Arkansas in 1868. The following year the Florida legislature, which consisted of thirteen carpetbaggers, twenty-one "loyalists" (Southerners willing to cooperate with the Federal troops), nineteen Negroes, and twenty-three white conservatives, established a single general-act charter for all Florida towns and cities. The municipalities were given nine months in which to reorganize under the general act if they were not to forfeit their charters and their status as municipalities.

The story of the Reconstruction in the Southern cities belongs largely to the next volume, however.*

Special Problems

Although American practices of English origin generally dominated local government institutions, the rapid growth of some areas that had a different tradition and only recently had become American territory sometimes caused temporary conflicts during the period of transition. California, for example, had been under Spanish or Mexican control for centuries and had passed into American hands only shortly before the great gold rush began in 1849. San Francisco, like many other Califor-

* Griffith, *A History of American City Government, 1870–1900: The Conspicuous Failure* (New York, 1974).

nia communities, had been dominated by the military governor of the presidio. San Francisco continued to be so ruled until 1835, in which year a new town government was established under the Mexican general code. The government was now headed by an *alcalde* (mayor). About three years later, it was ruled that the community did not have sufficient population for town government, and the existing officers were replaced by two justices of the peace. In 1843, when the community had a population of about two hundred persons, city status was restored by governmental decree.

In 1846, when California was conquered by the United States, too many important activities were taking place for the temporary American leaders to be concerned with a San Francisco that still had a population of less than five hundred. The *alcalde* continued to rule, but in 1847 he appointed a town council to assist him. The governor objected, and the *alcalde* relented, permitting the council to be elected. With the discovery of gold a short distance away in the foothills of the Sierra Nevada, the city of San Francisco was almost completely vacated by the rush to the gold fields. But this outward surge was quickly more than replaced by persons arriving by sailing ship in the great harbor that was so conveniently located for access to the new source of riches. Many people quickly learned that it was generally more profitable to sell supplies to the miners than to do the actual mining. San Francisco boomed, and by 1849 confusion reigned. Three different groups each claimed to be the real city council. As almost always happened in the Western boom towns, however, the Main Street merchants were anxious to have a stable government to protect their expanding businesses. A mass meeting was held at which a tentative city government was established. The office of *alcalde* was abolished, and its powers were transferred to the new position of police magistrate, but the governor overruled this action and not only re-established the office of *alcalde* but provided for two of them. Stormy conflict then arose among the first *alcalde*, the council, and the territorial governor over the matter of taxes.

As late as 1850, the year of formal incorporation, San Francisco still experienced difficulties in the transition from Mexican to Anglo-American practices. In that year, the city government protested against interference with local self-government by the governor, who was continuing to follow precedents of Mexican law, in which the concept of local governmental autonomy was weak. A short time later, the first legislature of California provided San Francisco with a special-act charter providing for an American type of mayor-council government. The legislature replaced this hastily drafted document the next year with a new one, followed by a third in 1855. The following year the San Francisco Consolidation Act was passed in order to combine the county and city governments. As far as possible, city officials were to exercise county functions, and those county offices that necessarily had to be continued were to be paid for by the city. The city council and county board of supervisors were consolidated, using the latter name and giving the city-county a different governing board from any of the regular counties of the state. The president of the board of supervisors was given a veto power and other characteristic powers of a mayor, rather than of the presiding officer of a county board, and the title was later changed to mayor. This act of consolidation by the state was logical on the basis of geography alone, for the city was situated at the tip of a narrow peninsula. It was hailed locally as a great success when it was found that, while the costs of the city and county operating separately in 1855 had involved a total budget of $2,646,000, the consolidated city-county had needed a budget of only $353,000 in fiscal 1857. The legislature had cooperated in throwing the rascals out.

The case of mining camps in the West, particularly those resulting from a sudden gold or silver strike, demonstrated the speed with which regular legal institutions and procedures were established. In California the confusion created by an enormous gold find and a rapid influx of population was compounded by the confusion resulting from the recent taking over of the area from Mexican control. In his classic study of the mining camps, Charles Howard Shinn tells us:

When, early in 1848, mining began at Coloma, near Sutter's Mill, Captain [John A.] Sutter himself had *alcalde* powers over the region. That autumn Mr. Belt was elected *alcalde* at Stockton [where only one house had stood the year before]. The two thousand Americans who were living in California in February, 1848, were nearly all in the mines before the end of June; and most of them knew what an *alcalde* was, knew that they had no legal right to elect any other officer, and knew that Colonel [Richard B.] Mason, the *de facto* governor, was the only other authority.[15]

The miners, however, generally took a highly empirical approach to local government. None at all was established until actually needed. Decisions were usually made by an assembly made up of all those who held a claim, irrespective of age. For trials, a judge would be selected by the assembly, and verdicts were rendered either by a jury appointed by the judge or by a vote of all the assembled miners. Assemblies also adopted any local ordinances that were thought to be necessary.

The rapid growth in population and in demand for mining claims and the expected surge of migrants the next year made it clear that the informal, pragmatic method would not do. Therefore,

. . . upon the coming-on of winter, the great majority of the miners returned to their homes in the towns. . . . They felt, as all Americans feel,

that the most important step they could take, and that most imperatively
called for by the wants of the inhabitants, was the establishment of a stable
system of government, which would command the respect and obedience
of the people whose property it protected, and whose rights it preserved.
Congress had adjourned without providing a Territorial government; and
the public had settled into the firm conviction that the *de facto* government was radically defective, and incapable of answering the public's
wants.[16]

By December, 1848, steps were being taken to organize a "provi-
sional Territorial government," but when a constitutional convention
met for this purpose it was decided that territorial government would be
inadequate and inappropriate. The members issued a call for a new
convention to meet and prepare a state constitution. This meeting took
place at Monterey the following September, and a year later California
became a state. The new legislature then promptly established a conventional relationship to local governments. Both the constitution and
the early legislative acts relative to municipal government borrowed
from practice in the other states, and particularly relied upon the Iowa
constitution of 1846.

Sharp, politically motivated conflicts between local officials and state
legislatures over charters and powers took place with increasing fre-
quency at the approach of 1870. As Chicago grew rapidly and became
more wealthy, it came to be subjected to increasing control by the Illinois legislature. Conflict over where the decisions should be made was
intensified after 1860, when the city and state governments were frequently in the hands of different political parties.

In 1857 Lawrence, Kansas, refused to accept a city charter from the
"pro-slavery" legislature, claiming that the legislature had been elected
by fraud. The city fathers then framed and put into operation their own
charter, but the governor demonstrated his objection to this unorthodox
move by having four hundred United States soldiers sent to Lawrence.
This was one of quite a number of situations in which the local residents prevailed in the end. After a few weeks President Buchanan ordered the troops withdrawn, and the next year the legislature repealed
the state-granted charter and legalized the one that was in use in the
city.

In 1860 and 1861 the new community of Denver experienced some
chartering difficulties. It was first granted a charter in 1860 by the extra-
legal legislature of the state of Jefferson. By summer this had disintegrated, and a vigilance committee established a new charter without
outside sanction. In 1861 the new territory of Colorado was established,
and it granted the city its first legal charter.

Notes

1. J. S. Kendall, *History of New Orleans* (Chicago, 1922).
2. George F. Robeson, *The Government of Special Charter Cities in Iowa* (Iowa City, 1923).
3. *Ibid.*
4. *Ibid.*
5. *State of Iowa* v. *City of Des Moines*, 96 Iowa 521.
6. J. F. Dillon, *Commentaries on the Law of Municipal Corporations*, 5th ed. (Boston, 1911).
7. State of Ohio, *ex rel. Knisely* v. *Jones*, 66 Ohio St. 453.
8. Robeson, *op. cit.*
9. Dillon, *op. cit.*
10. Eugene McQuillin, *The Law of Municipal Corporations*, 3d ed. (Chicago, 1949).
11. For Cooley's decision, see *Michigan ex rel. LeRoy* v. *Hurlbut*, 24 Mich. 44. For the weaknesses in his legal reasoning, see H. L. McBain, "The Doctrine of an Inherent Right of Local Self-Government," *Columbia Law Review*, vol. 16, March and April, 1916.
12. Robert J. M. O'Hare, "Cities Rush Home Rule Gate," *National Municipal Review*, 42:73–77, February, 1953.
13. Robeson, *op. cit.*
14. H. L. McBain, *Law and Practice of Municipal Home Rule* (New York, 1933).
15. Charles H. Shinn, *Mining Camps: A Study in American Frontier Government* (New York, 1884).
16. *Ibid.*

Chapter 3

INTERGOVERNMENTAL RELATIONS

DURING THE FIRST CENTURY of the Republic intergovernmental relations took place with a smaller volume of traffic than has been the case in the twentieth century. Yet the same kinds of relationships were to be found. Research, particularly by Morton Grodzins and Daniel Elazar,[1] has demonstrated that national, state, and local levels of government have always cooperated in dealing with many matters of public policy. States' rights advocates have long argued that the relationships among the levels of government and particularly between the national and the state-local levels are competitive in character. They see a situation in which the state and local governments lose whatever power is picked up by the national government. The Grodzins and Elazar researches indicate, however, that while rivalry and conflicts did sometimes exist, the basic pattern has been cooperation and shared decision-making.

Cooperation in the twentieth century has been encouraged by the professionalization of the bureaucracy at all levels of government. Because a professional in a particular field, say education or public health, tends to share the same values, standards, goals, and procedures as do other professionals irrespective of the level of government in which they operate or whether they are within government at all, they are often able to work together in harmony. Because bureaucracies in the nineteenth century and earlier were not professionalized, the pattern of interrelationships was quite different. The principal contacts were between members of legislative bodies, although sometimes members of the executive branch were also involved. And, indeed, there was more than a hint of the likely future pattern of interrelationships. For example, most of the available supply of civil engineers in the early nineteenth-century United States was to be found in the United States Army. These specialists were often lent to states and cities, where their specialized knowledge was essential to the solving of such problems as the building of a bridge.

In Loco Parentis

Although the states and their cities often worked together in harmony, the states made it clear that municipalities were their children and did not hesitate to exert parental authority, and the cities, like children, sometimes rebelled or at least resisted. In 1777, for example, in newly independent New York State, the legislature hastened to establish its authority by expressly reconfirming the colonial charter for the (then British-occupied) City of New York. The states asserted their control, particularly after about 1820, through the extensive use of special legislation to control the authority of municipalities. In 1828, for example, when Camden, New Jersey, was incorporated as a city and separated from Newton township (it then had a population of only 1,143), it was sharply restricted in its municipal powers by special legislation. Perhaps the legislators believed that such a small community could not effectively govern itself. In any case, practically its only powers were to license taverns, protect life and liberty, and abate nuisances. Other possible activities were not authorized, and certain actions were specifically forbidden. For example, Camden was the only city in the state that could not levy taxes on agricultural lands or buildings. Many of the powers that normally would belong to the municipality were instead assigned to the township. One writer noted: "So closely are the affairs of the city and township connected that it is difficult to always distinguish the actions of the town meetings, which were sometimes called on township matters and sometimes on city affairs." But this type of close check upon the powers of the municipality was usually quite short-lived. Thus, in 1844 legislative control was lessened over a community now much more populous. The mayor, instead of being appointed, was made popularly elective. Powers over streets were transferred from the township to the city, and in 1848 the township was abolished and its powers in the Camden area were transferred to the city.

Occasionally the legislatures would offend a particular community by offering it less status than it seemed to deserve, at least in the minds of the local inhabitants. This particularly occurred whenever more than one community was incorporated in the same legislative session. Thus, the Georgia legislature incorporated both Augusta and Savannah in 1789, indeed, in the same act. But the former, a smaller community, was given merely town status, while the latter was made a city. The inhabitants of Augusta were reported to be greatly offended. But the views of inhabitants sometimes changed when they discovered that a higher status often carried with it responsibility for carrying out additional functions, which meant higher taxes. The residents of Augusta probably objected with special vigor because between 1786 and 1795 their city was the state capital. No doubt to many this implied city status. In the legislative session of 1791, after many protests, Augusta was made a city. The title of "intendant" was changed to mayor, and the mayor's court was established with the same powers as those in Savannah. The practical financial meaning of city status was soon brought home to the inhabitants, and in 1795 the incorporation of the city was repealed as "incompatible with the interests and wishes of the inhabitants." But the community continued to grow, and in 1798 Augusta was again incorporated as a city.

In 1857 the New York State legislature revised the charter of the City of New York and refused to submit the changed version to a vote of the people of the city. Control of the police was removed from the city and vested in a board for the metropolitan district. The first members of the police board were appointed by the governor and subsequently elected by the legislature. The board had jurisdiction over the police of both the city and the adjoining (and then independent) city of Brooklyn, as well as some adjoining urbanizing territory. The plan was borrowed from the metropolitan police system of London. One writer noted:[2]

So unsatisfactory and even corrupt had been the management of the city's affairs [by Fernando Wood and the "Forty Thieves"], so insecure property and even life within its borders, that the Republican state government felt impelled to intervene. Hope of party advantage may have prompted its action, but its legislation had strong backing in public sentiment. Nevertheless, this legislation was not carried into effect without tumult and bloodshed, nor without intelligent opposition, for it involved nearly complete subversion of the principle of home rule, until then almost unbrokenly acknowledged. The city charter was radically altered; the election of all department heads except the corporation counsel and the comptroller was taken from the people and their appointment given to the mayor, upon confirmation by the common council; the city government was separated from the county government and a board of supervisors created to levy local taxes, canvass the vote and perform other county duties. For the ward . . . was substituted an arbitrary district so gerrymandered as to increase the strength of the Republicans in the board of aldermen. Councilmen were to be elected from senatorial districts. Charter elections were to take place the first Tuesday in December. Control of the police system was withdrawn from the city. A metropolitan district in imitation of the London system was established and there was created a police board, appointments to which were made at Albany. Later [1867], the government of the new Central Park was vested in a State Commission and a metropolitan fire district and health district also were formed.

This vast transfer of powers to the state government was tested in the courts (*People* v. *Draper*, 15 New York 532) and was sustained in the state supreme court by a bare majority.

The charter of 1857 was presented as a reform movement introduced by the state because the city had failed to clean out its own corruption.

It was more than that, however, for the Republicans, who had swept the preceding state elections, badly wanted to gain some power and patronage in the city. They got more than they had bargained for, however, because the new charter trod heavily upon the long-established and emotion-wrapped idea of local home rule. William Marcy Tweed, an ambitious local politician who was to take over New York City government in 1868 and become one of the first and perhaps the most notorious of all American city bosses, recognized the symbolic value of the home rule issue. Ostensibly it was his chief concern in city politics that power be returned to the local voters and officials. The "reform" charter was the vehicle that carried him to power.

Tweed, a Democrat, represented a threat to the Republican state administration, but he was an effective negotiator and opportunist in the stereotyped mold of big city bosses. In 1870 he managed, through the use of widespread bribery, to get from the legislature a new city charter that abolished the state appointments to boards of health, police, Central Park, and others. Control was returned to the city.

Special legislation (discussed in Chapter 2) was another means used by state legislatures to substitute their policy preferences for those of the city council and sometimes to control local patronage. It was the subject of increasing criticism throughout the 1830s and 1840s. Community leaders began to demand that state constitutions be changed to prohibit special legislation and to require that states adopt legislation relative to municipalities only on the basis of general acts that applied to all cities or at least to classes of cities.

The Imposition of State Will

The states sometimes acted in cases where communities apparently failed to do what was expected of them. In 1815 the North Carolina legislature prohibited stagnant ponds from being allowed to stand in seaport towns, presumably as a public health measure. It also forbade the accumulation of filth or dead animals within these towns and established a penalty of five dollars a week for each violation.

On rare occasions the state acted to abolish the very existence of a city by removing its charter. Thus the territorial council of Florida in 1835 wiped out Key West, a city of around 2,000 population. These kinds of extreme actions were, however, never successful for long. The council in this case soon re-enacted the charter in response to local protests.

The states did not hesitate to step in where local communities did not seem to react quickly enough to threats that were interpreted outside their boundaries—and sometimes within them—as endangering the entire state or a substantial segment of it. Thus North Carolina took steps to reduce the threat of yellow fever and other diseases to the extent that they were understood in those days, and other states did the same. After a yellow fever outbreak—a common and terrifying threat to port cities in the eighteenth and nineteenth centuries—the Louisiana legislature in 1819 abolished the New Orleans Board of Health, and the state governor was given quarantine powers over the port. The board had been established only two years earlier under a state act that included a health code. Among its many provisions, the mayor was given authority and responsibility for preventing the landing of anything deemed injurious, and the Board of Health was expected to protect citizens from the spread of communicable diseases. This board almost immediately encountered what has come to be a classic problem in conflicts between levels of government: When the higher level imposes responsibilities upon the lower level without offering to pay the costs of those responsibilities resistance can be expected to develop. Such was the case in New Orleans:

> The opposition to this body was unquestionably based principally upon the idea that its regulations hampered unnecessarily the growth of the port. There was also some resentment towards it as a creature of the state legislature, thus representing the tendency of that body to interfere in purely local matters. This interference was hotly resented at all times in the history of New Orleans. In the latter part of 1819 the Board proposed to levy the tax which it was empowered by the Legislature to impose and with that end in view made a demand on the City Council for the assessment rolls. The Council refused to supply the document on the ground that the Board had not been elected by the people of the city, or by the Council, and that the city charter "assured to the citizens the right to appoint the public officers necessary for the administration of the police of the city." It seems probable that the inability of the board to obtain funds as the result of the council's perfectly correct attitude was what led to the changes which resulted in the concentration of the quarantine power in the hands of the governor in 1819.[3]

The council, then, in attempting to defend the principle of the right of local self-government, had failed to provide financial support for the board of health but unknowingly had chosen to take this stand just in time for it to appear to have been a case of dereliction of duty. Councilmen were forced to assume the blame for the yellow fever epidemic. The result was the state assumption of responsibility for administration of what had been considered to be a local function. The quote makes it clear that some, at least, of the local citizens did not view a public activity as being a local responsibility simply because it was imposed by the state legislature. But in the early part of the nineteenth century matters of public health were gradually coming to be recognized as municipal responsibilities, and the unfeasibility of their administration by the state government became increasingly evident. The public health powers assigned to the governor in this case, characteristically, did not remain with him long. In 1821 the power of quarantine and other responsibilities of the Board of Health of New Orleans were returned to local control.

Conflict was most likely to center on the relationships between the state legislature and the largest city of the state. The 1870s represented a time when there were many demands for increased expenditures by municipalities as a result of rapidly growing populations, the backlog of demand built up by the Civil War, the destruction in some cities resulting from the war itself, and the increasing concern about contagious diseases—especially cholera and yellow fever—which became more common as populations concentrated in cities and as American trade to foreign nations expanded. To make matters worse, much of the 1870s was plagued by a nationwide depression following the panic of 1873. Under these circumstances, legislatures sought to control the taxing, spending, and indebtedness of their cities, particularly the large ones. The states were especially concerned about property tax rates, since they themselves depended heavily upon this tax. The Illinois legislature in 1872 carefully circumscribed both the manner in which city councils could appropriate monies and the content of appropriation ordinances. The restrictions were especially aimed at Chicago. Restrictions on spending were seldom completely successful, however. Although the millage levy of the property tax could be controlled through court action, this was less true in the cases of limitations upon bonding power and, in general, whenever the voters in the community would support increased expenditures, ways around the state-established restrictions could usually be found.

Other cities had experiences similar to that of New Orleans concerning state imposition of responsibilities upon municipalities whether they wanted to assume them and their costs or not. In 1855 the Illinois legislature established a Board of Sewage Commissioners in Chicago after a cholera epidemic. In 1867 the New York legislature established minimum standards for tenements in the absence of adequate building and zoning codes in New York City (such codes were then virtually non-existent anywhere in the United States). This Tenement Act was not effective, and New York's notorious slums continued to expand. As in so many cases of a state-imposed local responsibility, administration of the act was left to local officials, and those in New York and Brooklyn often did not attempt to enforce the provisions.

In 1865 the New York legislature abolished all volunteer fire companies in New York City and required that they be replaced by paid companies. There was some local protest, not only because of the cost involved but also because membership in volunteer fire companies was a popular thing, often something of a status symbol in the neighborhood, and the volunteer companies were also, to a considerable degree, frequently important political organizations. The protest in this case rather quickly died down, in part perhaps because community leaders generally felt that such a development was inevitable.

The early part of the nineteenth century represented a period of rapid development of the public schools in the United States. Generally, and especially outside of New England, the schools came to be operated by a special district of government, local in character but independent or nearly so of the municipality and subject to the state or territorial school code, which often provided for different administrative and legal relationships between state and locality from those provided for between the state and municipal governments.

The states and territories, with the help of Federal aid in the form of land grants, pressed for the establishment of public schools in all communities. While some of the states provided grants-in-aid, considerable cost was involved in the construction and operation of the school buildings. Sometimes there was local resistance, but schools were so important in the eyes of Americans of the day that state insistence prevailed. Thus, in 1826 Louisiana required New Orleans to open one secondary and two primary schools. There was considerable local sentiment in favor of this, especially as the law provided revenue to finance the schools from license fees.

During this period there was also a trend toward giving school boards independent taxing and bonding powers and thus establishing them as special districts. This development was most pronounced outside of New England but was to be found there also. In the 1830s professional school superintendents began to play an important part in urban education, and by 1870 every large city except Philadelphia had a superintendent and a school board. Although professional administration of the schools began to appear, there still was no meaningful concept of a teaching profession, and in smaller communities there was not even a full-time administrator. Sometimes the president of the school board acted as an amateur superintendent.

Occasionally there would be a direct conflict of incentives and goals between the state and the city. Where the state's interest was supported by public opinion, it was certain to win. Thus, in 1841 Maryland and the city of Baltimore disagreed over fees to be charged for the use of wharves in the city and owned by it. These fees were an important source of income to the city, but from the state's point of view—the states were often more zealous business boosters than were the cities—they represented a threat to the growing tonnage that passed through the port of Baltimore, which was engaged in lively competition with Philadelphia, New York, and others. The result in this case was that the state arbitrarily reduced the wharfage fees despite the protests of the city.

Where state boosterism involved what appeared to be an unnecessary expense—and an expense to be borne locally at that—the eventual winner was not so obvious. In 1832 Louisiana authorized New Orleans to lay out and dedicate many new streets, but little action was taken by local authorities. On the other hand, when the legislature three years later passed an act prohibiting gambling in New Orleans, local officials did not bother to enforce the law. Perhaps the cultural differences between New Orleans and upstate Louisiana produced differing images of effective boosterism.

Utilities Regulation

The period between the 1820s and the 1880s was the gaslit era of the American city. A gas-lighting system was first installed in Baltimore in 1816, shortly to be followed by Boston and New York and then other cities.

As in the case of water supply, gas was generally provided by private companies rather than by the municipality. During this era there was little control over the companies. The municipalities usually extended long-term franchises with few restrictions and little supervision. (These were not always monopolistic; competitive utilities were not uncommon, until they proved to be impractical and financially unsound.) There apparently was relatively little protest against such practices at the time, because citizens were anxious to have utility development. The major utilities scandals did not come until electricity made possible the lighting of cities and the operation of streetcars. Although utility regulation later became a major factor in intergovernmental relations, state supervision over gas companies did not begin until 1885, when Massachusetts asserted such authority for the first time.

State Removal of Local Officials

Sometimes state officials would remove local officials from office. This might take place for misfeasance, malfeasance, or nonfeasance in office; because state and local officials belonged to different political parties; or for other reasons. After the Civil War, state-municipal conflicts in the South often centered on the struggle for power between the carpetbaggers and the leaders of the recently freed blacks on the one hand and the old aristocracy on the other. The leaders of the Old South were often more influential at the community than at the state level, where the governor had the support of Federal troops. Thus, in 1870 the Alabama governor removed the mayor of Mobile. A few years later Mobile was forced to surrender control of the public schools to the state board of education, which was carpetbagger-controlled and was attempting to get Negro education under way.[4] The New York State superintendent of schools was given power in 1864 to remove school commissioners or officials for neglect of duty.

Substitute Administration: The Police

Probably the most dramatic and most important state involvements in local policy-making and execution concerned the police function. As American cities grew, the citizens' nightwatch was replaced by full-time policemen, and these were eventually required to wear distinctive uniforms (see Chapter 4).

Beginning around 1850 a strong trend developed toward state control over the local police. The police represented an important center for party patronage and the recruitment of party workers during campaigns. Transfer of powers from municipality to the state, therefore, often took place when the legislative bodies at the two levels were in the hands of opposing political parties. Concern about corruption and incompetence probably also was occasionally a factor. Shortly after the Civil War, when many state governments were characterized by corruption and ineffectiveness, at least by middle-class standards, local and sometimes partisan pressures brought the return of the police to municipal control in most, but not all, cases.

A typical example of the struggle for police control occurred in Chicago. In the election of 1860 the Republicans had taken control of the Illinois state government, but Chicago remained in Democratic hands. In the 1861 legislative session the Chicago police were reorganized and placed under a state-appointed commission. The governor appointed all Republicans to the police board. Two years later, during the "off-year" election, the Democrats recaptured control of Illinois. They shortened the terms of members of the police board from six years to three years and then named Democrats to one-half of the seats on the board. In 1864 President Lincoln, running successfully for re-election, carried his home state of Illinois, and the coattail effect gave Illinois a Republican state administration once again. This time the legislators tried a tactic that they hoped would provide more lasting success. They restored the six-year terms for the police board but provided that members were to be elected rather than appointed by the governor. The catch was, however, that they were to be elected not merely by the voters of Chicago, where the police performed their functions, but by all the voters of Cook County. In the 1860s, as in the 1960s and most of the years in between, Chicago was strongly Democratic while the suburbs and satellite communities surrounding it in Cook County were overwhelmingly Republican.

Many other examples of state action to control local police could be cited. In 1866 the New York legislature created the Frontier Police District, which included the city of Buffalo and its police department, together with a few adjacent towns. Members of the police board were appointed by the governor, and so for a two-year period while that office and that of mayor of Buffalo were in opposing party hands, the state controlled police patronage. As early as 1820 Baltimore residents were complaining that the legislature often made changes concerning the police without local consent. In Boston a movement was begun in 1861 to place the police under a state board. There had been some complaints that the police did not enforce the law to provide protection for groups with which they were not in agreement. In particular, it was complained that they had made no attempt to protect meetings of the Anti-Slavery Society. In this case the legislative committee that considered the matter decided to let Boston continue to control its own police until the need for a change was more clearly demonstrated. Two years later criticisms of a rising crime rate together with a prohibitionist movement added to the demands for a transfer of the police power. The issue of prohibition was one of many manifestations of the conflict between Irish Catholics and Yankee Protestants in Boston. A joint special committee of the General Court (the Massachusetts legislature) made the following observation: "Large classes, having the rights of citizens but not the welfare of government at heart, always run into large cities as the common sewers of the State, and are ready to make use of just such machinery as the present system affords to them."

Many citizens of Boston protested the move toward centralization, and a committee of citizens reminded the legislators that general laws administered in local communities by officers of their own selection had always been regarded as an essential principle of free institutions in New England. This group argued that police power should be left to the towns and municipalities, and it denounced the proposed change as an "imputation upon the loyalty to law and order of a community which has been always justly distinguished at home and abroad for the excellence of its municipal government." But in 1865 the legislature established a state police force, with the ordinary patrolmen carrying the title of "Constable of the Commonwealth." The state police were expected to operate primarily in the city of Boston and adjacent urbanized areas. This approach was intended to be a compromise between those who wanted a metropolitan police force and the political leaders of Boston, who insisted upon local self-government. State control over the police was to become a continuing issue in the government and administration of Boston.

We have already noted that New York State established a metropolitan police district under a state board in 1857. This was changed so that the governor of New York was authorized to appoint the New York City police commission under the charter of 1867, although this arrangement lasted only for three years, after which the city received a new charter. The police of Baltimore in 1860, St. Louis in 1861, Detroit in 1865, and other cities were also placed under state control. It is possible that this pattern might still prevail today in our large cities were it not for the sharp decline in public, and especially middle-class, confidence in state government in the years following the Civil War.

Local Requests for Authority

Boston in the 1860s had a good deal of difficulty in getting authority from the General Court (state legislature) to develop streets and to levy special assessments in order to pay for them. The necessary legislation was finally passed, however, in 1866. The request of Savannah, Georgia, in 1817, for state aid in fighting smallpox was not acted upon. Other cities, too, often asked for state aid in connection with the terrible epidemics that were common during this period. Such requests were often rejected or ignored. Indeed, the common legislative response to epidemics was to require the cities at their own expense to establish boards of health and for these boards to clean up the filth of the cities. Filth was blamed for all types of illnesses in the absence of scientific knowledge, for the germ theory had not yet been developed.

The general pattern of relationships was one of cooperation on a voluntary basis. (It was not until near the end of the period under study that state legislators became seriously corrupt and venal and sought to dominate local policy in profitable ways.) Legislators generally were quite eager to see the cities grow in wealth and productivity, for they associated this with the growth of the nation. Many kinds of cooperation could be cited. Perhaps the most common type was for the state to grant the necessary powers for a community to perform some function the city considered necessary but where state action was required because of the narrow interpretation given to municipal powers by the courts. Thus, in 1819 Mobile was given powers to regulate its harbor. In 1835 the New Orleans Municipal Drainage Company was incorporated by the state, with both the state and the city buying a portion of the shares of stock. When the city of New York was authorized in 1834 to establish a municipal water system because of the inadequacy of service provided by the privately owned Manhattan Company, legislative support was given, even though it was necessary for the city to build an enclosed aqueduct from Croton Reservoir, forty miles north of the city, and extending through the jurisdiction of numerous local governments, many of which were hostile to the project.[5]

In 1851 the New York legislature first authorized the city of New York to acquire land for what was to become Central Park. Perhaps the argument that such a large park in the heart of the city was in the interest of protecting public health and preserving some aspects of the beauties of rural America was effective. In any case, the legislatures of the mid-nineteenth century in New York and other states authorized the beginnings of park systems, often placing them under semi-independent governing boards established by state law, but locally administered and financed.

The states often sought to encourage local governments in the establishment of schools. Aid for construction was relatively uncommon and for operations nearly unknown. But some assistance was provided. In 1841, for example, Rhode Island enacted a statute allowing local communities to borrow from the state at low rates of interest for the construction of school buildings.

At that time many and perhaps most states followed a policy of accepting the wishes of any city government concerning additional powers or minor charter alterations. The dramatic power struggles were still between the national and state governments. The great amount of local legislation may have been a nuisance to legislators, but it was an entirely practical approach to the handling of state-local relations at that period in history.

Perhaps the eagerness of state governments to encourage the development of urban communities for the benefit of the state and the nation is best demonstrated by a quotation from the New Jersey act of 1784 that renewed the corporate powers of the city of Perth Amboy:

> Whereas the improvement of trade and navigation in this State is of the utmost importance to the well-being of the same; and whereas the prosperity of trade requires the collection of merchants together in sufficient numbers in order that the union of their force may render them competent to great undertakings, and that the variety of their importations and their wants may always furnish to the purchasers and sellers a secure and constant market; and whereas, it is necessary . . . to bestow on merchants peculiar immunities and privileges . . . : and inasmuch as commercial cities require a peculiar mode of government for maintaining their internal police and commercial transactions; require more expeditious and summary tribunals than others . . . and whereas . . . the inhabitants . . . have set forth that for many years previous to the late revolution, the said . . . Perth Amboy under and by virtue of charters . . . did hold . . . powers, privileges and immunities, which they found greatly beneficial . . . be it therefore enacted [etc.].

Perth Amboy, then a town of not more than 1,000, had been the capital city. Both its leaders and those of the state government were anxious to re-establish economic development after the war. But state-local relations were soon to become less cordial as state legislatures began to make policy in areas that many city-dwellers considered local in character.

Interlocal Relationships

Richard Wade, writing about frontier cities, has concluded that "virtually no major project was launched [in such places] without a close study of established urban practices."[6] Thus, in 1829 the St. Louis council asked its water works committee to get information about water mains and water purification from Philadelphia and New Orleans. When Cincinnati was considering building a sewerage system in 1827, a delegation was sent to learn of the practices and problems of the principal Eastern Seaboard cities. Pittsburgh, that same year, looked carefully into the practices of Baltimore and New York while planning for a system of gas lighting. That city's housing ordinance of 1828 borrowed directly from Philadelphia's of 1796. When an emerging frontier urban settlement sought to incorporate as a municipality, its leaders often proposed to the legislature a charter borrowed largely from the city from which they had come, or they wrote back East, asking for charters from communities they thought it appropriate to copy. Because Western state legislatures were simultaneously building up bodies of law based on older practices in the East, municipal corporation law and city charters came to be highly similar from one state to another, at least in terms of fundamental approaches. They usually differed for the most part only in detail.

Local communities that had common boundaries or were only a short distance apart were faced with a different situation from that facing frontier communities in their relationships with older communities across state lines. They found matters upon which to cooperate, but relationships under conditions of close proximity seem often to have been more competitive than cooperative. (The great majority of communities did not, of course, have any basis for direct interaction at that time in the development of the nation, for cities were generally well spaced.) Communities were often anxious to beat their rivals in the rate of population growth, the number of jobs available, or the rate of increase in the value of local real estate. Then, as today, residents outside the corporate city limits often benefited from—or were victimized by, depending upon one's point of view—nearness to the city and even from some of its services. In 1853 the city limits of Hartford, Connecticut, were extended over the bitter opposition of those whose property was to be taken into the city. Similarly, for the fifteen years following 1865, the city of Key West, Florida, made many attempts to annex territory outside of its city limits, but these efforts were opposed by affected property owners, who feared that annexation would increase their taxes without an offsetting increase in the value of services rendered. The state legislature refused to change the law, which required concurrent approval within both the existing city and the area to be annexed.

Sometimes a city would oppose the incorporation of another city adjacent to it. In the 1830s New York tried hard to block in the legislature the incorporation of Brooklyn. Although it succeeded for a time, a charter was granted in 1834. (The two municipality-counties, along with three other counties, were eventually amalgamated into a single City of New York in 1898.)

Federal-Municipal Relationships

While Federal-municipal direct relationships were rare in the period under study, and probably neither ordinary citizens nor leaders thought the national government had much business with cities as such, some developments were already taking place that were indicative of things to come. For example, cities benefited indirectly from Federal land grants for public education, policies for this being based upon the Northwest Ordinance of 1787, enacted before the adoption of the United States Constitution. We have already noted that the Federal government also extended grants-in-kind to cities by lending them the skills of civil engineers in the Corps of Engineers of the United States Army. As Daniel Elazar has pointed out, the need for internal improvements and for systems of public education were two of the three most important issues confronting Americans during this period (the other was to provide a national system of banking and finance, with which cities were not directly concerned or in a position to make policy). And, as Elazar has indicated, government at all three levels simultaneously attempted to deal with these problems.[7] Other developments, at least symbolically, indicated the shape of things to come. About 1818 the New Orleans city council sent several petitions—unsuccessfully—to Congress asking that the Federal government provide grants for the erection of public buildings in the city. Nothing was done at the time, but a similar policy was to be successfully adopted in the 1930s, nearly twelve decades later.

Closing Note

Intergovernmental relations in the period between the Declaration of Independence and the years immediately following the Civil War were characterized by both cooperation and conflict. The former appears to have been the dominant pattern, although some degree of rather infrequent conflict seems to have taken place between state and local units of government. Furthermore, while the Federal government was already beginning to make decisions that affected cities, Federal-municipal contacts were uncommon during this period. Although the states frequently sought to impose their will in local decision-making, especially when there was a conflict of political party interest between the state and local levels, the usual pattern was one of cooperation designed to encourage the rapid growth of population and development of the American economy, an interest shared by decision-makers at all levels of government.

Notes

1. Morton Grodzins, "The Federal System," in the *President's Commission on National Goals* (Englewood Cliffs, N.J., 1960), and Daniel J. Elazar, *American Federalism: A View from the States* (New York, 1966).
2. M. J. Lamb, *History of the City of New York* (New York, 1896), pp. 82ff.
3. J. S. Kendall, *History of New Orleans* (Chicago, 1922), p. 114.
4. For more on this, see Ernest S. Griffith, *A History of American City Government 1870–1900: The Conspicuous Failure* (New York, 1974).
5. Nelson M. Blake, *Water for the Cities* (Syracuse, N.Y., 1956), Chap. 7.
6. Richard C. Wade, *The Urban Frontier* (Cambridge, Mass., 1959).
7. Daniel J. Elazar, *The American Partnership* (Chicago, 1962).

Chapter 4

MUNICIPAL FUNCTIONS AND POLITICAL ISSUES: HEALTH, EDUCATION, AND WELFARE

THE CENTURY FOLLOWING American independence saw the pre-eminent development of the trading town. The industrial city was not to begin its great spurt of growth until the time of the Civil War. It was in the industrial center that the notorious city bosses and machines flourished, rather than in the modest-sized communities we are concerned with here. In the trading towns, interest groups and political parties, often including third parties, were important, but to a considerable degree the ordinary citizen could make his views on issues known directly to the mayor or, at the least, to his ward alderman.

The issues of those days varied in detail from those of the latter half of the twentieth century, but many troublesome matters of that period remain extremely familiar. Some items, of course, were probably of greater relative public concern then than now. Political issues included problems of pollution of the environment and the desired extent and quality of public education. The costs and possible abuse of public welfare were also debated. The protection of the consumer in those days was a problem for the city council rather than Congress. A leading problem was that of public health in an age of increasing urban population concentration. The need for adequate systems of water supply and sewerage was closely related to health.

By 1840 "reform" was in the air. It affected the programs in public health, the growth of the public schools, the treatment of the mentally disturbed (then called the "insane," which was a legal rather than a medical concept), jail and prison practices, the control of the sale of alcoholic beverages, and other matters. Evangelical Protestantism, which in the next decade was to be turned into a politically active form of anti-Catholicism, was a driving force behind these new concerns for the disadvantaged and for those who hoped to compete successfully within the rules of what was often their adopted country.

The public schools were considered to be a center for the teaching of moral values and behavior. Dorothea Dix was inspired to attempt to secure reforms for the mentally disturbed after she observed the conditions under which these persons were intermixed with common criminals in the Cambridge, Massachusetts, jail where she had volunteered in 1841 to teach a Sunday school class. Her subsequent investigation and her report to the state legislature in 1843 led to the establishment of mental hospitals first in Massachusetts and subsequently in many other states. Early concerns in the United States about the consumption of alcoholic beverages resulted in efforts to discourage the use of high-proof distilled liquors, thus the use of the term "temperance." The American Society for the Promotion of Temperance, founded in Boston in 1826, was strongly supported by many Protestant churches. By 1836 the organization had moved on to an endorsement of complete abstinence, and the battle for the prohibition of the manufacture and sale of all alcoholic drinks was under way.

Some issues of the day are no longer of much concern to us or, to the extent that they are, are fought in the state or national political arenas rather than locally. Examples are the prevention of communicable disease epidemics and the protection of consumers. Hovering over all of the issues that implied the raising of standards and hence the expenditure of greater sums of money was the ever present issue of how services should be paid for.

Public Health

As American cities grew larger and existing sewage disposal systems became more and more inadequate, the country was struck by wave upon wave of serious outbreaks of communicable diseases. In addition to the childhood illnesses, which carried off a large proportion of youngsters, adults often suffered from such potentially fatal diseases as smallpox and many viral diseases, particularly cholera, typhoid fever, and yellow fever. These would often begin in a port city and then spread inland. Cholera and typhoid fever are commonly transmitted by contaminated drinking water. Yellow fever, although primarily a tropical disease, is capable of spreading in epidemics to the temperate zones. It is transmitted by several types of mosquitoes. While cholera and typhoid fever are controlled through maintaining the quality of water supplies, yellow fever is controlled primarily by elimination or treatment of swamps, bogs, and other places where still water may be found. Many American coastal cities of the nineteenth century, particularly port cities, were nearly surrounded by swamps and bogs. Vaccination against smallpox, especially of school children, began about the time of the Civil War.

How serious communicable diseases could be may be illustrated by New Orleans in 1855–56, when the three leading causes of death were yellow fever (2,760), cholera (1,029), and tuberculosis (652). These included two-thirds of all the deaths of those under age thirty. Yellow fever was feared the most. The 1855–56 epidemic in Norfolk caused 2,000 deaths and left the city almost desolate. The worst visitation in New Orleans was in the summer of 1853, when more than 7,000 died. The Irish and German immigrants were particularly hard hit in the cities like New Orleans and Memphis, where they had settled in considerable numbers. The Irish were also unusually susceptible to typhoid, even in a "model" city like Lawrence. The poor suffered the most everywhere.

As garbage piled up and dead animals lay in the streets, as the open drains that served as sewers became more foul, and as epidemics swept across the land, people became increasingly concerned about public health. The germ theory of disease being as yet unknown, the tendency was to blame filth and hence to emphasize as part of a public health program the cleaning up of garbage and dead animals and the covering of sewers. How little was understood of where the dangers lay can be seen in a remark by John H. Wilkins, a prominent Whig politician in Boston. In 1845, commenting on the quality of the public water supply, he insisted that running water was purer than pond water for, he thought, it had fewer living organisms in it. By this he meant living things visible to the naked eye, adding, "For it is to such only that anyone can attach much importance."[1] In Philadelphia, around the beginning of the nineteenth century and stretching over many years, control of the board of health was a contest between the "contagionists" and the "noncontagionists," each advocating a different set of policies based on their assumptions.

The level of information about public health in the mid-nineteenth century is well demonstrated in the Griscom report of 1845.[2] John H. Griscom was a physician and a pioneer in the New York public health movement. Had he lived in Philadelphia, he would have joined the noncontagionists, who represented the predominant view of the day. The following was the basic theory of disease entertained by Dr. Griscom:

> Summer is the season generally deemed most prolific in diseases; the cause usually assigned for this is the heat of the weather acting upon animal and vegetable matter, producing more extensive and rapid decomposition, the gases from which are generally imagined to be so destructive to health and life. It is true that certain diseases prevail mostly during the hot months— these are Yellow Fever, Cholera Infantum, and the like, while Typhoid and Bilious diseases are frequent in autumn, the latter also attributable to the same cause. The quantity of these offensive vegetable and animal ma-

terials is, therefore, among other things, supposed to be, in a considerable degree, the generator, and regulator of the intensity of these diseases. But this is not by any means the whole of this subject. By a reference to some of the Annual Mortality Reports, it will be seen that sometimes as great a number of deaths occurs during the cold months as during the hot. These are mostly of those affections attributable to the influence of cold and of increased moisture, principally diseases of the Lungs.

Laymen had about as much knowledge of medicine as did physicians in those days, and they energetically joined the debates over the causes of epidemics and possible preventive measures. Thus, a citizen of Newark in 1807 wrote as follows:

At a time like the present when an epidemic has spread universally through our town, would it not seem well for us to enquire whether sufficient attention has been paid to the means of preserving public health? What is the situation of our streets? Are they freed from stagnant water, from putrid substances, or do they present a scene of filth and putrefication? The latter is the case; it is not infrequent to see dead animals in our streets and about our public market house the feet and heads of dead animals. These things are offensive; they pollute the air we breathe and have a sensible effect on our health. These gross violations call loudly for public interference.[3]

Demands for action triggered a trial-and-error approach to public policy-making that is characteristically American. The first efforts were taken before the end of the eighteenth century. New Haven, for example, adopted port quarantine regulations in 1794 and established a board of health the following year. The regulations posed a typical problem in urbanizing America. Quarantine laws involve fairly elaborate enforcement procedures if they are to be effective. These require a bureaucracy which in turn implies higher taxes. But increased levies are resisted. In New Haven this problem was solved when most of the work was done by volunteers, and direct costs were largely taken care of by gifts. Another problem was that rivalry among seaports was such that too-strict health and quarantine procedures were avoided in order not to drive commerce and shipping to other locales. The boards in seaport cities (and elsewhere) consisted almost entirely of physicians.

Soon after the turn of the century boards of health began to be established in many cities. Savannah named one in 1804, although it was abolished four years later and replaced by a committee of the council. Boards were established in New York in 1805, in Philadelphia in 1818, in Chicago in 1837 (only four years after it was first incorporated as a village and the same year that it became a city), and Memphis in 1838. In 1855, after a series of cholera epidemics, the Illinois legislature established a Board of Sewerage Commissioners for Chicago. In 1861 the sewers were put under the city's Board of Public Works. Progress was steady. The six miles of sewers in 1854 had grown to 140 in 1871. By 1879 it was reported that the death rate had been greatly reduced.

The early boards of health tended to reflect the simultaneous public demand for action relative to a problem, in this case epidemics, and for keeping taxes low. Characteristically, the boards operated on low budgets with very few personnel. Usually, they did little except during outbreaks when they would impose temporary regulations concerning sanitation and isolation. The public, although concerned and fearful, did not always offer its support. A board of health was established in New Orleans in 1817, and it attempted to use the quarantine technique against a yellow fever outbreak. The public objected to the inconvenience and argued that the quarantine was not an effective approach to the control of the disease. (In this case, the protestors happened to be right, though not for reasons they could have known.) Two years later the board of health was abolished and the governor was given the power of quarantine. In 1821, however, the board was re-established. Organized sanitation measures became more widespread after the United States Sanitary Commission was established in 1861.

Early sewerage systems in America were very simple or nonexistent. That of New York in 1789 consisted only of slaves, "a long line of whom could be seen late at night wending their way to the river, each with a tub on his head." The streets of American cities in the first half of the nineteenth century were filled with decaying garbage, excrement of man and animals, and stagnant pools in every low place. Around the edges of public markets were stacked the decaying, smelly leftover vegetables, meat, and fish. Indeed, the public markets were strewn with "the heads of sheep, lambs, &c. the hoofs of cattle, blood, and offals strewed in the gutters, and sometimes on the pavement dead dogs, cats, rats, and hogs." Until the fourth or fifth decade of the century, often until after the Civil War, there was little in the way of sanitation systems. New York in the late 1830s was called "one huge pigstye." Hogs and other scavengers, in fact, did more than the city government to clean up the mess, but they never were able fully to succeed. Boston, a city of 85,000 in 1840, had no sewers, and that was the accepted situation at the time.

Cities generally regulated the building of outhouses and established rules concerning their periodic cleaning, but these were not always enforced, particularly in rapidly growing cities. The coming of the indoor toilet, originally known as a "water closet," led to demands both for water systems and for sewerage lines. Shortly after taking office in 1801, President Thomas Jefferson had an indoor toilet installed in the White House, although no American patent was issued for such a device until 1833.[4] In the 1840s and 1850s, both the indoor toilet and the bathtub became matters of popular demand. Outhouses were not prohibited in cities, however, for a long time. As sewers replaced outhouses and cesspools, they ordinarily merely carried the sewage to a nearby body of water, where natural chemical action was assumed to take care of the purification process.

Gradually improved sewer systems proved a boon to the health of the city. But the most important health improvement involved the development of pure sources of water.

Water Supply

Issues of water supply during the first century after independence focused primarily on three matters: the securing of a pure supply, disputes concerning alternative sources of water, and private versus municipal ownership. Although bitter battles were fought before city councils and in the newspapers over the first of these issues, the problem was complicated by the uncertainty as to just what constituted pure water. This issue was tied in with the second, but the issue of alternative sources was often complicated by the pressures exerted by the owners of land dominating the access routes. The last issue was a "service-versus-profit" issue; the "service" side argued that water supply was so closely connected with the questions of public health and firefighting that its provision could not safely be left to private companies. The record shows that the American urbanite of the early nineteenth century commonly considered himself an authority on public water supply and did not hesitate to offer his opinion when the problem of a new source arose, which was quite frequently.

In Boston the issues of purity and source were kept alive and not finally settled for more than a generation. The public policy debate could be said to have started on April 7, 1825, when the city was ravaged by a great fire. The city council immediately began a series of inquiries, which produced, among other things, a recommendation for a new water supply. In the course of the long controversy four different sources were considered, with the final alternatives being between Spot Pond and Long Pond. The issue was aired before the city council, the state legislature, public meetings, and saloon bartenders. Pamphlets, newspaper editorials, and even poems were written in support of each side. Finally, by a referendum held on December 9, 1844, the Long Pond faction won the big victory. Two weeks later the council endorsed the public referendum and instructed the mayor to apply to the legislature for the powers needed to build the necessary aqueduct. Further controversy followed, and on one occasion a referendum was actually lost by the Long Pond faction, but finally it was victorious.

The new water source that was to be the salvation for Boston hardly bore an impressive name, but while the project was in the planning stage the water commissioners announced that they had engaged in considerable research and had discovered that the Indians had called the pond "Cochituate." They then explained, apparently with straight faces and an audacity that would give a contemporary representative of Madison Avenue pause, that the name meant, "an ample supply of pure and soft water, of sufficient elevation to carry it into the City of Boston, at a moderate expense."[5] The mayor proposed that Long Pond be known as Lake Cochituate, a suggestion that was happily adopted, and the Cochituate Aqueduct was constructed with relatively few important interruptions. The project was completed, and a great celebration in recognition of the opening of the aqueduct was held on Boston Common on October 25, 1848.

The greatest project in the first half of the nineteenth century was one designed to bring water from the Croton River above Ossining to New York City.[6] As was often the case, many citizens argued against such a daring project and instead favored a source much closer to the city and hence less expensive. There were advocates of, among other possible sources, the Rye Ponds east of Tarrytown and the Bronx River. The possibility of building a dam across the Croton River and creating a reservoir had been discussed at least in elementary outline as early as the 1820s. In the following decade, as New York grew rapidly, discussion focused more on the Croton, but the idea of building a dam and an aqueduct to carry water more than forty miles into the city seemed to many a reckless venture. In 1834, however, the Common Council voted to ask the legislature to authorize it to raise the funds needed for the project. The legislature, after deciding that a board of water commissioners should be established to take charge rather than leave it in the hands of the annually elected Common Council, provided the necessary authorization for the Croton project on May 2, 1834. A year later the voters of the city approved it by a vote of about three to one. It was supported in twelve of the fifteen city wards, the only exceptions being in the sparsely settled northern portions of the city, where wells were still performing adequately.

The project was a long time under way, both because of the necessity to build a substantial dam and because in early 1841 heavy rains and melting snows nearly destroyed the almost completed dam. Finally, on June 27, 1842, water from the Croton River reached the city. Celebrations were held then and again on Independence Day, but the greatest celebration occurred at the time of the formal dedication on October 14 of that year. The importance of the occasion and the fervor of civic pride in the nineteenth century is indicated by the fact that Columbus Day was begun with the salutes of one hundred cannon and the ringing of church bells. Later there was a five-mile-long parade led by the governor and mayor and including militia, fifty-two companies of firemen, the butcher's guild (on horseback), representatives of temperance societies, and representatives of workingmen's organizations. At every appropriate place, fountains were turned on to demonstrate the force and plenitude of the new water supply. The project cost more than twice the original estimate of $5 million; including distributing pipes, interest, and other costs, it eventually ran to about $13 million. But there were few citizens, once the project was completed, who doubted its desirability and, indeed, necessity.

Similar great proposals were debated in other cities. The controversies, particularly as fire losses skyrocketed, grew more serious as one moved westward. As one historian has noted:

> So long as towns remained small, rivers and springs were sufficient, but as building moved inland, shortages became critical. Even before 1815 some people saw the need for comprehensive service through reservoirs and pipes, but the cost seemed prohibitive. The denser cities, however, worried by growing property damage, could no longer postpone action.[7]

In the 1820s Cincinnati and Pittsburgh installed water systems, and St. Louis began to plan one. Considerable discussion and controversy also took place in Louisville, although construction there was still several years off.

In Lowell, Massachusetts, a new water supply project was approved in an 1869 referendum by a vote of 1,866 to 1,418. At that time wells were still used even in the most crowded parts of the city. One well, used by at least one hundred persons, was supplied by street drainage, and water from sewers and vaults that was filtered through only a few feet of earth. In 1864 Worcester, Massachusetts, approved its first modern sewerage system by referendum vote of 1,867 to 70.

In the Far West, water for cities depended upon the availability of underground sources in porous rocks at or near the foot of mountain ranges. Winter snows melted and sank into natural caverns or rock formations that could provide supplies for cities of considerable size, as it was later discovered. Those who understood that this situation offered a possible supply, essential to any kind of urbanization of the West, became the founders of Western cities. They built, as a first order of priority, a *zanja madre* (mother ditch) for their proposed towns, leading from shallow (but later ever deepening) wells at the foot of mountains to the desired town location. This system lasted for a long time as a satisfactory source of water. In Los Angeles, for example, it was adequate until the early years of the twentieth century.

Another controversy centered on the question of who should operate water supply systems. Except in Philadelphia, the early systems were nearly always first proposed and operated by private firms. Fire insurance companies often added their advocacy. The New York legislature in 1799 had authorized a private firm, the Manhattan Company, to supply water to that city. Boston also began with a private company.[8] As early as 1810 a private citizen petitioned the St. Louis city council for an exclusive franchise to bring water into the city, and similar proposals were under discussion in Pittsburgh and Lexington a few years later. The Baltimore Water Company lasted longer than did most of the other private firms because it made greater efforts to satisfy its customers. Critics of the privately owned utilities generally complained that they were undercapitalized, did not make sufficient effort to extend their services into newly developed areas, and were unconcerned about either quality or quantity. The most common and insistent objection, however, was "that the chief view of the Water Company was to make money out of the necessities of the people."[9] In general, the result was a shift from private to public ownership, often with only token payments to the vilified owners of the private companies. The increasing emphasis upon the relationship between water supply and public health made it easier to gain support for such transfers. In the cities west of the Atlantic seaboard, public ownership was well established as the basic approach even before 1815, and the pattern was generally accepted in the East within the next generation. However, even in the 1890s about one-fourth of the systems in cities of under 100,000 remained in private hands.

Water, as a basic human necessity, was the focus for many types of community conflicts. Before water systems were installed, the question of the number and location of town pumps was frequently a matter of controversy. Later, concerns about the pollution of wells led to demands for controls over outdoor privies and cesspools. Another issue centered on the type of pipe to be used. The earliest pipes were made of wood— hollowed out logs. These had one considerable advantage. In case of a fire where no hydrant was conveniently available, a hole could be drilled into the main and a hose connected. Afterward a wooden plug could be driven home to repair the damage to the main (this was probably the origin of the term "fire plug" for hydrant). But wooden mains rotted quickly, and new debates arose over the replacement of them by more permanent but expensive iron pipe.

Still another controversy centered on the types of pipe to be used to bring water from the mains into homes and other buildings. In a day when there was a shortage of skilled labor and before the development of modern copper and plastic plumbing, it was common to use lead for such purposes. Lead had the great advantage of being easy to shape, hence it required less skill to install than was needed for iron piping. It had the disadvantage, however, of being poisonous to human beings. After a great deal of controversy over whether it was actually poisonous, cities began to prohibit the use of lead pipe in water supply systems. But such action was a long time in coming. A common approach was that used by the Boston Water Commissioners, who decided to use lead service pipes except in cases where the customers specifically requested iron.

In the South the pattern of water development was much like that of the North. In 1823, for example, Nashville authorized the construction of a private waterworks system, but this approach was subjected to a great deal of public criticism. In 1830, therefore, the city acted to develop a public system and borrowed money for the purpose. The city purchased a number of slaves to do the major share of the work, and the project was completed three years later at a cost of $55,000, only $5,000 more than had been borrowed for the purpose. The additional funds were raised by selling all but a few of the slaves, all of whom had increased considerably in value during the construction period. Those who were retained continued to do the basic maintenance work of the system until the Civil War. As in New York, Boston, and elsewhere, the opening of the new waterworks was made the occasion for a parade and a great public celebration.[10]

Consumer Protection

In medieval times, cities had the power and responsibility to protect the consumer from adulterated foods, false weighing and measuring, and certain other misrepresentations of products offered for sale. Although enforcement was spotty, American city governments of the nineteenth century were similarly authorized by charters or other state law to prevent the sale of spoiled meat, vermin-infested flour, and other kinds of putrified, unclean, or adulterated foods. Indeed, during this period, the consumer may have actually received more governmental protection than he has had at any later time in our history.

Municipal governments also sought to prevent cheating in the sale of goods by misrepresenting weights and measures. They assumed responsibility for checking scales as well as measuring various kinds of products offered for sale. Communities even acted to fix prices in some cases. Rules concerning the size, weight, and price of bread were particularly common.

Savannah offers an example of controls. In the 1790s the city council regulated the prices of many kinds of articles and services. Food was regulated as to quality and price. Taverns were subjected to regulation of the charges they could make for board and the maximum price for drinks, as well as charges for the care and feeding of horses. In 1800 Savannah citizens complained of butchering practices in the city and the council thereupon ordained that, "the hind quarters [are] to be cut into two pieces, the loin from the leg, and the forequarters to be cut into three pieces, the shoulder to be taken from the neck and breast, and the breast to be cut from the neck if requested by the purchaser." Even the fees of ministers and cemetery sextons were prescribed, with a penalty of $50 assessed for overcharging.

Bread was particularly a matter of concern to the citizens and community leaders:

> Attended by the clerk of the market and the marshal, an alderman would visit the several bakeries and shops, weigh and examine the bread. Loaves not complying with the requirements were seized and distributed among the poor and the offenders brought before Council and fined, generally four [shillings] and eight [pence].

A new "assize of bread" was prescribed by the Savannah city council in 1800, outlining the required price and quality as well as measurements. A similar ordinance was adopted in Augusta in 1808.

Similar practices prevailed in the frontier cities. Ordinances were adopted to protect the citizen from adulterated foods, false measurements, and rigged prices.[11] In 1819 St. Louis adopted an ordinance that provided that "no person shall sell or expose to sale any blown, stuffed, unsound, unwholesome, tainted, or putrid meat or other articles or provisions or measly pork." Violators were subject to fines up to $20 for the first offense and twice that for subsequent offenses. Municipal inspectors checked to ensure that bushels, pounds, cords, and other measures were accurate. They fixed prices on some goods, and the eighteenth-century assize of bread, controlling its quality and price, continued to be used on the frontier.[12] Honest efforts appear to have been made in many cases to enforce these regulations. It was not until after the Civil War that the common-law doctrine of "let the buyer beware" became the undisputed rule of the marketplace in the American city. Even then, inspection of weights and measures continued.

As America became increasingly committed to the doctrine of "free enterprise" there was a gradual decline in the scope of business regulation exercised by the city councils. The notion that the buyer had to be responsible for his own decisions became increasingly accepted. As a result, some of the traditional controls over business, many of which had come down from the Middle Ages, were abandoned. Thus, in 1820 the Albany city council repealed the assize of bread statutes, although it continued to regulate the size and quality of the loaf. Councils in other cities followed suit. In 1818 Worcester, Massachusetts, closed its free public market after a one-year experiment. Other cities did so, too, although the public market was never completely abandoned.

Public Libraries

Although no intense controversy arose over the development of public libraries in the United States, persons of genuine intellectual interest and others who were status conscious and wanted to show how "civilized" their community was, were eager to see to the development of libraries that were generally available to the public. The first such libraries were supported not by public funds but rather by private subscriptions, although they were generally available for use by the public. The first such library was established by Benjamin Franklin in Philadelphia in 1731. Private libraries spread throughout the East and by 1815 existed in nearly every urban center as far west as the Mississippi.[13] In 1803 the Salisbury, Connecticut, town council set a precedent by voting funds to support a local library for youth. The first library to be supported by taxes was established in Peterborough, New Hampshire, in 1833. That state was also the first to provide by statute—in 1849—for public tax-supported libraries. The Michigan Constitution of 1838 encouraged the establishment of public libraries. The Boston Public Library was begun in 1852. The Civil War interrupted public library development, but only temporarily. Although there was some opposition to the use of taxpayers' funds for what some regarded as a private purpose—that of reading and learning—the public library eventually became a standard municipal institution, particularly in the Middle West and the Far West. In New England and the South, libraries were sometimes continued as private, nonprofit institutions under self-perpetuating boards of trustees. Aside from formal control, however, these were virtually public libraries, because they were supported by funds appropriated by the council or by a special property-tax levy. The self-perpetuating boards were subject to considerable control by the council, which appropriated a goodly proportion of the library's funds.

Very few tax-supported libraries of any size existed prior to 1850. Most of the development followed after 1870.

Public Education

Public education at the primary and secondary levels as a local government responsibility has been developed in many competent histories and will not be given detailed attention here.[14] By the beginning of the movement for Jacksonian democracy in the 1820s, it was widely believed that education for all was a necessary thing if we were to have government "by the people." Earlier, Jefferson had assumed that an educated citizenry was the key to the problem of making democracy viable, and he argued for equal opportunity for education for all free citizens. This was the essence of his "Bill for the More General Diffusion of Knowledge," which was introduced into the Virginia legislature in 1779. His bill was never adopted into law, but his ideas of education for citizenship available to all had a lasting influence upon American educational policy. So did those presented somewhat earlier by Benjamin Franklin who, in his "Proposals Relating to the Education of Youth in Pennsylvania (1749), suggested that education should be both vocational and college preparatory and that both be achieved within the same secondary school.

In the early nineteenth century, and especially after the Jacksonian "revolution" of the 1820s and 1830s, interest in public education increased rapidly and broadly. It came to be viewed—following Jefferson's ideas—as essential for an informed citizenry that would govern a democratic nation. The movement toward universal manhood suffrage was assumed by Jeffersonians to imply the need for an educated public. The Jacksonian idea that anyone of reasonable intelligence could serve in public office was also interpreted to mean that education was a necessity for those who might be elected to public office.

Advocates of universal public education also emphasized the need for schooling because of the growth of trade and manufacturing. As the nineteenth century advanced, the ability to "read, write, and cipher" became increasingly important and a basis for preference in job hiring. Similarly, some persons came to argue that only universal education could mitigate the tendency toward an increasing gap between those who profited from the wealth created by new business opportunities and the rest of society. Free educational opportunities, it was believed, would open up the channels for social and economic opportunity and thus diminish the possible conflict between able but frustrated persons in lower status positions and those who had "arrived" economically and socially. Horace Mann and many others felt a deep connection between ignorance and poverty and saw universal elementary education as greatly aiding in the elimination of poverty.

Social reform that became a matter of public concern following the acceptance of Jacksonian values also added emphasis to the need for public education. The "cult of the common man" insisted that the ordinary individual was capable not only of choosing his rulers but of himself ruling. But in order to do this, it was assumed, he should have a basic education. Hence, if government was to be by the common man, it should be by an *educated* man. Those who held to this belief did not doubt but that those who aspired to leadership could also learn what was necessary for the task.

Leaders in the movement for public education appeared and had their impact upon the "free" or "common" schools that became increasingly important as the nineteenth century advanced. Men such as Horace Mann in Massachusetts, Henry Barnard in Connecticut, Samuel Lewis in Ohio, and John Swett in California all supported the idea of free, universal education. New England, in particular Massachusetts, was the center of interest in the development of public education and the source of recruitment of leaders who became important throughout the rest of the nation.

As the public schools emerged as a commonplace phenomenon, they taught primarily "reading, writing, and arithmetic" plus spelling, good citizenship, and what was considered locally to be right and wrong— that is, moral education. The high school remained something in the future for most young people in the years before the Civil War. Even eight grades of education were considered a considerable achievement. Beyond that point the few who went on in an educational program usually attended an "academy." That was most commonly private but might have some public funds supporting it. High schools of the general type that later became common were slow in being established. The first was created in Boston in 1821. The early high schools were expected to meet Franklin's goal of providing both vocational education and precollege training for those who could not afford to attend private academies.

In 1827 a Massachusetts law established the framework for a system of high schools, and that state, which had led the way in public education from the beginning, long stood in the forefront of secondary education. The law required towns and cities, depending upon their size, to offer courses of the high school curriculum for all who attended, and the cost was to be supported by public taxation. Public high schools were supported in New York by the Union Free School Act of 1864 and later in other states. But the high schools were slow to appear. In 1870 there were 6,792,000 pupils in elementary schools in the United States, but only about 80,000 high school students in the entire nation.

The importance of public education was stressed to such an extent in the first half of the nineteenth century that the idea was gradually accepted that education was not only desirable but necessary in a democracy. Massachusetts in 1852 was the first state to establish compulsory attendance in schools, and this rule was quickly enacted in other states. Only a relatively few states, primarily in the South, did not adopt such a requirement until the twentieth century.

A major controversy over public education centered on the question of financing the schools. Traditionally, education had been considered a private matter. Only the very poor were eligible for free education on the basis of charity. But if education should be a universal matter and a necessity in a democracy, it was argued that it should be paid for from regular tax funds. This proposal was logical, given the assumptions upon which it was based, but many citizens were outraged at the thought that childless citizens, or those whose children were grown, should pay a part of the cost of those who had children, but no funds to pay for their education. Gradually, the idea that all citizens benefited from a program of public education and should pay an equal tax share regardless of their economic position or number of school-age children came to be accepted as the American approach to education.

The acceptance of this idea of "free" (tax-paid) public education was slow to be accepted, but by 1860 it was clear that this system was to prevail and that such education would eventually apply at both the elementary and secondary levels. It was also clear that, although state government would influence public school policy, local school board members would have an important voice.

In a society that was increasingly to be based upon achievement rather than ascription, broadly available education was seen to be necessary. Furthermore, it was widely believed that such education could not be derived primarily from institutions under sectarian religious control. If the ideal of separation of church and state were to be achieved and if persons of different religions were to live in close physical proximity to one another, education would have to be secular and, if not based on ability to pay, a governmental responsibility. This idea first grew in New England and then spread to the Middle Atlantic and Middle Western states, finally moving on westward to the Pacific Ocean. Only in the South, where a caste and class system prevailed and where population density was low, did it spread slowly. New Orleans was something of an exception. In 1857 the Whigs carried the city on a platform calling for (among other things) a better school system. By 1860 the city was spending $259,960 for schools. There had been three public high schools in operation since 1852.

By the middle of the nineteenth century, public school systems existed in at least elementary form throughout the nation. In many cases these schools were extremely sketchy and in many areas were operated for only a few months a year. Furthermore, many persons, such as the children of slaves, were offered no opportunity for education at all. Even after the Civil War, most blacks in the rural South did not attend school, although city dwellers had a fair chance. When they did, it was under a segregated system, except for some areas during the first few years after the war. Segregated schools existed as far north as Michigan through the 1880s, and in many other parts of the North until much later. It was not uncommon for black children to be excluded from schools in the North, with policy commonly determined by the local district. Even in the 1860s, however, legal action to force local school districts to comply with the law took place. Thus, in the mid-1860s blacks were not admitted to the public schools of Central City, Colorado. A petition to the legislature for a law to require admission was not successful. A team of attorneys finally secured admission of the blacks by resort to the Civil Rights Act. The Wyoming legislature provided for separate schools for blacks (1873) if more than fifteen were enrolled in a single district. (The same state had required equal treatment as to sex by a law of 1869.)

The financing of public education was traditionally through gifts, tuition, and other voluntary contributions or charges based upon services rendered. The first concessions toward the idea that every child should have the opportunity to go to school consisted of provisions permitting the children of paupers to attend schools without charge. Gradually the idea spread that all children, regardless of the financial position of their parents, should be provided with "free public education," that is, without the costs of such education being charged directly to the parents on the basis of the cost of such education or for the number of children the parents had in school at a particular time. Once this concept was accepted, legislatures generally authorized local school districts to levy property taxes as a basis for financing education if they wished to do so. As the idea spread, legislatures often provided grants-in-aid to local districts that were levying taxes of their own as an incentive both to expand their local tax levies and to induce areas without such taxes to impose them. Eventually, the process was carried to its logical conclusion by statutes requiring each school district to raise the funds necessary to provide a minimum level of education as prescribed by state law. This pattern began to emerge in the Eastern states, starting with Massachusetts in 1827, and spread throughout most of the East and Middle West before the beginning of the Civil War. Providence will serve as an example. Its school population increased 233 per cent between 1840 and 1854, about two and one-half times as rapidly as its population. The expenditure per pupil grew 65 per cent. Immediately after the war the states that had not yet acted in the North did so and were followed by the Southern states, where tuition or other levies depending upon the number of children actually in school disappeared last.

School reformers quickly recognized that mere local authorization, or later even state-required tax levies, would not be enough to assure an adequate level of education throughout the state and that gross inequities were certain to develop. Pressure was brought to bear upon state legislatures to provide forces for equalization. In addition to the use of the grant-in-aid as both carrot and stick, the states began to establish departments of public instruction under state superintendents of schools. New York was the first to take this step in 1812, and almost all of the Northern states had such an office prior to the Civil War's outbreak. State boards of education, consisting generally of interested laymen anxious to advise the not yet professional superintendent, also began to emerge. The New York Board of Regents was created in 1784, but it was not until the 1830s that similar boards began to be established elsewhere, beginning with Massachusetts and Connecticut.

In New England the early school boards generally were the town councils, with policy-making gradually becoming more concentrated in the school committee of the council. These committees, in turn, tended to become increasingly independent. In the South the typical pattern to develop (largely after the Civil War), was for schools to be controlled by the county governing board or an independent school board. In the remainder of the country the pattern was somewhat less standardized than is the case today, although the trend was from the beginning toward an independent board. Members might be appointed, elected, or *ex officio.*

The first board of education for the city of Detroit (1842), for example, consisted of two school inspectors from each ward, plus the mayor and the recorder. The inspectors, although not teachers or professional administrators but more commonly businessmen, acted in effect as the part-time principals for the ward schools. There was no permanent high school until 1858. (The Detroit schools, in the nationwide pattern, were segregated, with a "colored" school having been established in 1839 and with state funds appropriated to hire a teacher for it the coming year.)

Until the coming of the automobile and the motorized school bus following World War I, public education in the United States primarily involved only the elementary levels. The vast majority of "academies" and other college preparatory schools were private organizations with funds from gifts and tuition. The free public education concept was, however, slowly extended to the secondary level. In 1821 Boston established the first free public high school for boys; a female counterpart lasted only from 1825 to 1827. Although several hundred high schools existed by 1860, only a small portion of the school-age population attended them. Furthermore, the secondary schools were generally vocationally oriented and were not designed to prepare students for higher education. The issue of the college preparatory course in a free public high school did not arise seriously until after 1870, simply because no such expectation yet existed. But the idea of free public education was well established in the United States by 1870 and was no longer importantly controversial. In that year, only 11.5 per cent of whites, a large proportion of them foreign born, were classified as illiterate—but 77.9 per cent of nonwhites were in that deprived category. Only the often touchy details concerning curriculum, finance, purpose, equality of opportunity, and other policies remained as a basis for conflict.

Social Welfare

During the nineteenth century welfare remained primarily a responsibility of private organizations. These consisted for the most part of churches and private organizations led by upper-middle-class persons.

Near the end of the eighteenth century a "Patriotic Society for Promoting Objects of Public Utility" was organized in Newark. It was organized by prominent citizens and was concerned not only with poor relief but also with providing ladders for fire protection, aid to prisoners in the local jail, and the organization of schools for the poor.

Almshouses or poorhouses were organized by cities early in the nineteenth century and even before (New York City's dated from 1736). They were accepted as a community responsibility, being part of a welfare policy that dated back to the early seventeenth century in England. But it was not easy to persuade taxpayers to spend money on new almshouses, and skepticism on this point increased as American society became more heterogeneous. Thus in the second and third decades of the century a growing resentment emerged in the state of New York at the high incidence of pauperism and lawlessness among the Irish immigrants. Indeed, by 1795 one-half of the paupers in the New York City almshouses were foreigners. The idea of a general public responsibility for the protection of the poor was still a long way off, though programs were even then expensive by the standards of the day and there were quite harsh "reforms" in New York City (1817) and the state (1824).

In 1818 Savannah established a dispensary, following the lead of Charleston. Six aldermen were appointed as trustees, with the dispensary to be operated by a pharmacist and a panel of physicians. The project was abandoned the following year, however, as was a plan for providing free medical care for the poor at city expense.

The welfare burden remained heavy throughout the 1770–1870 period, as impoverished persons continued to arrive in America irrespective of the prospects for jobs. This remained the case in cities from the time of the great immigrations of the late 1840s until well into the twentieth century. In Brooklyn about 12 per cent of the residents received welfare aid (private or public) in 1868. The average for the following two years was 10 per cent.

Americans have always been suspicious of the poor and have been prepared to think the worst of them. The almshouse commissioners, as well as councilmen and mayors, were defensive about their roll in caring for the poor and the cost of society's nonproductive element. In 1789 the New York commissioners themselves complained that the almshouse was "too much of a common Receptacle for idle intemperate Vagrants," who "by pretending Sickness or otherwise" received aid to which they were not entitled.[15]

New York grew rapidly and was always a major port of entry for immigrants. Its almshouse was therefore almost constantly overcrowded. The original one was replaced by a new one built in 1796–97, not, of course, from tax moneys but from the proceeds of a lottery. It was immediately obsolete, and a new one was begun at Bellevue in 1811. Construction was delayed by the war that began the next year, but it was finished in 1816. The new location, on the edge of the city along the East River, was considered especially appropriate because it helped to make the poor less visible to the middle classes and to visiting dignitaries. The first two almshouses had been located at City Hall Park, and councilmen were frequently reminded by persons coming to do business with them that they were shocked "by haggard paupers and undisciplined children peering from almshouse windows, hanging on the fences, and wandering in the park."[16] In 1848 a new poorhouse was constructed on what is now called Welfare Island—another secluded location. The buildings at Bellevue were converted into a public hospital.

The nineteenth-century welfare program included both the "indoor relief" provided by the almshouse and "outdoor relief" for those in need of aid only temporarily. This type of relief involved home assistance. Disputes over which was to be used were endemic in the situation. In the short run outdoor relief was less costly and less disruptive of family and social life for the recipients. The politics of immigrant slum areas dictated its use. For a person or family more or less permanently on the dole, however, almshouse residency was less costly and hence preferred. It also carried with it the implicit condemnation of a "work-ethic" society. The individual was incarcerated, marked as a failure. But each able-bodied resident was put to work.

Outdoor relief grew rapidly in the first decades of the nineteenth century, provoking a great deal of protest from taxpayers. Benevolent attitudes toward the poor and efforts to eliminate poverty turned to cynicism; relative support levels were cut back in many cases; and private welfare was forced to assume a greater share of the burden. In all cases paternalism and stern moralism lay at the roots of the attitudes of those who dealt with poverty during this period. Increasingly, the trend was toward a "work test" where public funds were involved, leaving to private charity emergency situations for the ill and the aged. For orphans there came to be institutional care in either the almshouse or the orphanage. The latter was usually privately sponsored but with public subsidy.

New York State in 1823 conducted a great, statewide Poor Law Survey. It revealed a number of grave defects: costly litigation concerning residency, barbarous treatment when the poor were "farmed out," neglect of the education and morals of pauper children, and no adequate provision for employment. A principal recommendation was to rely on the poorhouse for the able-bodied. This was usually a county responsibility. The state gradually assumed more responsibility for special groups, such as the insane.

A special problem was the very great increase in the numbers of needy during the panic years. Here old assumptions that the individual himself was to blame if he was poor began to crumble, as municipalities organized work programs (usually for part-time work at subsistence wages), or the leading citizens would meet and underwrite an expansion of private charity. In the 1848 depression almost 10 per cent of New York City residents were on relief.

Notes

1. John H. Wilkins, *Further Remarks on Supplying the City with Pure Water* (Boston, 1845).
2. John H. Griscom, *The Sanitary Condition of the Laboring Population of New York* (New York, 1845).
3. Quoted in J. O. Raum, *History of New Jersey* (Newark, 1877).
4. Nelson M. Blake, *Water for the Cities* (Syracuse, N.Y., 1956), pp. 211-212. This is a history of urban water supply systems.
5. Generally, see *ibid.*, chaps. 6–8.
6. Richard C. Wade, *The Urban Frontier* (Cambridge, Mass., 1959), p. 294.
7. Blake, *op. cit.*, Ch. 11.
8. *Ibid.*
9. *Ibid.*
10. J. Wooldridge, *History of Nashville* (Nashville, 1890).
11. Wade, *op. cit.*, Ch. 9.
12. *Ibid.*
13. J. H. Shera, *Foundations of the Public Library* (Chicago, 1949).
14. See, for example, F. F. Butts and L. A. Cremin, *A History of Education* (New York, 1953).
15. Raymond A. Mohl, *Poverty in New York, 1783–1825* (New York, 1971), p. 82.
16. *Ibid.*, p. 84.

Chapter *5*

MUNICIPAL FUNCTIONS
AND POLITICAL ISSUES:
PUBLIC SAFETY, UTILITIES,
AND OTHER ACTIVITIES

Protection from crime and violence was a matter of considerable concern to city dwellers during the nineteenth century. Urban riots were common; so were theft, murder, and vandalism. To some, like the reformer Charles L. Brace of New York, American criminals were more violent than those of Europe:

> They rifle a bank, where English thieves pick a pocket; they murder, where European *proletaires* cudgel or fight with fists; in a riot, they begin what seems to be about the sacking of a city, where English rioters would merely batter policemen, or smash lamps.[1]

And this was a period when earnest attempts were made to protect the morality of the community through the use of "blue laws," which now seem quaint and nonproductive. Fire protection too was important, particularly in the East, where most buildings were wooden and fires were frequent, often disastrous, and always a serious danger.

During the nineteenth century a new phenomenon, public utilities, emerged. The potential effect of their organization as monopolies was not yet well understood. But gas and street railway services were urgently wanted, and in the desire to secure them franchises were often given away in order to induce firms to act speedily. Concerns about monopoly, corruption, quality of service, and undue profiteering were still in the future. But traditions were in the process of being formed—and in a manner such as to provide them with great powers of persistence.

Police Protection

In the small trading towns of early America, police protection was usually extremely simple and sometimes did not exist at all until a "crime wave" forced a change of policy. Even in rapidly growing communities police protection was generally minimal, unable to cope with even small riots—of which there were many in the first half of the nineteenth century—not to mention the commonplace problems of enforcing the laws relating to personal violence, theft, prostitution, gambling, and liquor. Indeed, in 1821 a resident of St. Louis sarcastically complained that the only existing night watch was that maintained by prowlers, thugs, and kidnappers.[2] Of course, that city's citizens protested against such conditions, and the council authorized action, but as was usually the case on the frontier, funds were lacking. After organized gangs terrorized the city for several years, a small night patrol was established in 1828.

The first development in a growing frontier community was usually provision for a night watch. Where this was established, all taxpayers were often required to take a turn at night patrol or furnish a substitute on penalty of fine. We can well imagine that many participated with less than enthusiasm or alacrity. Thus in 1793 all citizens of Savannah who were not subject to militia duty were formed into patrol companies for the night watch. The mayor and aldermen took turns heading these amateur operations. Such volunteer duty was seldom popular and sometimes in the North was abandoned or replaced by a very small paid watch. In 1811, the watch for the city of Philadelphia was described as follows:

> There are 14 constables, one for each ward; and until the present year, one high constable who is required to walk the streets with his mace in his hand and examine all vagrants and disorderly persons, and upon refusal to give him an account of their residence and appointment, for not giving a satisfactory account, to carry such persons before the mayor or an alderman to be dealt with according to law: To give notice of all nuisances or obstructions in the streets to the city commissioners or mayor; and of offenses committed against the laws in force.[3]

In the South the desire to enforce the curfew upon Negro slaves and the fear of possible slave uprisings made the night watch impractical, and often it was felt necessary to divert scarce tax dollars toward fairly elaborate approaches to policing. Three years after the Savannah patrol experiment began it was abandoned, and a paid guard and watch were established.

Despite its location on the edge of the South, Cincinnati had poor police protection throughout the first half of the nineteenth century. The council established a night watch in 1803, calling for citizens to serve in rotation. This plan was quite unsuccessful from the beginning, and the city gained a reputation for being crime-ridden. In 1823 the council publicly admitted that the unpaid watch was inadequate, but it was unwilling to raise the necessary funds for hired constables.

Even when members of the watch were paid, low wages and lack of opportunity in such a job did not make for reassurance concerning the quality of protection. In 1798 Lancaster, Pennsylvania, established a paid night watch, but it was abruptly ended a few years later. It seems that the captain of the watch, allegedly intoxicated, made the mistake of arresting the Grand Master of the Blue Lodge as he left the lodge one night.

Crimes against property, crimes of violence, and riots large and small (see the Appendix at the end of this volume) were commonplace in America in the first half of the nineteenth century, when wealth was increasing, population was mobile, and people of many cultural backgrounds were converging upon American cities. Despite the cost, fear of violence and loss of property convinced reluctant taxpayers that paid police forces were necessary.

The first uniformed force was established in New York in 1845, and its pattern was copied by several other Eastern Seaboard cities before the Civil War. In the South, with the possible exception of New Orleans, the fear was not one of nativist-immigrant clashes of the kind common in the East but of the rising danger of Negro rebellion or lawlessness. Thus Lexington and Louisville maintained relatively elaborate police forces, largely at taxpayer expense. Cincinnati and St. Louis, on the border of the South and with many black residents, were major exceptions to this pattern. New Orleans was also different in that throughout most of the first half of the nineteenth century it included free blacks on its police force. Only the mounting tensions and distrust that characterized the period just prior to the Civil War caused all blacks to be dropped from the force shortly before hostilities began.

Among the cities of the East, the pattern of development in Boston was reasonably typical. That city had the usual night watch prior to the great Broad Street riot of 1837. This riot, like others in that city, stemmed from the antagonisms between Irish-Americans and Yankees, with the religious difference a strong motivating factor. In that year an engine company returning from a fire met an Irish funeral procession. Apparently some members on both sides were willing and even eager to fight. A riot resulted in which perhaps 15,000 were involved. The homes of many Irish-Americans were sacked. The mayor of the city, reviewing the results, called for the establishment of paid personnel for both police and fire departments. He was successful in securing the latter, but he could get the council to agree only to a small supplementary police day force under the city marshal. This force was maintained independently of the 110 night watchmen and ten constables. Even so, between 1830 and the early 1840s, expenditures for police increased from 4.1 per cent to 8.5 per cent of the city budget.

In 1846 the Boston police force was reorganized and enlarged, although still kept separate from the night watch. In the continuing Irish-Yankee struggle, the Yankees turned toward the prohibition of the sale of intoxicating drink, and under Mayor Josiah Quincy, Jr., a Whig, all liquor licenses were refused. "When I left office [1849], there was no place where such liquors were openly sold," Quincy gloated. Yet two years later the city marshal stated that more than 1,500 places sold liquor, and he urged law enforcement, but the council did nothing. The next year the council began to grant liquor licenses again, but these were stopped when the state enacted prohibition. Drunkenness and crime were said to be on the increase.

In 1854 the dual system of day police and night watch was abolished. A regular police department with 250 men was established. In 1858 a standard police uniform was adopted, and something approximating a modern police force came into being, although it continued to be rocked by controversy and remained a central focus in the struggle between the Yankees and the Irish-Americans for municipal control.

In Philadelphia in the 1840s, a number of riots and other disturbances resulted from conflicts between nativists and Catholics. Catholic churches and other institutions were burned, nativists' meetings were disrupted, and many people were injured. After many such riots, the common council undertook to organize citizens by wards into "peace police." The difficulties in controlling the disorders were said to stem in part from the number of districts within the county, each of which had its own police with no jurisdiction in other districts. The police in each district were too few to deal with large-scale disturbances, and the constables were no longer of much assistance to the police, although the actual legal responsibility lay largely with them. By this time the constables were confining their activities chiefly to the serving of processes and other court papers, for which they received fees. The county sheriff still had the power of calling out a *posse comitatus*, but he had proved hopelessly unreliable.

Some reformers urged that the various governmental municipalities within Philadelphia County be merged and that the merger include the county government itself. This proposal was strongly opposed by many, and a meeting of protest was held. The Philadelphia council was also in opposition, fearing that "the old respectable and conservative methods of the city legislation would be overborne by the less formal methods of proceeding in the districts." Presumably this referred to the unincorporated parts of the county. Some further efforts were made at this time to strengthen the police department, but a modern force was not developed until the consolidated city and county of Philadelphia was created in 1854. By the middle of the century the police departments of the larger cities had grown enormously from what they had been two generations before.

In the Far West, particularly in the boom towns of the mining areas, the first police forces usually were the "vigilantes" or vigilance committees, ordinarily consisting of middle-class businessmen who were anxious to maintain order, since an orderly town was likely to be a profitable one. Thus, the year after the great 1849 California gold strike, such a group was formed in San Francisco. It was called the "Law and Order League." This group was dissolved, but another was formed in 1856, when the corrupt and inefficient government of the rapidly growing city was unable to police it adequately. Although both vigilance committees enjoyed the support of the local newspapers, they unavoidably came into conflict with the regular peace officers, and after August, 1856, the second committee became permanently inactive. At its high point its membership had totaled more than 8,000. Over a period of more than a quarter of a century, vigilante groups performed the police function on an irregular basis throughout much of the West.[4]

Jails during this period were not a source of much controversy, except when the public objected to building a new one. In early America jails often did not exist at all, and punishment normally consisted of flogging, hanging, or banishment. This was also true in the mining and shipping towns of the West. When jails were built, they often became places where "criminals and debtors, men, women, and children were indiscriminately mixed."[5] Sanitation facilities in them were minimal or nonexistent. Sometimes conditions would get so bad that reformers demanded action, but jails and their inmates were relatively invisible to the average citizen, so the proponents of economy usually prevailed. Sometimes, however, there was concern over the fate of children in such conditions, and a considerable movement developed for the establishment of "reform schools" for juveniles. Such a school was proposed in Louisville in 1854 and finally completed a decade later. Its purpose was "to prevent our youth from becoming adepts in crime and subjects for the penitentiary."[6] Later, somewhat more adequate jails were built, and women were segregated, but no really significant penal reform movement affected policies at the municipal level similar to those that influenced state prisons. Juvenile courts were not created until the end of the nineteenth century.

Most of the patterns of contemporary American crime began to emerge early in the nineteenth century. The widening gap between wealth and poverty in the cities encouraged many poor persons to enter a life of crime. At the same time "white collar" crime was developing among members of the middle class, although this was not viewed as a threat to society to the degree that crimes using or threatening force or violence were.

Youth gangs made their appearances, staking out their own territories, terrorizing neighborhood merchants, and committing crimes against persons and property for both fun and profit. The lack of schools and the failure to enforce the truancy laws where schools were available provided plenty of idle hours for troublemaking. As today, the gangs had colorful names: the Blood Tubs of Philadelphia, the Stringers of Baltimore, the Crawfish Boys of Cincinnati, and the Dead Rabbits of New York, among many others. The use of animal names—Buffalos, Crawfish, Snakes, Wolves—indicated that city boys of the day were only one step away from the country, but the pattern of behavior was essentially the same as that of the gangs that were to haunt American cities, and particularly the slum areas, up to the present.

Organized crime, with its tie-ins to the police and the respectable middle class, also made its appearance, although the highly organized pattern did not appear until after the large immigrations from Sicily toward the end of the century. The pattern appeared early, however. In the first decade of the nineteenth century it was discovered that Charles Vattier, a Cincinnati financier and apparently a solid citizen of the community, was a secret owner of gambling houses, taverns, and brothels. About the same time in the same city, a horse-theft ring operated much as does a modern professional car-theft organization. It was subsequently discovered that the ring included middle-class, supposedly respectable, residents of the city.

Illegal occupations made their appearance early and had their usual corrupting influence upon city government. Gambling was especially troublesome. Starting in Vicksburg about 1835, a wave of reform spread through the Mississippi Valley. St. Louis, for example, used an ordinance for the trial and punishment of all persons who could not show honorable means of livelihood. The reform wave enjoyed some modest short-range success. The reaction of the middle classes to illegal occupations and their attendant corruption was often one of outrage. The middle classes saw government as an instrument that could be used to teach its version of morality to the rest of society and perhaps particularly to the more recent immigrants. The middle and upper-middle classes not only were relatively well off and tended to dominate business and industry, but they were also the only ones with a good education (by the standards of the day), and above all they viewed themselves as virtuous. Deviation from their views and behavior patterns was considered to be immoral and was often made illegal.

George Hall was elected mayor of Brooklyn in 1854, largely on a platform calling for temperance and the observance of the Sabbath. In Cincinnati an 1824 ordinance provided for the observation of the Sabbath and outlawed the playing of such games as marbles, quoits, kite flying, hoop rolling, and shinny on Sundays. Reformers organized, under various names, "morality" societies and, especially from the 1840s on, urged the prohibition of the sale of liquor. The Irish immigrants quickly gained a reputation for brawling and hard drinking. The middle class's response was to attempt to control the sale of alcoholic beverages. Prohibition was advocated in many parts of the country, and for a short time the Yankees made Massachusetts "dry," but early attempts to prohibit the sale of liquor appear to have been no more successful than were those of the 1920s. On the other hand, the people of a city such as Denver showed no desire to enforce the state antigambling and antivice laws. Fines were so light as to amount to licenses.

Occasionally a middle-class citizen would make a dramatic gesture in an attempt to teach "proper" behavior to the citizenry. Thus, in 1835 Jonathan Child resigned as mayor of Rochester, saying that his conscience would not let him sign the liquor licenses. But such gestures were of little avail. The liquor establishments were much in demand and commonly operated without licenses, even in "wet" communities. Albany in 1851 had one grog shop for every sixty-seven residents. Of the total of 744, only 426 were licensed. In Natchez in 1803–4, the town granted twenty-six tavern licenses in the first year of its incorporation, one for every fifty-eight residents. Yet by 1870 the "Protestant ethic" of the middle classes was being modified and, in many cases, found wanting. The year 1866 saw the emergence of the most notorious of the great boss-and-machine combinations, when what was shortly to be known as the "Tweed Ring" took control of New York City. The pre–Civil War, police-based machine of Fernando Wood probably helped provide ideas for William Marcy Tweed. In 1851 the council had been known as the "Forty Thieves." In other cities the beginnings of machine government were also appearing, although only in incipient form.

The machine was made possible by two factors: First, there was the rapidly expanding opportunity in business and industry. Ambition and greed contributed to a tendency to reject or overlook middle-class values and to emphasize expediency. Because a large number of governmental policies served as constraints upon the businessman or industrialist, the temptation for bribery and other illegal activities was very great whenever the businessman wanted to ensure or speed up governmental cooperation. Second, there was the immigrant, usually poverty stricken and often anxious to use any means possible to advance himself economically or at least to stave off the greatest threats posed by poverty. The interests of the businessman and of the immigrant complemented one another. All that remained to be done was to bring them together. This function of broker was performed by the professional politicians, who emerged with the advent of the political machine.

The machines, of course, took funds not only from the legitimate, if sometimes unscrupulous, businessmen but also from those operating in

illegal areas. Payoffs for gambling and prostitution began well before the
establishment of the Tweed Ring. The advent of the paid, full-time police force increased the possibilities for corruption, for the public per-
sistently resisted proposed increases in the police budget. Earlier policemen, serving on a part-time basis, had less reason to be tempted. But
the new full-time policeman not only was constantly subjected to political influence from the mayor and council, which undermined his commitment to a full and impartial enforcement of the law, but his low
salary brought him to the very edge of poverty. The policeman had no
security of employment. He was often used as an arm of the party and
faction in power and was often subject to dismissal if the group in control lost an election. As a result, by the 1860s it was common for policemen in the larger cities to supplement their incomes with modest shakedown payments, some of them in kind. The illegal saloonkeeper, the
prostitute, and even the legitimate businessman often found it expedient
to pay minor tribute either to avoid harassment or to receive the ordinary protection that the law provides.

Indeed, the groundwork had been laid even before 1870 for the full
corruption of the police. As Alexander Callow has noted: "Under the
Tweed Ring, the police department became a patchwork of almost
independent kingdoms, where the Captain was autocrat and ruled, it
was said, by divine right. The Captain and his favorite subordinate often
took exclusive control of cases, removing the task from the patrolmen;
thus some cases would be dropped for political reasons. The honest policeman was relegated to the trivial cases."[7] The ordinary policeman and
his superiors, however, knew better than to challenge the general middle
class and its values. The police department enforced the general moral
principles of the middle class and limited exceptions to those areas of
illegal occupations that the middle class itself either secretly accepted
or considered necessary in order to placate and keep docile the working
classes and the ill-understood immigrant groups.

The typical middle-class citizen rarely had contact with the police,
except perhaps to ask directions from the officer on foot patrol. For the
working class, however, the policeman came to be seen as the individual
who was responsible in their area for the imposition of middle-class
values and the protection of middle-class property. For a short time,
there was conflict between the police and the new immigrants because
the police were from earlier immigrations. In the 1850s, however, young
Irishmen and later persons of other immigrant groups were recruited
into the police departments to patrol the immigrant neighborhoods.
The Irish, in particular, proved to be such effective policemen and so
suitable in terms of temperament, personality, and courage that they
soon were allowed to police all sections of the city. It was not long before the stereotyped policeman spoke with an Irish brogue.

Fire Protection

In the early years of the Republic every fire of any consequence was considered a community emergency, and all citizens were expected to render assistance, usually by joining the bucket brigade. Fires were common and often disastrous, for the great bulk of the buildings constructed outside New England were wooden. Some efforts were made to reduce the fire danger through building codes. As early as 1796 Philadelphia prohibited wooden buildings within the thickly settled parts of the city. This was helpful, but the commonplace use of wood, especially for homes, continued. Winter, with its cold and winds, offered particular dangers. People lived in terror of uncontrolled conflagrations, and these were indeed common. (Despite the great loss of life and property, fires also had some favorable side effects. A great fire in Portland, Maine, in 1866 for example, was followed by a decision of the city fathers to lay out Lincoln Park in the center of the city.)

The early notion of fire protection as a citizen's community responsibility was enforced to some degree by the levying of a fine if an individual failed to participate when needed. But this approach was not very satisfactory except in the village. As communities grew volunteer fire companies were formed.

The first voluntary fire company was established in Philadelphia in 1732. By 1811 the number in the nation had increased to more than forty. Others continued to be formed, including the all-black African Fire Association, which was organized in Philadelphia in 1818, but it was soon disbanded because of vigorous opposition from the white fire companies.

Often these companies received subsidies from the city, but they were independent of it, made their own rules, and did their own recruiting. Coordination and financial support were achieved because the leading officials and businessmen of the city commonly were members of the fire departments. Large numbers of more ordinary citizens also were eager to join, and the departments became important political forces. They also became competitive with one another, seeking the opportunity to put out a blaze in order to secure the payments offered by an insurance company. Many a building or even city block or more burned to the ground while volunteer companies battled one another for access to a well, stream, or hydrant.

The simple bucket brigade was soon supplemented by a hand pump and hose. This change vastly increased the supply of water to the fire. Early in the nineteenth century, after cities had begun to develop water supply systems, it was realized that water could be delivered to the pumpers much more rapidly than by bucket brigade if a hose were con-

nected either to a hole drilled in a wooden pipe water main or to a hydrant. All of these technological developments involved additional costs,
but taxpayer resistance was overcome by the politically powerful fire
companies.

In 1803 a man named Reuben Haines thought of the idea of attaching a hose to water main hydrants in order to supply the hand pumpers
with water. This reduced the time required in order to fill the supply
tank of an engine from fifteen minutes by bucket brigade to one and
one-half minutes. A number of young men met with Haines to talk
over forming a hose company operating under the new system but found
the costs greater than they could afford. They then sought assistance
from businessmen and others who owned real estate and from the insurance companies. The new approach was a success, and by 1811 nine
such hose companies existed. At that time, public funds were not directly used to support the fire companies or the hose companies. But a
municipal subsidy was not far off.

After a serious fire in Newark in 1797, a mass meeting was held at the
courthouse and a "Fire Association" was formed. Assessments were
levied against the members according to the value of their combustible
property, and a pumper engine was bought, but the fire company provided service only to members of the association. Another mass meeting
in 1810 resulted in the formation of the Newark Mutual Assurance
Company. It was instrumental in supporting the fire department and
gradually relieved members of the responsibility of contributing person-
ally to fire sufferers. This combination of fire company and insurance
company was common, but it did not do much to overcome the threat
of serious conflagrations, for it provided assistance only to those who
were willing and able to pay the insurance premiums.

The fire company itself was seen to be a device not only for protection
but also for moral instruction. A few years later it was noted that "only
healthy, athletic, and sober young men were admitted to the fire companies in the early days; abstinence from intoxicating drinks was one of
the standing rules." There were often other inducements besides social
and political prestige leading to service in volunteer companies. For example, exemptions from jury duty, militia (except in time of war), and
the road tax were granted in Chicago.

The next major technological improvement involved the application
of steam power to run the pump. The first effective steamer appeared in
1852. It was designed by Alexander B. Latta of Cincinnati. A great deal
of interest was immediately focused upon the new invention, but it also
became a center of political controversy. The volunteer fire departments
were well established as political powers, and they saw new equipment
as a major threat. This was especially true of the steam pumper, for the

complexity of the new equipment suggested the need for professional fire fighters. Political battle lines were quickly drawn. Against the volunteers was a powerful set of counter-interests, led by the insurance companies and the businessmen who had to pay the insurance premiums. For them, more efficient fire-fighting apparatus was an advantage.

Perhaps because it was Latta's home town, and because of the publicity resulting when two volunteer groups engaged in a brawl while the building they were supposed to be protecting burned to the ground, Cincinnati became the first city in the United States to provide for a paid fire department. The date was April 1, 1853. Establishing the new approach to fire protection was not easy, however. Volunteer groups tried to intimidate the city council while it was considering the matter. They were only slightly placated by explanations that the city was going to purchase an expensive and complicated steamer that could be operated only by trained personnel. The volunteers attempted to sabotage the first efforts of the new professional department, but they were frustrated as a result of the fact that the city had selected one of the most able and toughest of the volunteers to serve as the first fire chief. He was able to control the situation. Professionalism had come to fire fighting.

The Cincinnati approach attracted wide attention elsewhere. Representatives from Baltimore inspected the new system and inquired as to the advantages of a paid department. They were told: "First, it never gets drunk; second, it never throws brickbats."

Other cities also were quickly convinced that economic growth and paid firemen were interrelated matters. Sometimes compromises with the volunteers were worked out or they were co-opted, as in Cincinnati; but if this was not possible, the pressures for change tended to outweigh the political power of the volunteers. As an example of partial accommodation, New Orleans in 1855 disbanded several volunteer fire companies and called for bids. The fire-fighting contract was then awarded to the Firemen's Charitable Association for $70,000.

In 1855 a contest was held in New York's City Hall Park between a large hand pumper and a steamer. The former was actually able to throw water slightly farther, winning by 189 feet to 182, but after its firemen collapsed from exhaustion at the hand pumps, the steamer continued indefinitely. The city decision-makers were convinced. After their first use, the steamers were quickly improved in design to make them lighter in weight. Some of them were hand pulled by firemen, as had been the old mechanical pumpers, but as cities grew larger the greater stamina and speed of the horse as compared with man became important. By the end of the Civil War the famous matched teams of fire horses were well established in the cities of the nation. Major additional technological changes that would produce further important political conflicts did not take place until the coming of the internal combustion engine' in the second decade of the twentieth century.

The full-time paid fire department seemed to many citizens necessary for the rapidly growing cities of the mid-nineteenth century, but they were by no means universally supported. A taxpayers' revolt took place in Utica in 1855, particularly protesting the costs of the paid city fire department. A referendum on the question of providing additional fire equipment was rejected by a vote of 400 to 4. When the Republicans took control of the city government three years later, the paid fire department was abolished.

Professionalism was respected and became a source of envy in those cities that, for one reason or another, were not ready for it. When the city of San Francisco considered establishing a paid department in 1865, the Los Angeles *News* sneered: "By all means pay the firemen $100 or $200 per month; the taxpayers of San Francisco are rich and can afford it." The much smaller Los Angeles did not even establish a volunteer department until late in 1871, and a paid service had to wait until 1885. In many other cities the cost factor delayed adoption of what was clearly a superior system.

Criticism of professional full-time departments was, however, only an effort to postpone what was to become inevitable. Everywhere, the Main Street merchants who dominated the city councils wanted fire protection for economic reasons, and in the 1850s and 1860s full-time fire fighters and the increasingly elaborate equipment that these men demanded became commonplace in cities of any size.

Utilities: Gas and Electricity

Urbanites generally welcomed the technological improvements that offered better lighting for their homes and for the streets that they had to travel at night. However, controversy did arise over the granting of franchises to the private companies that supplied illuminating gas and that often seemed more interested in profits than in service. Certainly a major inspiration for corruption in the period following the Civil War was the beckoning opportunity for profits to be made by securing exclusive franchises that often ran for decades or even in perpetuity for the supplying of gas. Illuminating gas had first been supplied on a community basis in Baltimore in 1816. Its use was approved within the next few years in Boston and New York, but the main streets of both were lighted by whale oil lamps until after 1840. The effectiveness of gas lamps was limited by vandalism. Apparently, the destruction of gas lamps by rock throwers was a favorite evening sport in a great many American cities of the day.

Eventually utilities were considered to be monopolies and hence subject to governmental regulation. Their nature was underscored in 1844 in Chicago, when two competitive gas companies agreed on a division of territory. Rates were then increased.

At the time the use of gas for lighting came into general practice, cities were usually able to issue franchises on their own, although this was not universally true. In some instances, such as in Colorado, the state was the first instrument, but there in 1868 this power (including horse car franchises) was transferred to the municipalities. In general, however, only after major abuses had reached scandalous levels did state governments seek to take control over their issuance. Thus, in 1827 one man was given an exclusive franchise to supply gas to the city of Pittsburgh. The council agreed to pay $5 for each street lamp. The contract was to continue for twenty-one years, with the city having the option of taking over the responsibility at that time. Political controversy centered on the objection of many citizens to a monopolistic contract and to the fact that individuals were given no chance to subscribe to stock in a company that was almost certain to be profitable. Under such pressure the individual grant was transferred to a corporation. The enabling ordinance was drawn in such a way as to permit the entire corporate stock issue to be purchased by the city councilmen as soon as they adjourned after adopting the ordinance. Because they could buy the stock at par, which was considerably below its actual immediate worth, further strong protests were made. Finally, a third ordinance permitted all persons to bid on the stock.

In the years following the Civil War, competition surrounding the issuance of gas distribution franchises became a major cause for the corruption of city governments. The use of electricity for light and power, another opportunity for bribery in the securing and reissuing of franchises, did not occur until the 1880s.

Streets

In colonial times, streets were typically either unsurfaced, paved with cobblestones, or, less commonly, covered with wood blocks. In most towns, the first streets to be surfaced were the main street and the street connecting it with the wharves of the waterfront. For a long time, others remained dirt or mud, depending upon the weather. Stone blocks were used toward the middle of the nineteenth century, especially in the vicinity of municipal markets and the wharves.

Bituminous pavement was patented in 1834, but it was not much used until after the Civil War. It was expensive and not well suited to the wheels of urban vehicles prior to the development of the pneumatic tire. Bricks were first used for street surfacing in Charleston, West Virginia, in 1873. Concrete pavement was not made use of until near the end of the century.

Typically, paving took place only when abutting property owners— usually the state law required 60 per cent or two-thirds of them— petitioned the city for street surfacing. On the other hand, when St. Louis became a city in 1823, its first mayor, William Lane, at once took the lead for public improvements, including the paving and grading of streets. In most cases the entire cost was paid for by the property owners, although in some cases part of it became a charge against the city and was paid for from regular tax revenues. Curbs and gutters as well as sidewalks were ordinarily paid for entirely by the property owner and were optional with him. Hard surfacing was expensive, and efforts were constantly being made to find cheaper methods. In the 1860s, wood blocks, called Nicholson pavement, became very popular.

Street maintenance was generally neglected in early America, being to a degree at least postponable. The newspapers of the era, particularly in the letters to the editors, showed that the streets commonly were filled with manure, carcasses, and other filth, and a stroll along the public ways was often far from a pleasant experience. Gradually the cities began to spend greater amounts of money on street maintenance and street cleaning, but efforts were generally concentrated upon the business district. In attempts to lessen the cost of street cleaning, ordinances requiring the confinement of cattle, hogs, and other animals became increasingly common. Drainage was often a problem. Storm sewers were almost nonexistent, and roadside ditches were often not provided for or were blocked at occasional points along the way toward the nearest river or body of water. In 1823 a St. Louis resident in a sarcastic letter to the editor of the *Missouri Republican* commented that Main Street was "the only navigable watercourse through the city."

Street lighting was slow to be established. In some cases, porch lights were supplemented by privately owned street lights, but these were the frequent targets of vandals. Furthermore, if not properly installed, they also represented a fire hazard, and cities gradually established regulations concerning their construction and required permits for their erection. In time, lights were provided for the central business district and a few other heavily used areas, but for the most part the lighting of streets in residential areas awaited the coming of electricity. The whale oil lamp was in some cases replaced by coal oil (kerosene) and later by gas. In 1812 Lexington, Kentucky, became the first city west of the Alleghenies to have municipal street lighting. Eastern cities were somewhat ahead of the others. Some cities supplied the oil and provided the maintenance for street lights in an effort to encourage private property owners to install lighting. In general, most cities preferred private installation or property-owner-paid installation with municipal maintenance. In quite a few cases where gas was the source of power, however, the city had to negotiate with a private utility as the only practical way to achieve a desired goal, even though this approach often was not popular with citizens.

Even though streets and street lighting were slow to be developed, some of the special amenities that were to come were planned and construction begun during this period. For example, Chicago's excellent system of boulevards and parkways was begun in 1860.

Public Transportation

Horse-drawn omnibuses without rails were first used in New York in 1827, eight years after their initial appearance anywhere in Paris. This form of transportation represented an improvement; but it was too expensive for the workers, footing was often bad for the horses, and the ride was uncomfortably rough for the passengers. Even so, this form of public transit was adopted in many other cities.

The use of rails for the horse trolley represented a great advancement, for it could operate under almost all weather conditions and the reduced resistance allowed the horses to haul a much larger load than was possible with the omnibus. In 1831 the first street railway, the New York and Harlem Railroad Company, was incorporated. It began operations late the following year along the Bowery from Prince Street to Fourteenth Street. New Orleans, two years later, began to operate the nation's second street railway.

Elsewhere, the problem at first was to find enough customers who could afford to pay the fare, horses and their feed both being expensive enough to make the early public transportation systems a luxury item. Horsecar lines were opened, however, in Boston (1856) and Philadelphia (1858). A street railway franchise was first granted in New York in 1851, by which time it was becoming clear that unrestricted competition was not practical for a public utility that later came to be referred to as a "natural monopoly." A decade later, the California legislature authorized a franchise for the city of San Francisco.

In nearly all cases, transit systems came to be operated by private companies on the basis of franchises. In the early years it was often unnecessary to secure permission from the state government; the franchises being granted by the municipality. There was, furthermore, nothing resembling a public utilities commission to supervise these "natural" monopolies at either the state or local level. In this case too, the franchises, which were actually contracts, were often granted for very long periods of time, because this was considered necessary in order to induce private industry to organize and to make the sizable investment in necessary equipment. In Albany the 1863 franchise for the street railway company was for 1,000 years, although when a time period was specified it was more commonly 99 or 100 years. Typically a franchise made some minor provisions for the obligations of the utility, such as the maintenance of the street between and adjacent to the tracks, but these were often vague, and frequently no attempt was made to enforce their provisions in court. The street railway firms were often attracted further by promises of reduced taxation. For example, Mayor Doyle of Providence pleaded for tax exemption for street cars and railroads on the grounds that they benefited the city.

The early street railway cars were horse-drawn, except for the relatively few cable car systems. These were used especially in San Francisco and Seattle, but elsewhere as well, and were invented by Andrew Halladie, who introduced the famous San Francisco system in 1873. The electric trolley came in the 1880s. Subways were not built until the 1890s, but the first steam-driven elevated railroad was opened in New York in 1871.

In general, the idea of horse-drawn streetcars capable of carrying large numbers of persons from their homes to work or to the shopping areas downtown was so attractive that cities of any size commonly had community leaders who felt that almost any kind of agreement that would attract funds and the necessary organizational skills to the city was desirable. Little thought appears to have been given to the possibility that the streetcar franchise owners would exploit their monopolistic advantage for personal profit and that the quality of service might be a secondary concern. After a few years of development, street railways were indeed profitable, and they were established in even fairly small cities in the last half of the nineteenth century.

Ports and Harbors

In the early years there was no uniformity as to the responsibilities for developing and improving the port facilities of the seaport, lake, and river towns. Sometimes the state, sometimes the city took the initial steps. Usually the initiative and subsequent development belonged to the city for most of the period. Rivalry was intense. Costs were great, and private individuals and firms often constructed wharves and profited therefrom. By the middle and end of the period the assistance of the federal government was more and more enlisted, and the lineal sequence of the "Rivers and Harbors Bills" dates from this period.

Apart from construction and development, there were always problems for port cities of the visiting seamen and disorder and of quarantine. These have already been discussed in the sections dealing with police and health.

Parks

The fifty-acre Boston Common could be called the first park in the United States, but Governor John Winthrop established it in 1634 for "feeding of cattell" and as a "trayning field," hardly conventional park uses by later concepts. In the early part of the nineteenth century there was no great need for parks because of the small size of cities; nature was only a short buggy ride or even a walk away from one's home. As cities grew, however, the yearning for the memory, if not the reality, of rural America began to have its influence. Philadelphia, as early as 1812, set apart some land for a park. The Boston merchants who in 1845 planned the model city of Lawrence included parks and broad streets. Land for what was to become Chicago's Grant Park was set aside about 1840. The first real park of any importance, however, was Central Park in New York City. It was authorized by the state legislature in 1851. Because of its location in what was to become the heart of Manhattan, the proposal was vigorously fought by real estate developers and political leaders allied with them. On the other hand, some members of the council saw the political advantage of establishing such a park and the monetary possibilities in owning land on its periphery. The battle over land use in this case was a prototype of what later took place in many other cities. This was true both in regard to the reactions triggered when it was proposed to use land for something less than its most profitable potential and also in regard to the scramble for control of the lands immediately adjacent to the park.

Frederick Law Olmsted and Calvert Vaux, building and landscape architects, in 1858 submitted a plan for the design of Central Park and won first prize. Development began the next year under Olmsted's personal supervision. It was plagued all the way by political opponents but was a success, and he became the father of what came to be the City Beautiful movement. This was later developed by Daniel H. Burnham and was to become associated with the development of the Chicago World's Fair of 1893 and the period immediately following.

Although Olmsted seemed to be oriented toward the American county seat town of the period, his design was more on the order of an English country gentleman's estate. Writing in 1870, he described what he thought was the proper style of a park:

We want, especially, the greatest possible contrast with the restraining and confining conditions of the town, those conditions which compel us to walk circumspectly, watchfully, jealously, which compel us to look closely upon others with sympathy. Practically, what we most want is a simple, broad, open space of clean vistas, with sufficient play of surface and a sufficient number of trees about it to supply a variety of light and shade. This we want as a central feature. We want a depth of wood enough about it not only for comfort in hot weather, but to completely shut out the city from our landscapes.[8]

The Civil War slowed down the development of parks. In 1869, however, Chicago experienced an organized movement for a unified parks development. The previous year Lincoln Park had been planned along the shore of Lake Michigan and placed under the control of park commissioners. The commissioners of the South Park System were also established. They floated a $2 million loan to develop other parks, including Jackson Park, also on the lake front. In 1869 three park districts were organized with authority to issue bonds, the authorized amount of which was increased from time to time in future years.

In 1867 Baltimore began the construction of a 700-acre park. The movement spread rather slowly, but cities of middle and large size saw the desirability of developing parks. Olmsted was involved in the planning of a great many of them.

In the Southwest the tradition of a central square or "plaza," similar to that of the town square in New England, owed much to Spanish-Mexican custom. As American law came to dominate in this area, the midtown park was generally preserved and considered to be a valuable community asset. Los Angeles, for example, had a plaza in its original layout equal to about the size of two football fields (200 by 300 feet). As the city center moved toward the southwest, the old square fell into disuse, and the city established a five-acre plot as "a Public Square or Plaza for the use and benefit of the citizens in common." (The area is now known as Pershing Square.)

Blue Laws

In 1854 a cholera epidemic struck Newark. Many theories were offered to explain its cause, including filthy streets, drinking of liquor, and Sabbath breaking. The mayor announced that he would enforce the laws in these matters. The next year he was re-elected as the candidate of a "Law, Order, and Morality" Party. The "blue law" advocates were persistent in Newark. In 1869 they strenuously objected to the operating of horse cars on Sunday. The street railway company was cowed by the pressure, but the council called for a referendum, and Sunday transportation won by more than 64 per cent, 6,486 to 3,563. The company remained apprehensive of the power of an organized and highly motivated group but finally gave in to councilmanic insistence.

Newark had adopted a Sabbath-observance ordinance in 1798. In 1811 the following article had appeared in a Newark newspaper:

Melancholy! On Sunday last an apprentice boy named Mattias Edison who had gone into the River Passaick to bathe was in a moment of thoughtless security, drowned. His body has not yet been found.

Should not this alarming Providence, as well as other accidents that frequently happen to Sabbath breakers, be an awful warning to the youth, and at the same time lead parents and those entrusted with apprentices to be more circumspect toward those committed to their care? The profanation of the Sabbath by strolling apprentices and servants is among the crying sins of this town and loudly calls for a remedy.

St. Louis, despite a large "wet" German population, held a referendum on the Sunday sale of liquor in 1859. Those opposed to such sale won. The vote was 7,544 to 5,528, a "dry" margin of 57.7 per cent.

Philadelphia's post-Revolution charter noted that, in the uncertain status of the city after the end of the proprietary colony, it was "inadequate to the suppression of vice and immorality." By the time of the Revolution, Philadelphia had nearly ceased to be a Quaker city. The pressure for "blue laws" came chiefly from the hinterland. Still, in 1815 the common council memorialized the legislature to provide a means of repressing some 4,000 taverns and 1,800 tippling houses in the city and county. In 1855 Philadelphia's Mayor Conrad enthusiastically enforced a new law closing liquor establishments on Sunday. He was not up for re-election, but that fall all those supporting vigorous enforcement were defeated. The wet Democrats were victorious, and the next spring they elected a mayor. In 1859 Philadelphians debated whether to permit horse cars to run on Sunday, but the strict Sabbath lobby lost.

Entertainment or any kind of pleasure on Sunday was the heart of the controversy during this period. Gambling was not attacked as vigorously as it was to be later in the nation's history, and the lottery conducted by the government to raise funds for public construction was common, although each such lottery commonly required specific authorization by the state legislature. Thus lotteries were conducted in Rhode Island during the first decade of the nineteenth century to build bridges at Coventry and Wickford and an academy (high school) in Providence. In 1789 the Philadelphia Common Council authorized a lottery to raise money for a new city hall. The Florida legislature in 1834 authorized St. Augustine to operate a lottery to provide funds for a free public school. More than one thousand state or local lotteries were conducted during the nineteenth century.

As the American city grew, it began to develop centers of vice. New York had its Five Points District and the Haymarket, San Francisco its Barbary Coast, and other cities their own versions. Issues of law enforcement levels and policies were commonplace, as were periodic cleanup campaigns. But, as in the city throughout history, not all available services are legal, so conflict and controversy reign.

Annexation and the Boundary Problem

Throughout American history city leaders have desired to annex adjacent territory that is showing signs of urbanizing or is viewed as having such potential. Until the twentieth century, when technological developments made it possible for suburbs to supply certain essentials such as water, sewage disposal, and gas or electricity either by themselves or through privately owned utilities, persons on the "outskirts" of town were usually eager to be annexed by the core city.

The conflict between the city and the surrounding area is very old, as is seen in an early nineteenth-century "memorial" addressed "to the honorable, the legislative council and general assembly of the state of New Jersey," from the mayor, aldermen, common council, freeholders, and other inhabitants of "this city and freeport of Burlington." The petitioners or memorialists noted that they had seen a petition from "the freeholders and inhabitants of the township of Burlington, exclusive of the Corporation" in which they asked "that a law be made to separate them from the said city and Freeport." The representatives from the central city objected that the petition contained "allegations utterly unsupported, but upon the other hand in direct opposition to Acts of Assembly, resolutions of town meetings and the testimony of several of our most ancient and respectable fellow Citizens, which now to specify might be deemed trespassing upon your time to the injury of other important business of the public, though should your Memorialists be indulged with a hearing, they pledge themselves to support this statement of the subject to the satisfaction of your Honorable Body, while they defend the undoubted rights and immunities of this Corporation and the granting which will be acknowledged as a favor of your Memorialists, for themselves and their Constituents."

As in contemporary America, emerging communities of the nineteenth century often attempted to protect the life style of the community against external pressures. In 1826 Camden, New Jersey, experienced a movement toward incorporation as a city as the result of complaints against "lawless elements" who came across the river from Philadelphia on Sundays to the "beer gardens" of Camden. These Pennsylvania citizens were looking for an opportunity to avoid the "blue laws," which for many decades characterized Pennsylvania. Incorporation offered to Camden a number of opportunities for greater control of the "lawless," including conditions of liquor sale within the city.

When adjacent and competing cities began to grow together in the early nineteenth century, annexation was somewhat less common than it is in contemporary America, but the pattern of response was not much different. In 1833 the City of New York opposed the incorporation of Brooklyn as a city and was successful in the legislature. The Brooklyn village charter, however, was modified as something of a consolation prize. Some citizens of both New York and Brooklyn wanted to see the two cities consolidated, apparently considering growth and size to be important factors in attracting industry and immigrants. The competition between the two cities continued until the end of the century. It was not until 1898 that what became the five boroughs were consolidated into a single city of New York. Although this resulted in a huge metropolis that was later to become, for a while, perhaps the largest city in the world, one of the consolidated city's mayors, William O'Dwyer, was later to say that the decision was probably a mistake.

Laws in most of the states during the nineteenth century provided that annexation could take place only after a referendum had been held and the areas to be annexed had approved of such a move. In addition, it was often required that the core city that was to receive the new urbanizing area approve in a separate vote. The assumption behind such provisions was based upon the existing technological conditions. It was assumed that what are ordinarily considered urban services would not be available outside of a municipality and that, once a developing area approached metropolitan life styles, its inhabitants would wish to become annexed. These assumptions were valid for a number of decades, but they were eventually defeated by changing technology. Once it became possible for suburbanites to enjoy the advantages of urban living without sharing in the costs involved in maintaining the older and more highly concentrated sections of the city, annexation became unpopular. Local pride and a desire to have a distinctive and prestigious name for the community, combined with a desire for a tax system less expensive than that of the central city, led to the popularity of independently incorporated suburbs. Although large-scale annexations in order to secure urban services continued into the 1880s, the suburban attitude of independence and a preference for isolation from the social and economic problems of the core city began to assert themselves immediately after the Civil War.

Closing Note

Many other areas of political conflict existed in the early nineteenth century. Tax rates, of course, were a hardy perennial and will be discussed in Chapter 10. The extension of suffrage to the urban poor was also an issue that lasted for a couple of generations.

Other areas of issue conflict included questions of street paving, the materials to be used, how such surfacing was to be paid for, whether sidewalks should be built, and policies for controlling the galloping of horses or the herding of animals through the streets. The most colorful issues of the early nineteenth century, however, and the ones that strike the modern reader as being quaint, were those centering on the so-called blue laws. The restrictions on the activities and penalties for Sabbath breaking were perhaps strictest in Pennsylvania, where traces of them remain today. But they also were enacted in other states.

The issues of the first century after independence were traumatic to the citizens of the day, but they do not—for the most part—seem foreign or quaint to the contemporary citizen. Urbanites of all eras have been and continue to be plagued with problems of subcultural conflict, transportation, communication, education, the preservation of health in an artificial environment, the care of the poor, the preservation of order, and the protection of the peaceful citizen.

Notes

1. Charles L. Brace, *The Dangerous Classes of New York and Twenty Years' Work Among Them* (New York, 1880).
2. Cited in Richard C. Wade, *The Urban Frontier* (Cambridge, Mass., 1959), p. 289.
3. James Mease, *The Picture of Philadelphia, Giving an Account of its Origin, Increase and Improvements* (Philadelphia, 1811).
4. George R. Stewart, *Committee of Vigilance* (New York, 1964); Wayne Gard, *Frontier Justice* (Norman, Okla., 1949); and Charles Howard Shinn, *Mining Camps: A Study in American Frontier Government* (New York, 1884).
5. J. S. Johnston (ed.), *Memorial History of Louisville* (Louisville, 1896).
6. Brace, *op. cit.*
7. Alexander B. Callow, Jr., *The Tweed Ring* (New York, 1966), p. 147, and bibliography.
8. Frederick L. Olmsted, "Public Parks and the Enlargement of Towns," *Journal of Social Science*, III:10 ff., November, 1871. See also Laura Wood Roper, *FLO: A Biography of Frederick Law Olmsted* (Baltimore, 1973), especially chaps. 12 and 13.

Chapter 6

THE SUFFRAGE, CANDIDATES, AND CAMPAIGNS

THE CENTURY FOLLOWING American independence was one of great change in the political process. First of all, it was a time for the concept of government by the people. Although Jefferson argued in support of the right of the governed to reject their rulers, he did not make clear who, precisely, should be allowed to make such decisions. He saw all men as being created equal, but their right to equal political participation was not granted in his time. As had been the case at least from the age of Aristotle, democracy was still viewed with suspicion. Yet at the time of Jefferson's death in 1826 the term "democracy" was emerging as not just acceptable but something to be proud of. Government by the people, although still given many different meanings, was beginning to mean by all free, white males who had passed their twenty-first birthday. And as Jefferson's life approached its end, the first populist movement, of which many more were to follow, swept across the United States in the form of what we now call "Jacksonian democracy."

Although at the time of American independence the suffrage was generally more liberal at the municipal than at the state level, that pattern was later to change as the states moved toward universal manhood suffrage. But cities often retained property ownership requirements for eligibility to vote on proposed special tax levies or bond issues. During this period the concept of a freeman of the city, a basic notion since medieval times, lost its meaning.

The period up to 1870 also produced a change in the political style of American municipal election campaigns. Through the first few decades of the nineteenth century, municipal, like national, campaigns were normally humdrum affairs with little competition and hence little electioneering. In Presidential elections, really strong and uninhibited campaigning did not take place until the 1828 Jackson-Adams conflict, and the prototype modern campaign did not come along until the 1840 contest involving Martin Van Buren against "Tippecanoe and Tyler, too." Busy persons of some stature in the community were often prevailed upon—virtually drafted—to run for the council or the office of mayor. The idea that municipal public offices were worth fighting for generally awaited the sharp differences in economic interests and ideologies that were to follow from the accumulation of urban wealth and the arrival in this country of persons of varying ethnic and cultural backgrounds.

The Popular Suffrage

In the colonial and post-Revolutionary periods not all adults could vote. Restrictions on blacks and females are easily documented, but difficulty arises in assessing the position of adult white males. Traditionally, the interpretation of historians has been that relatively few such men could vote prior to the liberalizing of the suffrage in the Jacksonian 1820s and 1830s.[1] Some historians have challenged this interpretation.[2] They have argued that the property requirements common during this period were relatively slight and had little effect upon the outcome of elections in a society in which most men owned the necessary amount of land, or the alternative requirement in personal property. The argument essentially has been that the intent and effect of the law was only to exclude paupers and others who were not able or willing to contribute to the accumulation of society's wealth. A plausible argument can be developed that the great majority of adult white males could vote in colonial times and that the liberality of the suffrage requirements expanded at a greater rate than did the immigration of the poor from Europe. This expansion can be interpreted as continuing until universal white manhood suffrage was achieved in most parts of the nation at some time prior to 1840.

This theory confronts a number of difficulties. For one thing, there was certainly a good deal of agitation, particularly by Jacksonian Democrats, for expanding the suffrage and eliminating property requirements. It seems unlikely that such activity would take place unless a substantial portion of the electorate were still excluded and hence potentially available as Democratic voters. (Of course, this pool of possible supporters may have been small in colonial times but may have increased rapidly after American independence.) A similar indication that the question of the suffrage was, after all, important was provided by conservatives. Certainly they viewed with considerable alarm proposals for allowing individuals who had no direct stake in the cost of government to participate in elections. The fact that the issue of the extent of the suffrage was a matter of controversy throughout most of the last half of the eighteenth century and beyond the first half of the nineteenth is an indication that, even though a majority of white male adults could vote, those who were disfranchised continued to represent a significant number of persons and a pool of potential voters worthy of the attention of both idealists and the politically ambitious.

The privilege of voting in the American colonies was based upon a centuries-old British principle, the forty-shilling freehold. It was from this rule that all struggles for liberalization in England and the United States moved. Parliament, fearing riots or at least lesser disturbances, and annoyed at the presumptuousness of persons who claimed, despite their lack of wealth, the right to a voice equal to that of knights and country squires, had decided in 1430 that no person should be allowed to vote unless he possessed a freehold (real property held in fee simple) and had an annual income of at least forty shillings.[3] This rule, however, did not apply to municipal corporations. In the case of voting for borough officers, qualifications were determined either by the municipal charter, local custom, or a special act of Parliament. In general, the right to vote in municipal elections was somewhat less restrictive than that for the general suffrage, but it was normally extended only to persons of property and freemen, that is, men who had been granted the privilege of enjoying the benefits of the municipality, in particular the right to do business there or to membership in craft guilds.

Universal Manhood Suffrage

Until the Jacksonian era the right to vote was associated with property rather than with citizenship. Thus, in New Haven in 1784 the suffrage belonged to adult males who had a personal estate worth forty pounds, or real estate renting for at least two pounds per year. Of the approximately six hundred adult males in the city, 343 were qualified to vote as freemen. Of those, 261 actually took the freeman's oath; only 249 voted for mayor that year,[4] but this was 76 per cent of those eligible—a comparatively high proportion. In Providence in 1831 there were only 1,200 freemen in a population of about 17,000, and 54 per cent of them voted on the question of adopting a city charter.

As with other aspects of the Jacksonian ideology, the idea that voting was a right attaching to membership in the body politic rather than a privilege stemming from the need to protect one's property was strongest along the frontier. Vermont, today scarcely thought of as a frontier state, was first to establish universal manhood suffrage in its original constitution of 1791. New Hampshire followed the next year, as did Kentucky. The 1792 constitution of the latter granted the suffrage to "all free male citizens of the age twenty-one years, having resided in the state two years, or the county in which they offered to vote one year before the election." Seven years later this provision was amended to

limit the suffrage to members of the white race. This action was significant, for in general the right of free blacks to vote was more generously
extended in the years just after independence than just before the Civil
War. Although black Connecticut citizens of property could vote in
1784, they could not do so after the adoption of the constitution of
1818. In 1838 Pennsylvania, while broadening the suffrage for white
males, disfranchised all black males. Blacks of property were few and
not much of a status threat to anyone in the early years of the Republic.

The Kentucky universal manhood suffrage provision, in effect, substituted stable membership in the community for property as a requirement to vote. The lengthy residence requirements were later to become
particularly popular in the South, which retained, on the average, longer
residence requirements than did the rest of the nation, and did so far
into the twentieth century. Tennessee in 1796 carried the idea of the
right of the free adult white male to vote to its final triumph, providing
that a man "being an inhabitant of any one county in the state six months
immediately preceding the day of election shall be entitled to vote."
The completion of the suffrage by extension to blacks, Indians, women,
and youth remained for a later age. Other states quite rapidly adopted
the Tennessee or Kentucky principle, but with numerous variations in
the residence requirements. In 1800 Maryland did so under the leadership of Edward Lloyd, who was only twenty-one, but who had already
inherited a large estate from his father. (Neither Lloyd nor any other
major reform leader advocated a voting age eligibility less than that of
the historic legal age of adulthood, twenty-one.)

The original states, the action of Maryland to the contrary notwith-
standing, were generally less willing than were those of the frontier to
accept universal manhood suffrage, for they were more tradition-bound
and had different patterns of property ownership. The frontier was dominated by the yeoman farmer and the small merchant, neither of whom
was either very rich or very poor. In the older states the broadening of
the suffrage may have been hurried in part by the growth of cities with
their anonymity, for it became increasingly common to evade the property requirement for voting. Normally one was required only to swear
that he was eligible to vote. If he swore that he had the required amount
of property, it became less and less practicable to challenge him. In
some areas people accepted universal white manhood suffrage simply
because it had become the only administratively feasible approach, while
the resistance of conservatives weakened with the spread of the populist
ideology.

By the time New York came into line in 1825, the state constitutional
amendment was adopted so easily that "hardly a voice was raised in protest."[5] This was so even though at the state constitutional convention,
held four years earlier, universal manhood suffrage had been rejected.

At that convention, however, delegate David Buel stated the new ideology: "Our community is an association of persons—of human beings—not a partnership founded on property." (Buel, like Jefferson, defended the extension of the suffrage on the mistaken notion that universal education, another principle that was then emerging, would create an informed electorate. He argued: "The universal diffusion of information will forever distinguish our population from that of Europe.")[6]

Despite the easy victory in New York, not all people were convinced that Jefferson and Buel were right. The Frenchman, Alexis de Tocqueville, traveling in the United States in the early 1830s and talking principally with well-to-do urbanites and gentlemen farmers, was highly doubtful that urbanism and universal suffrage were compatible. He feared that, once the common people could control the growing cities and their governments, educated people and those of property would have to rely on the state militia for the maintenance of order. He thought such a militia should remain under the control of "the majority of the nation" (America was then overwhelmingly rural), and would have to be "independent of the town population and able to repress its excesses."[7] It is true that riots in cities were far more common in the early nineteenth century than they were in the latter half of the twentieth century (see Chapter 10), but the evidence does not show that the extension of the suffrage was a crucial factor, even though there were some election-day riots. Major ghetto disturbances occurred in New York and Philadelphia while de Tocqueville was in this country, and he gained some fairly direct evidence concerning them, but although they were a product of poverty, slum conditions, and inter-ethnic conflicts, the suffrage itself was not a direct factor.

The adoption of universal manhood suffrage was most strenuously resisted not in the more urbanized states, as de Tocqueville might have expected, but rather in those that were the most tradition-bound, especially in the South, where deference to an aristocracy was a powerful influence. It was not until 1830, deep into the Jacksonian era, that Virginia expanded the traditional forty-shilling freeholder requirement for suffrage to include leaseholders and householders if they paid taxes; and not until after the Civil War did the Old Dominion accept universal manhood suffrage in theory. It was very much later before it would approximate it in practice.

There was one other major holdout: little Rhode Island. That state had refused to ratify the United States Constitution. It now also resisted change in the suffrage. Agitation for broader voting rights took place there, too, of course. A Rhode Island Suffrage Association was formed with Thomas Dorr as its head. In 1841 a so-called People's Convention instigated by the association was held. The document drawn up provided for something considered to be universal manhood suffrage, but even it—regarded as a radical document by the social and economic leaders of the state—limited the vote to whites and excluded paupers. Under this irregularly adopted constitution, a governor was elected and attempted to take office simultaneously with the governor elected under the regular suffrage requirement, which limited voting to men possessing a freehold worth at least $134. Dorr's Rebellion followed. It failed, and it was not until two generations later (1888) that universal manhood suffrage came to Rhode Island. Even then, municipal councils were not included.

Remaining Restrictions

Restrictions of various kinds remained for the suffrage. Sometimes these appeared to be minor, but they had the effect of disfranchising nearly all black and some white men. The Florida constitution of 1845 gave the vote to free white males who were citizens of the United States and residents of Florida for two years or more, but there was the additional provision that they must also be enrolled in the state militia. In 1856 Massachusetts required a voter to be able to read the Constitution and write his own name, a change that was a result of pressure from the antiforeigner American party. In 1859 this policy was carried further through a constitutional amendment providing that no foreign-born person could vote until two years after he had been naturalized.

Gradually the United States approached universal manhood suffrage. The religious requirements for voting, stipulating that an individual must be a Christian or even a member of a particular church, were gradually removed. Some of these restrictions, however, continued into the Jacksonian era. A "Jew Bill" in Maryland was debated vigorously and often bitterly for many years before it was finally passed in 1825. It removed all religious disqualifications from voting. Although the feeling against non-Christians (it was not primarily the secular anti-Semitism so common in the twentieth century) was a powerful emotional issue, there were probably fewer than two hundred Jews in the state of Maryland at that time.

Restriction by race increased after the second decade of the nineteenth century until, at the beginning of the Civil War, only the New England states and New York did not have a color bar at the polls. After the war the Fifteenth Amendment prohibited further discrimination on this basis, but the effect in the North was quite different from that in the South. In the latter, after Federal troops were removed in 1877, various ways were found by which to disfranchise blacks. In the North many states moved to eliminate the racial barrier even before the Constitutional amendment was adopted in 1870. Illinois, for example, granted Negro suffrage in 1865. In the North generally there were relatively few efforts to keep blacks from the polls after that time.

Throughout the nineteenth century women were generally excluded from the suffrage because men were considered to be the spokesmen for their households and the guardians of the family interests. Voting formerly was considered to be a defense of property, so it was logical that the man should vote on behalf of his family. In any case, women were generally considered not to have an interest independent of their fathers or husbands, any more than did children. Even the Jacksonian perspective of the suffrage as an indication of membership in the polity did not change this attitude toward women. It was not until the twentieth century that sex was completely eliminated as a criterion for voting.

The movement to give women the vote was active from the early days of the Republic. By the late 1840s it was fully under way. State constitutional conventions and legislatures were thereafter bombarded by women's groups demanding the suffrage. Kentucky—that pioneering commonwealth on such matters—had allowed women to vote in school elections under certain conditions as early as 1838. The New Jersey constitution of 1776, apparently by oversight, gave the vote to all inhabitants who were "of full age" (twenty-one) and owned property in the amount of fifty pounds. Some years after adoption, it came to be recognized that this provision would permit widows and spinsters owning the necessary property in their own names to be legally eligible to vote. Apparently some women did so. This development did not set a precedent, however, perhaps in part because of an unusual and dramatic political accident. In 1806 violent controversy took place between Newark and Elizabeth concerning the location of a new courthouse for Essex County. The special election on the referendum question was wildly corrupt and irregular. There is no indication that women were guilty of any more irregularities than were men. Nevertheless, the incident provoked a demand for change in the election laws, and some of the male political leaders, seeing a dainty foot in the door, chose this opportunity to end the right of any female to vote. In that same year a new election law accepted the then favored notion of letting any male taxpayer vote irrespective of property value. The New Jersey franchise was extended for men but eliminated for women.

In 1869 the Territory of Wyoming granted white women the right to vote on the same basis as white men. The following year women served on juries in Laramie and Cheyenne and Esther H. Morris of South Pass City was elected the nation's first female justice of the peace. Women were relatively few on the frontier and respected for their stabilizing influence upon a crude society. And so Wyoming was ahead of its time.

A few years earlier, in 1867, at a time when the suffrage was being ex-

panded in response to the issues of the Civil War, the male voters of
Kansas rejected a constitutional amendment that would have permitted
women's suffrage. A number of states did give women the vote in school
elections in that period. Minnesota, for example, did so in 1875. But
universal suffrage for adults irrespective of race or sex on a statewide
basis was not achieved until it was provided for in the Wyoming constitution of 1889.

The Municipal Suffrage

Throughout this period the old English practice of making exceptions and special provisions for municipal corporations continued. In
Massachusetts after 1736 the suffrage for towns was based upon paying
a tax equal to at least two-thirds of the poll tax, while the commonwealth continued to have a property ownership requirement. In the
other New England states the town suffrage was also broader than that
for the state, except in Rhode Island, where the municipal suffrage, except for mayor, was until 1928 restricted to persons owning taxable
property.

In the Middle Atlantic states, suffrage in municipal elections was also
generally broader than for the state. In New York persons who were
made freemen of the cities of Albany and New York thereby gained the
right not only to engage in trade in the city but also to vote. The freedom of the city was not easily gained, however. The suffrage regulation
for the city of New York in 1784 provided that it was to be confined to
those born in the city or to persons who had served a seven-year apprenticeship, or who had paid a graded set of occupational license fees.
Those born in the city or who served apprenticeships there had to pay
a small fee when sworn in as freemen. And although the right of suffrage within the city was more liberal during the colonial period than it
was for the colonywide elections, this pattern changed after independence. The act of 1784 was more restrictive than that which applied to
statewide elections. Electoral changes in 1804 resulted in the dropping
of the freeholder or freeman requirement and permitted any male to
vote if he paid taxes on property with a rental value of $25 a year. At the
same time Tammany Hall went on record as favoring universal manhood suffrage. (A decade later Augusta, Georgia, eliminated its prop-
erty-owner and leasehold qualifications for voting, and suffrage was
made uniform with that of the state. In 1841 Chicago specifically accepted universal manhood suffrage in its charter.)

The importance of the role of freeman declined after it ceased to be
a basis for suffrage rights, and by 1807 the restriction of trade to freemen had fallen into disuse. By 1815 it was extinct except for the practice of granting the freedom of the city to distinguished nonresidents.

(In 1784 New York observed the traditional practice, as it still does to-day, of granting "freedom of the city and address" to well-known citizens. That year it recognized Revolutionary war heroes Lafayette, von Steuben, Washington, and others.) Although the State of New York adopted universal manhood suffrage in 1825, the city continued its taxpayer requirement for municipal elections until 1842, when the leaders of the Whig and American (Know-Nothing) parties united in agreement for its elimination.

In New Jersey tenants and householders could vote in municipal elections from colonial times. In Annapolis nonfreeholders could vote if they had served a five-year apprenticeship, had been registered as freemen for at least three months, and were inhabitants of the city. Norfolk, Virginia, had a similar provision, but voters in Richmond had to be freeholders. After the advent of universal manhood suffrage for state government elections, cities also generally accepted this principle. Sometimes they were required to do so under state law or the state constitution. Many cities, however, continued to restrict the suffrage to property owners on questions of the issuance of general obligation municipal bonds or the levying of a special millage in excess of the regular property tax. Some continued to have such special provisions into the twentieth century. In a few cases where taxpaying requirements had been allowed to lapse, they were revived during the Great Depression.

During the first century after American independence, then, the suffrage changed its theoretical basis from property, the right of the property owner to participate in decisions that might affect the value and use of his property, to the right of every adult man to participate. In the transitional process, the emphasis on property was transferred temporarily to an emphasis upon community stability, with residence requirements sometimes being as much as two years. (Pennsylvania had a two-year residence requirement during the colonial period, but this was atypical.) The belief that residence in the community for some period of time in order for the individual to identify with it, its issues and political personalities, as a necessary prerequisite for voting persisted into the twentieth century.

The Ballot

Changes in the method of voting occurred during the first half of the nineteenth century. The common early practice was for use of the voice vote, but this was gradually replaced by a show of hands. This method continued to be used as late as 1844 in New Brunswick, New Jersey. But the idea of a secret ballot became increasingly important as cities grew, consensus declined, and at least the possibility of intimidation of the individual voter increased. The written ballot appeared in Baltimore as early as 1801 and in New York City three years later. Yet in St. Louis *viva voce* voting for judges was not replaced by written ballot until 1842. For a long time, however, subtle means of influencing or intimidating the individual voter continued through the use of traditional practices. For example, in New Orleans in 1814 the polling places were still located in the homes of prominent citizens rather than in neutral public places, such as the city hall, fire stations, or public schools. Throughout the first century of independence, however, the ballot continued to consist of pieces of paper upon which the individual voter wrote his own choices. Sometimes they were premarked and supplied by various political parties or other interested groups. The so-called Australian or secret ballot, in which each ballot was of the same size, shape, and color, was printed at government expense, and was available only at the polling place from an election official, did not make its appearance in the United States until 1888.

During most of the first century of independence balloting usually extended over several days. For example, the polls in the city of New York in 1834 were open for three days. In an age when working hours were extremely long, excuses for absences were not easily accepted, elections were not always held at completely predictable times, and methods of transportation and communication were poor, such arrangements made a good deal of sense. But they also lent themselves to corruption, and the amount of suspense created in controversial elections must have been a factor in encouraging violence. Gradually there was a transition to the modern practice of having a single election day, with the polls open from early morning until into the evening. This was required by New York state law in 1840. In that same voting law revision, New York provided for the registration of voters. Modifications were made in the law two years later. But requirements for the adequate identification of eligible voters and precautions against the abuse of the suffrage by multiple voting did not spread rapidly. Its acceptance and effective enforcement did not come until the twentieth century.

The corruption of the ballot box began early, well in advance of Jacksonian populism. In the 1807 battle between Newark and Elizabeth, New Jersey, over the location of the Essex County seat—a valuable prize both economically and in terms of status—5,039 votes were cast in Newark township, even though it had a total population of fewer than 6,000 persons.

Once the Jacksonian movement had introduced universal manhood suffrage and the older pattern of noncompetitive local elections had given way to seriously contested campaigns, ballot fraud became increasingly evident. Thus, in Augusta, Maine, with 1,294 voters eligible, a suspicious 1,259 ballots were cast in 1850.

Election frauds were never uncommon in a competitive society based upon achieved status. Certainly, during the first three generations or so of the nineteenth century the emphasis was, as it later continued to be, upon winning. Corners were cut and moral principles were shaved even while most people continued to believe that the electoral process was "sacred" and not to be tampered with—at least not openly. Certainly the big city machines of a later era or modern techniques of political espionage were not something without precedent dating back to before the Civil War. Still, up to 1870 most elections were without any trace of fraud, if for no other reason than that they were polite contests of status and popularity between candidates who differed little in their approaches to local problems and had little, if anything, to gain from agreeing to serve for a while in public office.

Types of Candidates

During the years of restrictive suffrage, candidates for both mayor and councilman tended to be established, conservative members of the community, particularly Main Street merchants. In the older Eastern cities the beginnings of a genuine American aristocracy had begun to emerge, and it was from this group, with its sense of obligation to the community, that candidates for mayor sometimes emerged.

When the first city charter of Boston, in 1822, provided for the popular election of the mayor, the initial incumbent was undistinguished and made little attempt to provide leadership. His successor, however, was Josiah Quincy, a member of the Boston aristocracy. In many ways, he provided the prototype for the active, effective leader in the office of mayor, exercising influence where he did not have authority and always seeking to provide leadership in attempting to meet the major problems of the city. Quincy "was like an accomplished actor who takes a small part and makes of it a great one."

Quincy's successor, Harrison Otis, served three one-year terms, showing little innovation but attempting to carry out Quincy's policies. His successor of two terms, Charles Wells, was a kind of middle-class representative of protest against the magnificence of Quincy and Otis. His main goal was to prevent an increase in the municipal debt and, essentially, his was a do-nothing administration. Quincy, the aristocrat, acting as the guiding hand for the community conscience, represented a type of candidate that sometimes appeared in American municipal politics, but he was far from typical.

Of the mayors of Boston during the first half-century following incorporation, only Josiah Quincy, his son of the same name, and Samuel A. Eliot came from the city's most distinguished families. This was a common pattern: A member of the top elite would serve occasionally, but persons a notch or two lower in status were more usual officeholders. During these decades mayors were generally viewed as well qualified.

The first mayors of Newark "were picked from among the leading men of the community. Politics played their part then as now, but the head of the city government was always one who had already achieved much for the advancement of the community and was looked up to as representative of the best and highest expression of citizenship as it was then understood." During the first two decades after the city was incorporated in 1836, the Whig Party dominated. (The first Democratic mayor, Moses Bigelow, was not elected until 1857.) In 1837, Theodore Frelinghuysen was elected mayor. He was a former United States Senator and later became a candidate for the office of Vice President on the Whig Party ticket with Henry Clay. He also served as Chancellor of the University of the City of New York and President of Rutgers College. His family belonged to the early Dutch aristocracy of New Jersey.

Councilmen continued to be selected for the most part from among Main Street merchants of modest wealth and education, but with a considerable interest in public order, low taxes, and the preservation of the rights of property. Mayors, on the other hand, tended to come from a somewhat higher social status. But even among them the trend was toward the common man. In 1838 Key West elected a mayor who was a grog shop proprietor and an illiterate. Two years later New York elected Mayor Varian, whose administration was considered to have been effective and capable.[8] A principal basis for his popularity appears to have been the fact that he had been a "fire laddie" and that he enjoyed the campaign support of the members of the fire companies. But after 1842 there were complaints of a "marked decline" in the caliber of men elected to the council and to other city offices.[9] These complaints, however, coincided with the extension of the suffrage and may have been intended as protests against that trend.

During the period between 1857 and 1860, and again in 1865, John Wentworth was the mayor of Chicago. He was a picturesque character, vigorous in his efforts to establish an orderly community. He represented another type of mayor common throughout American history, one who wanted to resist the extravagances of his predecessors. Wentworth was able to reduce both the city debt and budget during his terms in office. He was a lawyer and a member of prominent city clubs. Other Chicago mayors were also able. One local pundit said that between 1848 and 1869, twenty-five of the twenty-seven candidates for mayor were men with "enviable standing in the business life of the city."

The first elected mayor of Philadelphia was John M. Scott, an attorney. During the violent riots that plagued Philadelphia during the 1840s he supported the forerunners of the police, the night watch and constables. A particularly interesting mayor was Richard T. Conrad, a member of the Native American Party, who sought to suppress the behavior of the immigrant groups and who viewed them as the source of all disorders within the city of Philadelphia. He contributed to the tension between the Protestant native-born citizens and the Irish by appointing only natural-born citizens to the police force. He also vigorously enforced the Sunday "blue" laws relative to liquor sales and, as a result, encountered the enmity of native-born and foreign alike and was forced to retire from office after only one term. After him came Richard Vaux, an aristocrat who defended the common man and his interests in a pattern familiar from the time of Jefferson to the Kennedys. Whether it was his personal preference or an affectation, he adopted many of the life patterns of the common man, walking rather than taking the streetcar and going without a coat, even in cold weather.[10] He had, however, been defeated for election as mayor many times in the past, and he served only one term, being defeated for re-election in 1858 by a Whig. As Sam Bass Warner, Jr. has indicated:

> Vaux's 1856 election resulted in large measure from a successful coalition of local bosses and firehouse gangs. To maintain such a coalition, lines of supporters seeking jobs had to be given work with the city. Neither Vaux nor his opponents could ignore that need. The price of such a pattern of professional politics is well known to American history; weak, corrupt, unimaginative municipal government.

During this period, mayors had fewer and fewer opportunities to demonstrate outstanding municipal leadership. Increasingly, they had to compromise with the parochial interests of neighborhood political leaders, and, although they did not recognize what was happening, they reluctantly and often unwillingly came to perform the brokerage function that was later to become the professional hallmark of the political boss and the machine leader.[11] At the same time the outstanding leaders of the social and economic segments of society tended to retreat into the background, and the mayors, as had generally been the case with councilmen throughout the nineteenth century, increasingly were selected from among the competent but undistinguished members of the middle class, particularly from among the Main Street merchants.

The turnover rate for mayors seems to have varied from one community to the next, reflecting local political styles but no particular pattern. The mayor's office was made elective in Wilmington, Delaware, in 1850, and the immediate result was a sharp increase in the rate of turnover. Nine different men served as mayor during the first decade. But in Mobile the mayor commonly served many terms, even after the coming of universal white manhood suffrage. Between 1826 and 1859, over a span of thirty-four elections, there were thirteen mayors. Austin, Texas, drew its aldermen from a great variety of occupations. Poughkeepsie, another small city, in the 1850s selected 60 per cent of its aldermen from the business and professional group, 32 per cent from artisans and workingmen. The identical pattern existed in Springfield, Massachusetts. Troy, New York, had a few councilmen who served long periods, except immediately after its incorporation as a city in 1816 and again for a time after the Civil War. In general, those who served in public office commonly seemed to consider a year or two a sufficient indication of their sense of civic obligation. The professional politician at the local level, with rare exceptions, belonged to the future.

Campaign Issues

Until after about 1850 municipal campaigns were generally conducted in a low key. The conflicts of interest among those who could vote in the period prior to universal white manhood suffrage were relatively few. It was often more a question of convincing some merchant or professional man that it was "his turn" to run than it was of planning strategies that would permit one's candidate to win in a competitive situation. Political activity was generally constrained by the notion that those with the greatest stake in society should rule—the propertied classes and, in particular, the Main Street merchants. Much of politics and political participation was ceremonial in character. Until after the Civil War, in most cities local politics did not develop the entertainment potential that was found in state and national elections.

New Orleans politics of about 1820 offers an example of the politics of the day in many cities. At that time it was customary for the candidates merely to announce modestly in the newspapers that a number of friends had considered the particular candidate a proper person to fill the post in question. There were no party nominating conventions or primaries to be overcome. Even the mayor was customarily re-elected with little or no opposition.[12] With the coming of universal white manhood suffrage and the conflicts engendered by increasing wealth and the widening disparity of wealth among members of the community, this pattern could not be expected to persist, and the image of public office as a public service was almost certain to be replaced by the idea that public office served as a basis for providing the services and establishing the policies demanded by a particular segment of the voting population.

Nonetheless, political campaigning in the early nineteenth century was minimal. There were no primaries, and the choice of the caucus or convention could ordinarily count upon party loyalists to turn out. Campaign oratory was unlikely to have much effect upon voter choice. In those days, "after nomination, there was little electioneering as we understand the word. To canvass for votes was looked on as betokening a lack of modesty."[13] But this attitude changed toward the end of the 1820s. During the 1850s, and leading up to the critical election of 1860, the controlling Democratic coalition was breaking down, and so party loyalties were dissolving and strenuous campaigning became increasingly worthwhile, even in local elections.

Issues that could become the basis of conflict began to appear early, of course. In the elections of 1822 (for legislature) and 1824 (for council) in Annapolis, conflicts arose over the question of the desirable method of nominating candidates for public office. The dispute was between advocates and opponents of a caucus for the nomination of a party's candidate. This conflict emphasized the new competitive pattern. Earlier the problem had been one of inducing a desirable person to run for office; now the dispute became one between those who were willing to accept such office and those who wanted to increase their chances of winning through organized activity. This type of competition led within a few years to a problem that was to plague American elections into the indefinite future. In 1830 a number of Annapolis citizens pledged themselves to vote for no man who had given drink, money, or any other valuable considerations as an inducement for a voter to cast a ballot in his support. Though by no means for the first time, the problem of bribery had reared its ugly head.

In the 1830s it came to be recognized that universal white manhood suffrage and a large immigration rate were affecting the outcome of municipal elections. Charges began to be made that "corrupt" politicians were seeking the vote of the new citizens in order to acquire control of municipal governments and to manage municipal affairs for their personal profit. Elections began to center on charges that municipal political machines had been organized to the detriment of good, fair, and honest municipal government. Although the effective formula for the boss and machine was not to be developed for another generation, the machine had emerged as a campaign issue and the target of middle-class businessmen and their allies. At that time party loyalties were very strong, and campaigns tended to become emotional name-calling affairs, sometimes with little or no debate over issues. As a happy Whig commented after Rochester's first city election (1834): "We have no pestilence, although we once had Jacksonianism and cholera."

Conflicts began to arise, sometimes ironically as a result of efforts to avoid political issues. In 1851 the Boston council refused to make Faneuil Hall available either to Abolitionists, who were feared as radicals, or for a reception for Daniel Webster, a conservative. These decisions, particularly the latter, cost both the mayor and the aldermen re-election. In that same year antislavery became an issue. The city was legally required to hold fugitive slaves for return to their masters. Abolitionists strongly opposed this practice and sought to prevent or at least disrupt it. In that eventful year of 1851 the police force became politically active in Boston. Many members of the force, including the chief marshal, worked for the election of the challenger to the incumbent, and they were successful. After the new mayor, Benjamin Seaver, took office, he practically guaranteed that the police would remain active as a result of his policies. At that time members of the police force were appointed annually. Seaver made some changes, which the chief marshal criticized; he was promptly replaced by the mayor, and the police from that moment, if they were not already, became a politically active group.

In the early years of the nineteenth century New Orleans politics was characterized by animosities between the Creoles and the Americans. In order to mitigate the tensions and to permit the Creoles a degree of self-government, New Orleans was divided into three quasi-municipalities, with the Creoles living in the old city area, now known as the French Quarter, and the Americans in the other areas. This plan was abandoned with a new charter in 1852, by which time local observers reported that conflicts between the two groups had largely disappeared. But under the old charter other kinds of problems had piled up. There were "fiscal confusion, badly managed finances and a large debt," as the debt commissioners that year reported, and "the people were disheartened."[14] However, within the year the new commissioners had reorganized and reduced the debt and made it manageable.

During the 1850s a new political pattern emerged as a result of intense emotions that were associated with single issues. These led to Whig disintegration and Democratic fractures. Free Soil and Anti-Slavery, Know-Nothing, and Temperance groups were among the most divisive in their effect upon the old alignments. These groups constantly sought to influence municipal elections, even though only the latter two had actual municipal relevance. As the Civil War approached, the Republicans and Secessionists cut across traditional and new groups alike. In Kansas City in 1860 about 23 per cent of the population voted in the national election. How high this was may be seen by comparison with the 13 per cent voting in St. Louis. (In the latter city about 9 per cent of the population had voted the year before in a local referendum on the sale of liquor on Sunday.)

A number of cities elected mayors and councilmen who were members of the Native American (Know-Nothing) Party during the 1850s. The huge migrations from Europe to America after the revolutions and famines of 1848 helped to provoke deep resentment at the immigrants. This resentment was partly cultural, partly economic. Sometimes the Know-Nothings would ally themselves with the dying Whig Party against the Democrats. Some of the Know-Nothing mayors were quite conventional, but others were colorful, if often ineffective, leaders. Thus in Boston in 1853 Mayor Seaver was replaced by Jerome V. Smith, who was described as a hard worker but was never quite taken seriously by the community elite. Know-Nothingism was, of course, a populistic movement, and its leaders sometimes featured proposals for expanding political power in the neighborhoods. These proposals were often greeted by scorn or alarm on the part of the community elite. Smith, for example, recommended a police board to consist of one man elected from each of the twelve wards, this board to make annual police appointments, subject to the approval of the mayor and aldermen. (The 1850s, of course, saw a considerable movement toward the use of commissions to head departments, even in cities not controlled by the Know-Nothings. This development was a transition from control of departments by city aldermen to the professional administrator, who was to come along a few generations later.) In the following year the Know-Nothings carried Massachusetts. They also scored heavily in the populous states of New York and Pennsylvania as well as in the South. But the party, like the Whigs, was unable to agree on a policy toward slavery, and it declined rapidly after 1856. It did not last even that long in Boston. After one year Smith had outstayed his welcome, and his opponent, Rice, was elected mayor.

By the time of the Civil War, the ethnic vote was no longer by any means simply that of the Irish immigrants. In the Newark municipal elections of 1865, the vote of German-Americans was largely responsible for the Republican victory. At this time, Newark was to a considerable extent a German town. In fact, the attitude of the German immigrants toward their new country was ambivalent. In 1869 there was a strong move to teach German in the grammar schools of Newark, and this effort was nearly successful. Had it been, it is likely that the assimilation of German immigrants and their advancement in terms of income and status would have been considerably delayed. The failure of this short-sighted effort redounded to the advantage of all German-Americans.

Three issues dominated the New York City election of 1854; nativism, temperance, and municipal reform. Although the Know-Nothings did not last long as a party, they greatly raised the conflict levels in cities and caused considerable political chaos. In New York they dominated the organization of both the Whig and the Temperance parties and represented a strong faction within the Democratic party. Even some of the municipal reformers, generally drawn from the upper middle class, were nativists. The tactic of the Know-Nothings was to attempt to capture control of the nominating conventions. Both of the major parties nominated Know-Nothings, Fernando Wood for the Democrats and John Herrick for the Whigs. The Temperance party nominee, James Barker, did not at first claim to be a Know-Nothing but later apparently found it to his advantage to admit that he was. During the campaign

. . . each nominee on the tickets of the older parties found it to his interest to seek support from the adherents of one or more of the organized movements [the nativists, temperance groups, and municipal reformers]. The result was a marvelous criss-cross of influences, which divided the former compactness of the older groups into subdivisions on new lines of cleavage.[15]

In a close vote, Wood was elected. Charges of election fraud were freely made, and many of them no doubt had a basis in fact. The nativists, in power, began an effort to have foreign-born city employees discharged. This effort was never carried off, and within a year the Know-Nothings were greatly weakened through internal dissension, particularly over the slavery issue. Fernando Wood, who was ambitious, clever, and sometimes daring, kept his job for two more terms. He carried the masses with him against a badly divided opposition. The Know-Nothings broke up into a number of organizations; those who were anxious to save the union began to gravitate toward the Republican party. In 1857 the Know-Nothings joined in a fusion ticket with the Republicans, but the combination was badly beaten by the Democrats. The closing years of the 1850s were represented by an enormous amount of confusion, as the Whig party died, the Republican was born, and third parties rose and fell. In 1858 the Democrats were, in turn, split over slavery. The Republicans won their first New York municipal election, with the support of what was left of the Know-Nothing groups.

Know-Nothingism was the issue in New Orleans elections during the late 1850s. In the parish election of 1855 there was widespread violence. A Native American mob seized and burned the ballot boxes in two precincts, and about 900 ballots were destroyed. In 1857 the state created the office of Superintendent of Elections for the parish of Orleans and especially for the city. It was given full power to prevent violence and intimidation, which had become so rife that, according to the governor, nearly one-third of the voters had been prevented from going to the polls. For nearly a year before the 1858 election there had been sporadic outbreaks of violence, chiefly anti-Irish and anti-German in character.[16] Crime was believed to be on the rise among the immigrants. Tensions were high enough to justify an expectation that the election would again involve violence and the destruction of ballots. A secret vigilance committee was formed, consisting of about 1,000 people. It was interested primarily in an orderly election and did not become involved in the selection of candidates. The Native American party nominated a candidate. The Democrats did not, but there was an independent ticket headed by former Mayor Beauregard, who was seeking a return to office. He made the police an issue. (Two years earlier, when the Know-Nothings won, there was considerable bloodshed, but police were now forbidden to carry arms and many resigned. A volunteer armed citizens' group then policed the election.) On June 1 a small mob, apparently made up of Know-Nothings, seized the office of the registrar of voters and began to revise lists to eliminate as many Whigs and independents as possible. The next night, the vigilantes, under the leadership of J. K. Duncan of the United States Army, went into action. They issued a manifesto calling for citizens' support. Mayor Waterman attempted to get the vigilance committee to disperse. It refused to do so unless the mayor agreed not to swear in the group as a special police force until after the election. He refused and called out the militia, which refused to respond. The mayor then allowed the mob to arm itself and issued a warrant for the arrest of Duncan and his associates, but it could not be enforced. The next day the mayor accepted Duncan's terms and agreed to swear in the vigilantes. This made the Nativist mob angry, and they set out to attack the Duncan group.

The mob was dissuaded with difficulty. On June 5 the agitation against the mayor came to a head. A heavy rainshower broke up the crowd around the city hall, but Waterman decided that the only safe thing would be to put himself at the mercy of the vigilance committee, and that morning he left the city hall. Despite urgings, he refused to return even to swear in the vigilance committee, but he did sign a paper authorizing the city recorder to do so. The council then impeached the mayor for refusal to perform his legal functions and appointed an acting mayor, who appointed a new police chief. Order was soon restored. Under these circumstances, the vigilante committee disintegrated. The election was orderly. Stith, the Know-Nothing, won the election by a vote of 3,581 to 3,450. The city council was also dominated by the Know-Nothings, although some independents were elected. Despite the furor, the actual voting turnout was unimpressive. Stith proved to be a capable mayor. His leadership was described as "effective," and he was the first mayor to have a definite and successful policy concerning public improvements. During his term, for the first time, considerable progress was made in the paving of streets and sidewalks, as well as in other permanent improvements.

Surveying the policies and administration of the Know-Nothing city governments over all, they were often considerably more ruthless than those of the other parties. This showed itself in the use of police, of political spoils, and of terror in elections. Fortunately, they soon faded out in the even more intense emotions aroused by the issues of slavery and secession.

Except for San Francisco, the issues typically confronting a Midwestern or Western city were far less unsettling, disruptive, or even interesting to the typical citizen. In contrast to the storms raging over the older cities, the ordinances introduced in Omaha in 1857, the year of the city's incorporation, were chiefly these quiet-preserving items: One, to define the duties of city recorder; two, to protect the city marshal in the performance of his official duties; three, to divide the city into wards and establish their boundaries (this could have been dynamite but was not); four, to prevent hogs from running at large; five, to establish a city pound for stray animals; six, to create the office of city engineer and define his duties; seven, to regulate billiard rooms and bowling alleys; eight, to regulate the sale of intoxicating liquors; and nine, to suppress gambling.

By the middle of the nineteenth century the United States was no longer by any means entirely dominated by the Protestant Ethic. In 1858 the Naturalization Association of Newark, an association of "hyphenated" Americans pledged its members to vote only for those candidates who would openly declare themselves in favor of "a liberal Sunday, meaning thereby, a Sunday not devoted to a puritanical observance but a day of rest and decent, respectful enjoyment." Members were also required to declare themselves in favor of the existing naturalization laws, against the extension of slavery into new territory, and in favor of the revision of the existing land laws. The Whigs were, at that time, advocates of strict Sunday "blue" laws and strict enforcement of the liquor laws, which did not appeal to the Germans. The Democrats tried to keep the Germans within their party fold, arguing that the party was opposed to the Nativists. Despite this effort, however, the antislavery sentiments were too strong among the Germans, and they moved into the Republican party.

As the Eastern cities grew larger and the functions their governments were called upon to perform expanded, concerns about costs became increasingly evident as campaign issues. By the time of the Civil War the beginnings of the Efficiency and Economy Movement that was to dominate middle-class urban politics from the 1880s on were evident. Thus in Boston between 1863 and 1867 Mayor Frederick W. Lincoln served four one-year terms, always emphasizing economy. (The mayor's name, in a city where the Civil War was generally popular, could not have harmed his candidacy.) He campaigned against the "growing extravagance" in his predecessor's administration, and he did succeed in checking the trend toward larger budgets. In many other cities the call for a rein upon expenditures was heard, along with some talk about the need for more effective administration, although the concept of a professional bureaucracy had not yet had any significant impact upon America.

Notes

1. Kirk H. Porter, *A History of the Suffrage in the United States* (Chicago, 1918).
2. Most notably, Robert E. Brown, *Middle-Class Democracy and the Revolution in Massachusetts* (Ithaca, N.Y., 1955).

3. William S. Holdsworth, *An Historical Introduction to the Land Law* (London, 1927), and Porter, *op. cit.*

4. H. W. Rogers, *Two Centuries' Growth of American Laws* (New Haven, 1901), and Robert A. Dahl, *Who Governs?* (New Haven, 1961), Ch. 1.

5. C. G. Lincoln, *Constitutional History of New York* (New York, 1906).

6. *Memorial History of the City of New York* (New York, 1892), vol. 3, p. 378.

7. Alexis de Tocqueville, *Democracy in America*, many editions; originally published 1835 and 1840.

8. *Memorial History of the City of New York*, vol. 3, p. 378.

9. *Ibid.*, vol. 3, p. 384.

10. Sam Bass Warner, Jr., *The Private City* (Philadelphia, 1968), p. 98.

11. Harold Zink, *City Bosses in the United States* (Durham, N.C., 1930).

12. J. S. Kendall, *History of New Orleans* (Chicago, 1922).

13. Abijah Ingraham, *A Biography of Fernando Wood* (New York, 1856). See also, William L. Stone, *History of New York City* (New York, 1872).

14. Kendall, *op. cit.*

15. Ingraham, *op. cit.*

16. Kendall, *op. cit.*

Chapter 7

POLITICAL ORGANIZATIONS AND THE REFERENDUM

IN THE EARLIEST YEARS of the Republic the assumption seems to have been quite general that it would be possible to avoid the creation of any kind of political party system, or perhaps it would be more accurate to say that large numbers of persons had no clear idea of what such a system would consist of and therefore thought in terms of a politics without organized political parties. By the beginning of the Jacksonian era in the 1820s, however, a great change had taken place, and it was the political party that was expected to be the coordinating unit not only among the three branches of government but also among the three levels of government—national, state, and local.

National Parties in Local Elections

During the Jacksonian era national parties emerged on the local scene and were deeply involved in municipal elections, particularly in larger cities. Thus national themes dominated the Cincinnati elections in 1824. The 1833 election in Boston was joined between the Jacksonian Democrats and the National Republicans. That year and in the following years, the Jacksonian candidate for mayor, Theodore Lyman, Jr., was victorious. At this early time, as later, national issues were not in themselves sufficient in a large-city local election. Lyman, for example, renewed an earlier local agitation for a comprehensive city water supply system. In Newark, which was incorporated as a city in 1836, all of the early mayors were Whigs. So long as the Whig party survived, the essential contest was between it and the Democrats.

Party loyalty was extremely strong in the nineteenth century, with commitment to the party much more powerful than it is possible for most contemporary people to understand. The result of Jacksonian populism and its deep commitment to political party at all levels of government was nicely summarized by a New Orleans observer in 1830: "In general, [there was] only a very small floating vote which could be swayed from one side to the other. People were Democrats or Whigs, and there was no possibility of inducing a man to change. Adherence to party was a matter of family tradition as much as principle."[1]

The partisan municipal election carried with it the traditional party conflicts and rivalries. The first election for mayor in Augusta, Maine, after its incorporation as a city took place in 1850. The Whigs argued that they should have the honor of providing the first mayor of the city in light of the fact that the Democrats had formed the chief element opposing the new city charter. The Democrats, on the other hand, thought that it was desirable to have the mayor selected by the most popular party. Even at this time of the Jacksonian emphasis upon national parties as coordinating institutions, the local political party was making an important appearance. In addition to the Whig and Democratic candidates in Augusta, there was one sponsored by the "Citizen's" party. Three elections were needed before the Democratic candidate finally secured a majority of the vote, as was required by the charter.

New Orleans offers a further example of national issue involvement locally. In 1843 the mayor resigned, and the subsequent special election was a contest between Whig and Democratic organizations. The Whigs were well organized and won the election by a vote of 1,289 to 974 in spite of the use of state and federal employees on behalf of the Democratic candidate. The New Orleans Whigs charged that pressure had been placed on federal officeholders to work in the election. One of the victorious Whigs called the result "a rebuke to the traitor, [John] Tyler who has brought the patronage of the government into conflict with the freedom of elections and whose officials in this quarter have openly taken the field and resolved to support the Loco Foco candidate for mayor." (Loco Foco was a nickname that had been given eight years earlier to the radical faction of the Democratic Party in New York. The term referred to stick matches. The Whigs were particularly angry at the incumbent President, John Tyler. Although a lifelong Democrat, he had been elected on the 1840 Whig ticket with William Henry Harrison. When Harrison died thirty days after taking office and Tyler succeeded him, he decided to make his a Democratic administration.)

One person, commenting on the local New Orleans political scene during the 1840s, made the following observation:

> In politics, this was a time of transition. The lofty ideals of an earlier day began to give way to a hard materialism. From this time onward, organization in the parties became increasingly efficient and superseded the personal leadership of the first part of the century. Hence, in city elections State and national issues figured more and more; and the disorders which were occasional at an earlier date became the regular feature of the municipal election day as of the State election day.[2]

This was a very different New Orleans from that of the late 1820s, when another observer noted:

Political conventions and "regular" nominations were unknown quantities in the science of electioneering. The usual practice was for every man looking for a local job to make the race on his own individual merits and partisanship was often laid aside in the general scramble. Hence, the one who had the most friends was invariably the winner, and became, in fact, the choice of the community.[3]

Local Political Parties

The insinuation of national issues into local politics by the national parties helped to generate demands for local parties, demands that already existed as a result of local issues, competing elites, or traditions stemming from the preparty days. In 1868 Nathaniel B. Shurtleff was elected mayor of Boston. He had been a lifelong Democrat but paid so little attention to the party's interests and wishes that when he ran for his third one-year term in 1869 he was opposed by his own party and was elected on a "Citizen's" ticket.

Two local parties were formed in Annapolis in 1822. They were known as the Caucus and Anti-Caucus parties. In that year, the two parties ran candidates only for the legislature, but two years later they had candidates for the municipal offices of mayor, recorder, and others. The issue at the time was the method by which candidates for office should be nominated. The view of the Caucus Party was obvious. The Anti-Caucus group preferred to have each candidate run on his own with no organizational approval required. A decade later the city experienced the creation of a Young Men's party, a group that protested the "disposition to deprive" them of any "participation in the political benefits of the city." But these local parties of Annapolis were later pushed aside by national organizations. By the mid-1840s national parties dominated Annapolis city elections.

In 1829 a significant radical third party, not strictly local, appeared in New York. It was the Workingmen's party, known as the "Workies." Although agrarian in origin, it was co-opted by New York workers who wanted to resist the lengthening of the working day. The party's motto was: "All children are entitled to equal education, all adults to equal property, and all mankind to equal privileges." Like radical parties throughout American history, it was plagued by factionalism and defections. The party accomplished little directly, but it made some penetration into Tammany Hall and had an effect upon Democratic party positions. It quite surely had an instrumental effect in increasing appropriations for education in the City of New York and in bringing about state legislation to provide for a mechanic's lien law and the abolition of imprisonment for debt.[4]

In 1836 the usual contest in New York between the Whigs and the Democrats was modified by the emergence of another third party, the

Loco Focos, or the Equal Rights party, as it preferred to be known. The party entered a local ticket, but in a pattern that was to become commonplace when a major American party splintered it was defeated at the polls, and the only important result of its efforts was an increase in city hall representation for the Whig party.

In Baltimore differences between the Know-Nothings and others reached a high in the level of conflict in 1858. Conditions became so bad that at noon on election day the independent candidate opposing the American party withdrew rather than further jeopardize the lives of his supporters and create further excuses for disorder. The city was known in newspapers of other communities as "Mob City." Cobblers' awls were the favorite weapons of political activists. One observer commented that "every trick and stratagem which thought could invent and every extremity to which violence could resort, were successfully employed for the purpose of electing the 'American' candidate."[5] Following this election a local party, known as the "City Reform Association," was created with the goal of eliminating ballot frauds and preventing the intimidation of the owners and managers of private industry. As time for the 1859 election approached the association, together with allies, issued a call for a "town meeting." The meeting was attended by about 10,000 people. It resolved to nominate candidates for such offices as fell vacant and to bring pressure on the mayor to safeguard or delay elections. The Know-Nothing mayor declined to respond to association demands, and the most aggressive among his supporters held a parade, displaying the awls with which they had in the past stabbed any of the opposition who tried to vote, and which they openly boasted they would use again. The local reform group succeeded in electing a few councilmen, but in the state elections held a few days later they had to abandon their poll watches by 2 P.M. in all but one of the city's wards. The following year the state legislature passed reform bills at the request of the association and declared the 1859 election null and void, expelling the sitting members of the legislature from Baltimore.[6] A new police commission was named and, perhaps aided by the quick decline of the American party then taking place nationally, restored order to the city. More than four years of virtual anarchy came to an end.

During the chaotic 1850s, while the national political party picture was in flux, local parties appeared in many cities. Thus in Boston, after the American party had fallen into disrepute, Alexander H. Rice was elected mayor on the Citizen's ticket. In 1857 the contest was between the Citizen's party and the Faneuil Hall party, and Frederick Lincoln, the latter party's candidate, was the winner. These two contesting groups kept themselves largely divorced from national issues.

A decade later the Citizen's ticket was revived in the third candidacy of Mayor Shurtleff. The party label was itself largely meaningless so far as a continuing organization was concerned, but it did imply a non-partisan, antiparty, or coalition type of organization.

In New York the deterioration of the national party system reached its peak in 1855, when at least sixteen local tickets entered the field. Most of these had split off from national political parties, but not all of them, and, furthermore, in the actual elections there were many intergroup alliances and considerable cross voting.[7] The various factions included the Nativists; hard-shell Democrats; soft-shell Democrats; half-shell Democrats; German Democrats; Whigs; the Republican Movement; the City Reform Movement; the Temperance Movement; and the High License Movement. In the midst of this confusion, Fernando Wood, the incumbent, was re-elected as mayor.

After the Civil War local parties became useful in the South, where the Democratic party symbolized the rebellion while the Republican party was not acceptable to members of the old elite. Thus in Little Rock in 1866 ex-Confederates listed themselves on the ballot as "Conservatives," and they succeeded in taking over the municipal government without incurring the disapproval of the commanding general of the Federal troops in the area. The Conservatives were strongly oriented toward low taxes and the preservation of property values.

The Fire Company as Political Organization

From the time volunteer fire companies were first organized, they had political influence. This was true in cities and villages of all sizes. Often they were the most effective and best organized political groups in the city. They differed from the organization of the political machines in many respects, but particularly in that they were often fiercely competitive, while the effective boss forced subordinate politicians to keep their differences secondary to the citywide concerns of the machine.

The fire companies were naturally equipped to become political organizations. Among the members of the companies a camaraderie existed, a pattern of friendship and trust. The companies had interests in the policy decisions of the city government, they had many opportunities to talk politics, to plan and scheme, during routine times in fire fighting and while cleaning and repairing the equipment. Later, when firemen were paid and full-time, idle hours at the firehouse could be taken up with matters of politics. No laws or ordinances prohibited political activity. And the firemen gained status because their job was seen as glamorous:

> Every man, woman and child got a tremendous kick out of a good conflagration. . . . All local ennui was banished by shouts of "Fire! Fire!" accompanied by the clanging of bells; the rattling of engines; the sound of running feet; the lurid reflections in the sky; and the wild excitement of

the volunteer firemen, who fought with each other while failing to extinguish the blaze. Those were happy days for everybody but the property owner.[8]

The firemen were not above using their highly visible activities and their political influence for their personal pleasure. The companies were social organizations for both the members and their families, and the city was often expected to pay for their recreational activities. In Somerville, Massachusetts, for example, the firemen went on strike in 1853, demanding a "pay" increase of from $1.50 a year to $12.00. But the purpose was not personal income—it was to establish an entertainment fund.

Sometimes the fire companies were infiltrated by hooligans looking for fun and plunder. This damaged the firemen's reputations and political power, so they often fought back. This was easier to do after the companies came to be coordinated through city control. Thus in Newark some of the engine houses by 1854 had become a rendezvous for many rough characters, and companies were demoralized. The common council then seized the houses, locked them, and disbanded and reorganized the companies, eliminating the "roughs." The new system was partly on a paid basis and was rated as more effective than the old.

The companies lost some of their political influence in some cities after they went on a paid basis, because professionalism produces pressures for costly equipment. In Utica, for example, there was a taxpayers' strike in 1855, and a referendum to provide more fire equipment was voted down by 400 to 4! Three years later, when an economy-oriented Republican slate took over the government the paid fire department was abolished.

In general, however, the words "fireman" and "politician" were closely interwoven in the nineteenth century, and the companies were powerful in state planning and highly active during campaigns. Many a councilman and mayor came directly from fire companies or were elected as a reward after they became too old for the heavy work of fire-fighting. Even William Marcy Tweed had been a "fire laddie" and was proud of the fact.

The Beginnings of the Machines

As the nineteenth century progressed there were increasing indications of corruption, especially in the cities along the Atlantic Coast, but it was not confined to Eastern cities. Cases of serious corruption developed in Milwaukee, Memphis, and San Francisco, to name a few. As early as 1807 complaints were made about frauds in Essex County, New Jersey. In 1806–7 corruption in Tammany Hall was uncovered, and the city controller, among other officials, was removed from office. That did not end the problem. Toward the middle of the century, corruption became still more common in the older cities. Thus in 1854 a commentator noted:

> The truth must be confessed, that now for many years, the municipal government of New York has been perverted to an increasing extent for purposes of private advantage, while its functions have been growing less and less effective for their legitimate results of public peace and security. Many offices have been rendered enormously and absurdly lucrative by extortionate constructions of fee-bills, while it has seemed impossible to procure proper legislation to check the evil. The doings of the Common Council have been dictated by private interests and influences; and it is generally believed that bribery, direct or indirect, has been employed to an alarming extent. The number of persons connected with city government, whose financial condition has become greatly changed immediately upon their obtaining office cannot be accounted for but on the supposition that public station has been made unduly subservient to private emolument.[9]

Prior to 1830 council committees supervised the administration of New York City functions. These committees met for "unreasonable and costly suppers at the city's expense," at which they were also served "such wines as they never in their lives [had] tasted before." They were criticized for "wrangling over appointments and cribbing at the public treasury."

Many of the complaints of the time, however, seemed to center upon inefficiency and lack of service rather than dishonesty. But these concerns were representative only of a prelude to the problems that would plague major American cities during the last half of the nineteenth century. Corruption and inefficiency, later to be identified in the propaganda of middle-class reform organizations as characteristic of the urban political boss and machine, were largely the result of the fact that city populations and service demands had exceeded the growth rate and competence of the bureaucracy. The near absence of professional administrators and technical specialists created such limitations. These phenomena were the result of factors quite independent of the development of the city boss and machine. The machines were, in fact, a product of the blending of the social and economic needs of working-class persons, the reliance of businessmen upon government for many services, and a desire of political leaders to achieve power (or, less often, wealth). The machine belonged to the industrial city rather than to the trading town. The political machines developed primarily during the period of rapid organization and industrialization that coincided with the Civil War and were not characteristic of the earlier years of the century, although their beginnings can be traced to that era.

The immediate ancestor of the classic American boss and machine is usually seen as Tammany Hall, the Democratic organization for Manhattan, and it is as likely a parent as any. The Society of St. Tammany was named for a Delaware chief (the "Saint" was jocular), by way of the Sons of St. Tammany, a Revolutionary War group of "hawks." The usual date given for its founding is May 12, 1789, but it held an annual banquet as early as May 1787, and this was probably not its first meeting in New York, though one of the earliest. Credit for establishing the society is generally given to one William Mooney, an upholsterer. Indian titles were given to officers. There were sachems and a grand sachem.

At first the society had a middle-class and upper-working-class orientation. It opposed domination of New York or the nation by the aristocracy, and, although its leaders used rhetoric associated with the ideas of Jefferson, it was an early "nativist" group, denying membership to the foreign born. The Irish fiercely opposed Tammany Hall. Gradually the society's desire for political power triumphed over prejudice. The more prosperous saw that their businesses would not benefit from confrontations with the Irish and they brought pressure for change. By the early 1820s the Irish were being naturalized. They became a major source of Democratic votes and eventually came to dominate the organization. Tammany then pressed for universal manhood suffrage.

The election of 1800 provided the society with considerable patronage, for Jefferson, the practical politician, recognized the effectiveness of the organization. Tammany Hall theoretically existed separately from the Democratic party, but the organizations and officers ran parallel. Tammany Hall itself was given a charter of incorporation by the New York legislature in 1805 as a benevolent institution. Through the two organizations, urban politics became a blend of political power, welfare, recreation, personnel administration (patronage), corruption, profiteering, and an institution for the coordination of social and economic institutions.

The first full-blown urban political machine in America was the Tweed Ring, which dominated Tammany Hall and the city of New York from 1866 until 1871. It was the classic example of the urban political organization of the last half of the nineteenth century, the period when Irish Catholic politicians came to dominate large American cities. William Marcy Tweed, a grand sachem of Tammany Hall, was the prototype of such politicians, even though he was of Scots-Presbyterian origin. The Tweed Ring overreached itself and was destroyed. Tweed went to prison in 1871 and, after a brief escape, died there. But Tammany continued apace. Tweed's successor, John Kelly, introduced reforms and persuaded well-known men of unquestioned integrity to become sachems—August Belmont, Horatio Seymour, and Samuel J. Tilden among them. But Tammany itself did not change much. This pattern—a veneer of middle-class respectability and rectitude covering corruption and other behavior unacceptable to the middle class—characterized many of the machines.

The machine primarily found its voter support among the poor of the urban slums and the money it needed to operate from among the business and industrial firms of the city. It provided jobs, burial funds or bond money if needed, welfare support during times of unemployment, recreation and entertainment activities, and many types of housing and welfare services. Tammany raised the funds needed for such activities by acting as a broker for the city's services. To the businessmen and industrialists who had the money that was needed, the machine sold permits, licenses, franchises, and other authorizations. Sometimes it succeeded in raising money simply through the use of blackmail and the shakedown. Large amounts of money were raised and large charitable activities were engaged in. During Tweed's peak years more than 60,000 patronage positions were controlled by him, and the city may well have been robbed of at least $200 million. The machine persisted (even though some individuals were sacrificed to the reformers), because so many saw it as beneficial to themselves: Businessmen were ahead because it cost less to go along with the machine than to fight it; for the urban poor, it performed invaluable services; to many, politicians and others, it was a source of wealth; to the national political parties, it was a guaranteed source of votes and of the spoils of office.

Political machines have always been associated in the middle-class mind with corruption, but some of the machines were run with considerable honesty, and many bosses were interested in power rather than wealth. Furthermore, corruption existed in city government both before and after the days of the big machines. A new chairman of the New Orleans finance committee in 1830 conducted an investigation that showed an enormous number of tax bills in default, some for seven years. He could not go back any further, because the books were missing. As the investigation continued, one official absconded, another committed suicide, the finance committee chairman was challenged to duels, and two attempts were made on his life. The financial controls for the city were casual in nature, and it is very possible that for this reason many improprieties never came to light.

Another example of the technique of the machines appeared early. In 1811 residents of the Washington poorhouse were brought to the polls where candidates or their friends paid the 25-cent poll tax. (This activity was protested, however, and the following year Congress provided that to be eligible to vote one's poll tax had to be paid at least two months before an election. The payment of the poll tax, direct payments for voting (bribes), and a free drink before and after voting became common after the poor were given the vote.

Just how much corruption took place in the years before 1870 will never be known with any degree of certainty. Much of the evidence is missing (as it was in New Orleans). Bookkeeping practices were often careless and performed by nonprofessionals. State governments did not demand accountings and did not audit the books, as they later did in some states. Collusion probably sometimes took place between auditor and other officials, although this can no longer be determined. But in most cities before 1870 city taxes did not raise enough money, and the typical part-time official was a Main Street merchant who wanted economy in government and was not seeking to line his own pockets. Irregularities there were, but the age of big-time theft had not yet arrived.

The political machines did exploit, although they did not invent, the patronage system. When Thomas Jefferson became President in 1801, he sought to achieve a balance in the bureaucracy between the Federalists and his supporters, but he did not call for a system of rotation in office. Even by that time the "spoils" system was making its appearance in local government. Indeed, patronage existed in colonial times, for under a system of government dominated by "friends and neighbors" politics the few jobs available—often on a part-time basis and almost invariably low paid—were quite naturally passed on to those friends who had worked for a candidate or those who showed a particular interest in local government. At least as early as 1816, Tammany Hall and its opponents made full use of the "spoils" system, dismissing the opposition's appointees whenever political control changed hands.

It was the Jacksonians of the 1820s and 1830s, however, who conceived of the typical patronage system that was to dominate municipal personnel policy for more than a century. They did so in part to avoid the creation of a professional bureaucracy dominated by conservatives of the upper classes. They believed that those who were to carry out the daily routine of administrative operations should be a reflection of the policy-makers who had been chosen by popular election.

There were other reasons, too, and they were nicely expressed by Andrew Jackson, anticipating the later ideas of Max Weber on bureaucracy, in his first message to Congress in 1829:

> There are perhaps few men who can for any great length of time enjoy office without being more or less under the influence of feelings unfavorable to the faithful discharge of their public duties. Their integrity may be proof against improper considerations immediately addressed to themselves, but they are apt to acquire a habit of looking with indifference upon the public interests and of tolerating conduct from which an unpracticed man would revolt. . . .
>
> The duties of all public offices are, or at least admit of being made, so plain and simple that men of intelligence may readily qualify themselves for their performance; and I cannot but believe that more is lost by the long continuance of men in office than is generally to be gained by their experience.

It is true that most jobs in the pre–Civil War period required relatively little education, training, or skill. They were routine tasks. Of course, we may assume that many a supporter of Jackson and other populists of the day believed in the patronage system out of pure self-interest. They worked for the party, and they believed it proper for them to be rewarded with jobs.

In the cities the municipal payroll was found to be a convenient instrument by which to reward the lesser laborers on behalf of the party and thus to help finance the high costs of operating a modern political party. It was early recognized that a dutiful worker could be repaid at no expense to the organization by putting him on the city payroll in some position appropriate to his skills or lack thereof. Before long it was recognized that it was also possible to place a person on the payroll without necessarily assigning him any duties.

It was Senator William L. Marcy of New York who, in an 1832 speech, gave a name to this particular form of personnel administration and, at the same time, a simple justification that the most simple-minded party worker could understand. As he said, "to the victor belong the spoils of the enemy." In the years before 1870, the spoils system reigned virtually without challenge.

As the spoils system developed, the stakes in elections correspondingly increased, and along with this came intimidation, ballot box stuffing, impersonations, plural voting, and bribery. State machines often had a malign interest in local elections. If the issues espoused were deeply felt, such as were slavery or nativism, national parties provided a further rationale to their supporters for corrupting local elections. Selective police enforcement, the politicizing of the police, rivalry of railroads for local favors, land interests—all of these were factors leading to unscrupulous ballot practices. Those who profited thereby needed no other justification. In time, an honest election came to be rare among the large cities.

Some cities, such as San Francisco, were lawless and corrupt from the beginning. Others, for example, Kansas City and Chicago, were tied in with bribery of and by railroads. Still others, including New York, Memphis, and Milwaukee, were associated with police graft and selective law enforcement or land deals or contracts, or intense feelings with regard to national issues expressing themselves in election frauds. In these and many other cities, the spoils in appointments were factors even earlier. In contrast, in Boston the only suggestion of graft before the Civil War was that some of the shopkeepers on the independent Board of Overseers sought election so as to sell their wares.

The Referendum

Although the use of the referendum did not become as popular as it was to be later, during the first century after independence it came to be used increasingly. In Massachusetts, a state that did not succumb to populism as much as others, the referendum proved to be popular when used. Between 1780 and 1907 fifty-seven questions were submitted to the voters of Massachusetts. Of these, thirty-nine were approved and eighteen rejected. Popular interest in them varied enormously, as is indicated by the fact that the number of persons voting on the issues varied from 101 per cent to 3 per cent of the vote cast for the office of governor.

The populistic ideas of Jacksonian democracy presaged the coming of "direct democracy," under which it would be possible for the ordinary citizen to vote not only for the principal state and local legislative and administrative officers but also on questions of public policy. The referendum and the initiative were developed during the nineteenth century. The former requires that an ordinance or a charter amendment, before adoption, must be approved by the voters. The initiative permits the bypassing of the legislative body through petitions for proposed legislation. If the required number of signatures are secured, the initiative is voted upon in the same manner as a referendum. The initiative seems not to have been used in an American city until after its provision in the San Francisco charter of 1898. It did have precedents, however, in the occasional petitions to councils for the calling for referendum votes on issues of the day. (This procedure was later known as the petition referendum.)

The referendum was much older. It was first required in Connecticut in 1818 for the adoption of legislative proposals for constitutional amendments. Earlier it was, in effect, the standard practice in the New England town meeting, where proposed budgets and major substantive legislation were subject to approval by all eligible voters attending the annual meeting. Maryland in 1825 authorized a referendum on the question of establishing a public school system.

An early use of the referendum was for the approval of city charters. These generally were adopted or at least had to be ratified by State legislatures, but they were sometimes submitted to local referendum for approval before they could be put into effect. Such a referendum was held in New York City in 1830. (It was framed by a local convention, approved in a referendum, and enacted into law by the state legislature.) A similar question in Newark in 1836 produced a favorable vote, 1,870 to 325. In 1852 the Louisiana legislature insisted upon a local referendum to approve a New Orleans Charter before it would authorize the document.

The referendum became commonplace in some cities after the Jacksonian influence upon American political behavior. In the decade following 1837 there were two referendums on free elementary schools in New York, and others on the establishment of municipal police, the Croton Aqueduct and a free academy (public high school).

The idea of requiring a popular vote spread to other areas of proposed policies. For example, in 1839 Salem voters authorized the city to construct sewers. Boston voters were asked to express their views on questions of water supply in referendums conducted in 1836, 1838, 1844, and 1845. Baltimore voters approved a proposal for a water supply in 1853 by a total of 9,927 to 307.

The use of the referendum spread into still other areas of substantive policy. For example, in 1849 the Trenton common council was forbidden to borrow money except upon referendum approval. Twenty years later voters in that city were asked whether horse cars should be allowed to operate on Sundays. Their answer was in the affirmative by a vote of 6,486 to 3,563. Although precise data are not available, most referendums appear to have secured a favorable vote. In some cases, as in the Trenton Sunday horse-car vote, it is doubtful if the council would have had the courage to do what the voters did.

Concluding Note

The years 1770 to 1870 were of vast importance in the development of the American urban political style. The Main Street merchant as an individual community leader was largely replaced by the political party organization, and that began to be converted, in turn, into the awesome structure of the boss and machine. During this time period a system in which questions of policy were seldom voted on directly and relatively few men (and almost no women) could participate in the selection of municipal officeholders was converted into one in which universal white manhood suffrage was approximated and both prospective leaders and many proposed public policies were subjected to the preference vote of the citizen, rich or poor. The full extremes of populism were not yet reached, and many remained without the franchise, but the century after independence shaped what was to become the American urban style of politics.

Notes

1. J. S. Kendall, *History of New Orleans* (Chicago, 1922).
2. *Ibid.*
3. *Ibid.*
4. Howard P. Nash, Jr., *Gadflies of American Politics: A Short History of Third Parties* (Washington, D.C.: 1956). On the parties of the era, generally, see Arthur M. Schlesinger, Jr. (Ed.), *History of U.S. Political Parties* (New York, 1973), especially volume I.
5. Baltimore American, *A History of the City of Baltimore* (Baltimore, 1902).
6. *Ibid.*
7. *Memorial History of the City of New York* (New York, 1892), vol. III.
8. W. A. Whitehead, *Proceedings Commemorative of the Settlement of Newark* (Newark, 1866).
9. Quoted in W. L. Stone, *History of New York City* (New York, 1868).

Chapter 8

INTEREST GROUP ACTIVITY

Political scientists and historians have long been interested in the organized groups that seek to influence public policy, both in its adoption and in the way in which the rules are administered. This interest has also extended to the general public and has found a place in American folklore, in which "pressure" groups are commonly viewed with suspicion, if indeed they are not considered an unmitigated evil. Each of the waves of populism since Jacksonian times has been particularly suspicious of interest groups. (Populists, of course, have tended to view themselves as "the people" rather than agree that they, too, are an interest group.) Nonpopulistic groups, such as merchants and bankers, tend to see their own interests not as selfish but as things that are "good for the country" or "good for the community."

Political scientists have sometimes approached interest groups as selfish power and privilege seekers that ignore a more general "public interest," but most serious scholars have accepted the notion that the interest group is an important and probably an essential means for aggregating individual views and concerns in a democracy. It is upon this assumption that we approach the subject here.

If we are to compare urban interest groups of the period ending in 1870 with those of a century later, we would find many similarities. The main differences would perhaps be two. One was that there was a greater consensus among groups in the earlier period, with a greater acceptance of the notion that deference should ordinarily be paid to the wishes of the merchants. The assumption tended to be that the prosperity of the entire community depended upon its growth, and that growth in turn meant that public policy should not be allowed to stand in the way of the merchants, bankers, and land developers. A seeming anomaly, but actually in part a result of the power of the business groups, is the second principal difference, the much greater neglect of city government by the elite, in earlier times. Partly as a result, a class of relatively low-status professional politicians—the forerunners of the men who were to lead the great city machines—were often allowed to run the government, and there was a great deal more overt corruption than is the case today. The leadership of the chief interest groups would occasionally clean house if the corrupt practices became too much of a nuisance, but, especially along the frontier, businessmen were characteristically more alarmed by lawlessness and disorder (which threatened the rapid and orderly growth of the city) than by corruption.

Yet even in this period examples of a hardening of class lines appeared here and there. Municipal elections sharply differentiated the merchants, and those who supported their viewpoints through deference or agreement, from the labor and immigrant groups and other poor. These working- and lower-class groups achieved successes in New York and New Orleans. In the latter city in 1860 identifiable groups among the foreign born were Irish 24,398, German 19,675, French 10,564. There were also 24,074 disfranchised blacks. The total population was 168,675.

Elsewhere a few members of city councils might bear witness to class embitterment. However, the Know-Nothing issue tended to split the working class, through adding resentments among the workers themselves against the "shanty Irish." Another factor that tended to lessen the likelihood of a successful immigrant-based machine was the comparatively greater mobility of these groups. Not much research has taken place in this field, but in Boston in the 1850s the total population turnover was 40 per cent a year. In the small city of Poughkeepsie the rapid outward movement of the foreign born was clearly delineated.

The key characteristic of the period ending in 1870, however, was a pervasive consensus concerning how a city should be run. As a result, elections did not often center on deeply felt local issues, and in between elections people were often scarcely aware of varying and competing interests. The interests themselves were sporadically organized, usually only under emergency situations, although general booster groups like the Chamber of Commerce were common by the 1820s. Because thinking about politics did not center upon the interaction of interest groups, the writers of the day did not leave an extensive record of their activities, although enough remains for the researcher to delineate the pattern.

Merchants

The needs of the Main Street businessman were always a matter of top priority for the cities. Because they were able to claim that the prosperity of the community depended upon their progress, the merchants often had no need to bribe councilmen or to recruit and finance the campaigns of persons who would be sympathetic to their cause. Much of the general working population appears to have accepted the argument made by the merchants. Their concerns were, therefore, given the highest priority. For example, during an economy wave in Nashville and a cut in the expenditure budget in 1854, the city constructed a large cistern in the public square to provide for added fire protection for the city's merchants.

The merchants viewed the city government from the perspective of the producer, even though most of them were really only middlemen. They commonly supported a policy of unabashed boosterism, seeing, of course, a growth in business as accompanying population increase. The goals of the city and the means of accomplishing them were generally matters of basic agreement during the period. Merchants (the term "businessmen" did not come into vogue until later) were commonly willing to serve on the city council and, indeed, often made up a majority of the membership. Even when they did not, they indirectly dominated it most of the time. Sometimes the most successful merchants were willing to serve. Thus, in Cincinnati in 1819 the average councilman on the eighteen-member body held property that would place him among the fifty wealthiest people in town. But this was not always the pattern, for often the merchants were so busy building and expanding their businesses that they left the council and even the mayor's office to minor characters, and this often meant saloon keepers and small-time professional politicians. There were almost no men of prominence in the San Francisco city government in 1851. That was the year that the famous "Committee of Vigilance for the Protection of the Lives and Property of the Citizens and Residents of the City of San Francisco" was formed. Some of the city officials were fearful of being brought before the committee, but they had an exaggerated sense of their own importance; the committee simply ignored them. Although it has been estimated that corruption in City Hall was costing San Franciscans $100 for every dollar taken by thieves, it was thieves and arsonists about whom the committee was concerned, for these criminals were threatening the good name and the very existence of the city.[1]

Like all property owners, the merchants were concerned about the tax rate and the level of services that had to be paid from property tax funds. They could control the agenda through their ability to agree upon the order of priorities, and they strongly favored expenditures that would enhance the city's commercial capability (wharves, water supply) over consumers' amenities. Often they preferred use of the special assessment or even of private industry for community services that would benefit business such as street lights and hard-surfaced streets. As utilities were developed, all except sewerage were paid for on the basis of the cost of service rendered.

The merchants were interested in policies relative to many of the traditional functions of local government. These included the administration of public markets and policies relative to licenses and permits. Through much of the period the traditional "assize of bread," that is, the ordinance controlling the weight and price of bread, continued to prevail. The merchants were interested in public health on a sporadic basis. Whenever an epidemic of communicable diseases occurred, the merchants would be among those demanding an active program for the maintenance of the public health. But in normal times they were not willing to spend much on this, and even in times of crisis they often tried to get the state to assume the responsibility and cost.

The merchants favored the growth of public utilities and often supported private ownership, in part because they were anxious to invest in the companies. They often favored long-term franchises for 50, 100, or even 1,000 years. Many of them must have recognized that this was not good business practice, but they were often more interested in rapid development than in avoiding future problems for the cities and, indeed, utilities were developed more rapidly in American cities during this period than was the case in Western Europe. During this period city councils could grant franchises (as well as licenses for the operation of saloons) and this opened up great opportunities for graft and corruption. Corruption, indeed, did result and eventually led the states to take the franchise power away from the cities, but these developments largely took place long after 1870. The utilities managers themselves, of course, were necessarily active lobbyists, for they were concerned about rates, taxes, and many other things in addition to franchises.

There were already at this time a number of examples of businesses from outside the city extending favors and bribes to a city's decision-makers. Chief among these were the railroads, but such influence might also be exerted by publishers of school textbooks.

All of the above and other matters, too, were important to the merchants, but their overarching concern then, as throughout American history, was with law and order. The ability of the police to protect the merchants' inventories and the good name of the city so that it might grow and prosper was their greatest preoccupation. This was particularly true in the first years after a town was founded and again during spurts of rapid growth.

Although the merchants were willing to tolerate a certain amount of gambling, prostitution, and even thievery, if it did not become notorious, whenever the situation got seriously out of hand they were almost always among the leaders favoring precipitous action. Committees of vigilance, or vigilantes, existed under one name or another at one time or another in all parts of the country. Sometimes they came into being because the town government had not yet been established and no local law enforcement office existed. Many vigilance committees were created as towns were founded at the division points established along the routes of the great transcontinental railroads. After a division point was determined, merchants would arrive to establish businesses. But they often found that, in addition to the railroad workers, the town had a goodly supply of professional gamblers, prostitutes, pickpockets, and muggers anxious to relieve workmen of their pay. The vigilance committee would then come into being. Its tactic commonly was to make an example of a few persons, thus encouraging other undesirables to leave town. (They would, moving on to the next new division point, where the entire drama was repeated.) The vigilance committees in California mining towns after the discovery of gold were usually dominated by the miners themselves rather than the merchants,[2] but the famous two in San Francisco were merchant-dominated. The most common characteristic of these committees was that they had very short lifetimes. For example, the 1851 committee in San Francisco, perhaps the most famous of all of those romantic if highly illegal organizations, was active for only one hundred days, and that was probably a relatively long time for such a committee. The merchants were always anxious to return to the normal legal processes, for men of property always respect the legitimacy and importance of law and order.

Realtors

The land developers and realtors had interests compatible with those of the merchants and enjoyed the strong support of the latter, in part because it was the land developers who advertised the new city in the East, calling for more settlers. Thus, in 1830 a man from Clinton County, New York, founded the village of Marshall in Michigan. He advertised the town as a "steamboat center," even though it was located on the small Kalamazoo River and at first was nothing more than a stagecoach stop between Detroit and Chicago. The developer, later joined by other realtors, worked hard at achieving growth and thereby enhancing his own investment. Commonly new communities fought hard to secure the county seat for their town. Being the county seat meant growth, because it attracted the then small but still significant bureaucracy and the persons who often worked at the courthouse, such as attorneys and abstractors. Besides, the persons who came to town to do business at the courthouse or to attend trials tended to bring their trade with them. Marshall succeeded in winning designation as the county seat, and the developers tried very hard to secure for the city the state capital, which was to be moved to a more central location from Detroit, but in this they finally lost out to Lansing in 1847. Meanwhile, many small industries were attracted to the town and this, in turn, brought two railroads. Marshall was never to become one of the state's large cities, but it was not for lack of trying, and this kind of effort was deeply appreciated by the merchants.

In popular image, land developers are often seen as rather evil persons who profited from the good luck of getting to a place shortly before great demand for land was created by those who were going to make real use of it. While some developers did become immensely wealthy, they were all engaged in a highly risky business. The developer had to guess at which among many likely sites would develop into a viable urban community. For every village that has survived until today, several either were plotted but never developed or became ghost towns. In other cases the community survived but, like Marshall, never grew to any size. In such cases the profits were probably relatively modest.

The land developers and realtors, along with the bankers, were the urban planners of this period and continued to be well into the twentieth century. They were commonly well represented among the members of the city council. The original developer typically surveyed and laid out the townsite, usually using the gridiron pattern because the modestly skilled surveyors that were likely to be available found that the easiest. This tendency was reinforced by the Northwest Land Ordinance of 1785, which called for land descriptions based upon a simple grid system. Rural roads were laid out along section lines, and these later became major city streets at right angles to one another. The developer chose a location, normally near a stream or body of water, for the central business district and, adjacent to that, an area where he hoped industry would develop. If the city grew beyond the original plat, the realtors and bankers would dominate the further development. Since these developments were normally financed locally, and since the banker would accept only the plans that seemed safest, most of the small and middle-sized cities of America had a certain sameness about them. Although critics have often remarked about this, the regional sameness to be found in the United States is not unlike that of Europe, where there is a rather basic style for Northern and for Southern Europe. The simple gridiron plan was reasonably efficient and lent itself in later years to the automobile better than did the radial-upon-grid, as in Detroit and Washington, or the haphazard street arrangement, as in London.

A note of caution: Not all city planning was in the hands of those who could most immediately benefit from it, nor was profit the only consideration of some of the town founders. Most were interested in immediate respects of payoff, but some were willing to consider the longer view. When George Rogers Clark and the original settlers laid out the town of Louisville (1779), the entire area between the banks of the Ohio River and Main Street was reserved as common land. Later, however, all of this land was sold off in order to retire some municipal debts. Moses Cleaveland (as he spelled it), in laying out his city on Lake Erie in 1796, kept in mind his native New England and provided for a village green, but he used a street grid.

The land area for Paterson, New Jersey, was purchased in 1791 by

Alexander Hamilton and his Society for Establishing Useful Manufactures. He asked Pierre L'Enfant and Nehemiah Hubbard to design the city for industrial rather than the then commonplace commercial uses. This was done, centering upon the falls of the Passaic River as a source of power. The planners proposed to accommodate to the uneven terrain rather than insist upon a right-angle grid. Unfortunately, the plan has not survived.

L'Enfant's Washington plan, symbolizing the grandeur that many Americans saw in the future of their country, was imitated in a number of places. Judge Augustus B. Woodward's 1807 post-fire plan for Detroit represented an improvement over that for Washington, cutting up the land less while still preserving green spaces. The plan, which was to have been expanded indefinitely, was abandoned for the conventional grid in 1818, in part because of animosities generated between Judge Woodward and other decision-makers. (The original layout, between the Detroit River and Grand Circus Park, still exists.) Other cities using the radial-on-grid for all or part of their design included Indianapolis, Madison, Sandusky, later parts of Cleveland, and parts of many other cities, as well as all of some small towns.

Thomas Jefferson, that man of endless curiosity and seemingly limitless talents, also tried his hand at city planning. His basic plan, proposed in 1800 and again while he was occupying the White House, called for a checkerboard approach, with alternate squares left permanently as vacant land. He advocated this in conversations with and letters to William Henry Harrison, Governor of Indiana Territory, and William C. C. Claiborne, Governor of Orleans Territory. Jefferson's aesthetic sense once again was combined with his pragmatic goals, as he made clear in an 1805 letter to the Comte de Volney:

> Every square of houses will be surrounded by four open squares, and every house will front on open square. The atmosphere of such a town would be like that of the country, insusceptible of the miasmata which produce yellow fever. . . . But it is only in case of enlargements to be made, or of cities to be built, that this means of prevention can be employed.

Jefferson's plan was used for Jackson, Mississippi (1821), and Jeffersonville, Indiana (1802), where it was modified by radials. But it could not survive the land pressures placed upon vacant portions of growing cities, and all traces of Jefferson's attempt to combine goals of public health with pristine beauty soon disappeared, in the latter city by 1817. Most of the frontier pragmatists did not even try to think of aesthetics or the future, which they believed would take care of themselves. To the typical realtors, land developers, and bankers, "highest and best use" meant the most immediately profitable use.

Industrialists and Railroaders

Most industry in America was quite small in the years preceding 1870, although there was a great deal of it, chiefly in small plants. There were firms for meat packing, textile manufacturing, buggy making, brewing; the manufacture of furniture, stoves, tobacco products, and patent medicines; iron and glass works, and the milling of flour, for example.

The budding industrialists had one interest in the police beyond those that concerned the merchants. This was in having the police side with management in the event of strikes and even serve as strike-breakers. Strikes were not as common in an age when the manufacturer was seen as a job-giver, but they did occur, both in those cases where trade unionism was beginning to make itself known and in other cases. The police could be very useful in intimidating workers and protecting industrial property during disorders. In the absence of federal or even state legislation, the greatest concern of the manufacturer often was with local government, and particularly with keeping the policemen, with their working-class background, on his side.

Nothing prior to the commercial railroad had offered such a prospect for industrial and population expansion in either the East or along the frontier. More than 1,000 miles of track had been laid and put in operation by 1835. By 1850 this figure had increased ninefold, and the railroad building boom was in full swing. In 1870, 52,922 miles of track were in operation. Cities and villages that had earlier sought canals as a connecting link with the rest of the world now courted railroad companies or formed their own. There was nothing a city would not do to entice a railroad to include it in the system. Land was given to it, its will as to route was accepted without question, and cities bought railroad stocks and bonds, using the willing taxpayers' money, often with little assurance that the funds would ever be returned. In many instances those who controlled the railroads were themselves principal landowners in the towns along their routes.

Sometimes urban residents, usually with the aid of the city government, would subscribe to and even build their own railroad. Cincinnati was one example, and Denver, with a population of less than 5,000, built the Denver-Pacific Railroad between 1867 and 1870. The rise of the railroads and utilities did much to change the character of city politics, regardless of whether their leadership was local or national.

On the frontier, the railroads themselves often founded towns, for it was necessary to have division points at suitable intervals. These new towns provided merchants with opportunities. Existing cities vied to become division points, since these provided additional jobs.

The railroads, having huge amounts of assessable property, became active politically at all levels of government. Many other decisions of governments affected their costs, so they felt impelled to continuous political activity. They also discovered that city leaders who would spare no effort to attract a rail line would sometimes forget their gratitude once the road was in operation. Harried taxpayers sometimes thought of the railroad as "rich" and hence a likely target for taxation.

Although the railroads concentrated on state governments and the national government, they could not ignore the local assessor in most states. The "railroad candidate" appeared in many city election contests, and sometimes a company developed a full-fledged political machine. One of the most notorious was the Central (later Southern) Pacific, which came to dominate the government not only of California but of all major California cities along its routes. In the 1852 election in Chicago behind-the-scenes rival railroads were the real competitors.

Bankers

Banks are essentially businesses, but bankers are a special kind of businessman in that they make decisions that may strongly influence whether other businesses are to flourish or decline. Because bankers wish those businesses to which they have lent money to prosper, their interest typically coincides with that of the merchant and manufacturer. In urban governments bankers therefore often lent their prestige to the causes of these other interests. But bankers had and still have additional interests. They often held mortgages on premises used for illegal purposes. They were interested in city government decisions. Revenues from taxes and other sources were deposited by the municipality in the local banks. The money was available to the bankers to use for their own profit until it was withdrawn. It was not uncommon for favored banks, perhaps in return for campaign contributions, to pay no interest on the deposits. Until the time of the Civil War, banks were controlled by state rather than federal law and were often subject to little supervision. Some banks were established to benefit from what amounted to an interest-free loan from the city and would be in shaky financial condition without that subvention. For example, agitation in Utica in 1857 finally resulted in the transfer of city funds from one bank to another that would pay interest. The first bank collapsed shortly after the municipal funds were withdrawn.

Banks often assisted in the marketing of municipal bond issues before the development of the municipal bonding houses and received a commission for handling them. In those days, before modern debt retirement techniques were developed, banks also had a considerable interest in municipal sinking funds. Sinking funds were accounts into which money was paid, either from utility revenues or from taxes, until such time as a municipal debt came due. The principal was then paid from the fund. These idle monies were commonly invested in bonds, and the bankers received a commission for arranging the purchases, or funds might be deposited in a special account in the bank. Obviously, the bankers had an interest in urging support for sound financial management by the city government, the growth of the community as a trade center, and the growth of population in the area.

Newsmen

Newspaper editors are also a special type of businessman. They are fundamentally interested in producing a product that will have the maximum possible sale, but they have a special advantage in their attempts to influence public policies that will further their private goals. Editors then as now were enthusiastic boosters of community growth, for a larger population meant not only the sale of more newspapers but also of more and more expensive advertising space. The newspapers of the era were even more unabashedly supporters of community growth and more outspokenly parochial in their editorial position than are editors of today. Furthermore, journalism of the day was not highly professionalized; rather, it was often highly personal, and no inhibitions were felt about editorializing in the "news" columns. Furthermore, the business was highly competitive, for even small cities commonly had several newspapers.

Editors and other newspapermen took strong positions not only relative to public policy but also in supporting candidates for local office. In addition, many a newspaperman himself served on the council or became mayor. Often the editors were allied with reformers, because reform was usually intended to encourage community growth. In New Orleans the local press aided greatly in the successful move to consolidate the three municipalities into a single city in 1852. Newspaper publishers also suffered from certain inhibiting selfish interests which at times muted their criticism of the *status quo*. Loss of municipal and other advertising and fear of increased assessments were the chief examples.

Municipal Employees

Municipal employees represented another major interest group in the community. In a day before the development of the merit system the city employee's job often depended upon his being politically active. He was recruited by an elected official or some political leader, and if his party or faction were to lose an election he could reasonably expect to lose his job. We have already noted the importance of the fire companies in local politics. In addition to the usual motivation of city employees, the full-time, paid firemen also had large amounts of time on their hands, time that could be used either for developing political strategies or for running political errands. The police were also very active in local politics. In a day when the "cop on the beat" knew all or at least many of the residents or merchants in the area he patrolled, he could be a highly effective campaigner. The police of the day were not professionals and, indeed, ordinarily received their only training on the job. They were commonly corrupt to one degree or another, but those who were astute recognized that their behavior should not attract notoriety, for they could easily be replaced. Their best hope for a reasonable amount of security was to ally themselves with the incipient political organizations of the day or, in some cities and the smaller towns, to ingratiate themselves with the merchant elite.

Reformers

Most of the great urban reform movements took place after 1870. The coming of the boss and machine had caused the merchants and their allies to lose control over city government and to be forced to negotiate with the machine. Although the reform movements were, in part, ideological, they also represented an effort to restore the almost complete control that the merchants had enjoyed before the Civil War. Even so, reform activities of one kind or another were frequently to be found earlier in the nineteenth century.

Sometimes the reformers were insincere, naïve, or incompetent. In 1851 the San Francisco Whigs ran a "throw the rascals out" campaign against the Democrats and won, but once in office they did not succeed, or even seem to try very hard, in bringing a crime wave to an end or the city's shaky financial condition into better shape.

Reform concentrated upon securing both "honest" government and various social changes. Persons opposed to the use of alcohol were active in local politics because the city controlled saloon licenses. Even on the frontier such groups as the Sons of Temperance were active. And throughout American history there was interest in various educational reforms. Organizations began to appear on a statewide basis, with the Florida Educational Association appearing as early as 1831. Ten years later the first appropriation was made in the North for Negro schools, and the education of blacks was encouraged, particularly by Abolitionists. After the Civil War reformers sought to end segregation of schools. In the South this lasted only until Federal troops were withdrawn in 1877, but in the North it was a longer struggle. As Negroes dropped off the "Underground Railroad" that extended north to Chicago and then around Lake Michigan and across the state of Michigan to Canada before the Civil War, segregated schools were established. Segregation continued after the war and was generally ended on a North-to-South basis. Even such a small town as Three Oaks, Michigan, along the underground route, continued to operate its segregated school system long after the Civil War. Legal desegregation did not take place in Ohio until 1887, and segregation continued in the cities of southern Illinois until the 1950s, despite the efforts of reformers.

Some reformers were interested in improving the lot of the poor through providing for better public health measures. Some control over building regulations to protect the health of slum dwellers resulted from the activities of such groups as the Council of Hygiene in New York during the 1860s. There were reformers who sought to control what we would now call communicable diseases, and there were sharp if largely uninformed controversies between the contagionists and the anticontagionists. Some reformers sought to provide their cities with healthful water. Others, in an effort both to control disease and to help protect water supplies, urged the development of sewer systems. The latter group contained many who were also concerned about aesthetic factors. They objected to the filth that littered the streets of the day and offended the eye and nose as well as threatened health. These reformers, precursors of the City Beautiful movement that developed in the last decade of the nineteenth century, were also interested in the development of city parks. Many parks were simply gifts to the city from wealthy persons, but others were planned by city officials. The original plan for Washington called for 275 parks, most of them small. The layout, with a grid superimposed upon diagonal streets, resulted in numerous outlots, many of which could not effectively be built upon. After about 1850 an increasing number of influential citizens pressed for parks, boulevards, and beautification in other ways. As people found themselves increasingly separated from the rural life that has always been romanticized in the United States, the desire for greenery and the preservation of the small-town look became more intense. Realtors sometimes supported, sometimes opposed such parks—depending upon the location of their holdings.

Immigrants and Laborers

Although working-class people and the marginal poor were not of major political importance in the years prior to the Civil War, increasingly they could not be ignored. Ethnic-group politics made its appearance after the Irish potato famines and the liberal revolutions in Europe in the late 1840s brought in large numbers of non-Anglo-Saxon immigrants.

The Irish had the advantage of already knowing the English language.

Their culture seemed to allow them to adapt easily to American urban politics. They produced large numbers of men with outgoing personalities. They showed a love of combat, a willingness to negotiate and compromise, and an ability to survive that had been learned through centuries of British rule of their island. As a result, the Irish soon learned the secret of political power at the ward level.

The Germans, often predominantly artisans, were less politically minded, but they increasingly organized against the Sunday blue laws. They were less inclined than the Irish to use their political power for personal advantage. The time was not far off when the Irish would serve as the common denominator for the working-class machine candidature, while merchants and reformers would frequently turn to a German to lead the city.

Both Germans and Irish migrated from the East in considerable numbers to the cities of the Midwest and to Memphis and New Orleans. In these two cities, the Irish outnumbered the Germans. In 1850 about 43 per cent of the population of Milwaukee was German-born, a higher percentage than in New York.

French-Canadians began their migration to the New England communities toward the end of the period. They were not as yet politically active.

All Southern cities were the homes of considerable numbers of slaves prior to emancipation. Their principal impact upon city government was their frequent ownership of and use by the cities themselves for the hard but menial municipal labor in unskilled work on the streets. Corporations as well as individuals owned them. Free blacks also congregated in considerable numbers in cities outside of New England. They were an almost entirely overlooked component of the population until after the Civil War. Slavery itself was disintegrating in the cities and existed only nominally in St. Louis and Louisville. The presence of numerous ordinances dealing with the "off hours" conduct of the slaves witnessed the difficulties.

Although blacks did not become politically important (except during Reconstruction in the South) until decades after the period under study, the movement of blacks from the South into Northern cities, particularly Washington and Philadelphia, immediately after the Civil War presaged the rise of racial politics.

The beginnings of the activities of the political machines as welfare agencies could be seen at least as early as the efforts of Tammany Hall during the 1837 economic recession.

Laboring groups have always been of some importance in American urban politics. Strikes go back at least as far as 1741, when bakers in New York stopped work in protest against the price established by the assize of bread. The first trade union was created by the shoemakers of

Philadelphia in 1792. From the beginning, trade unions (perhaps for the same reasons as manufacturers) took an interest in local politics and sought to influence local public policy. The first of a series of labor parties, the Workingmen's Party, was created in Philadelphia in 1828. Organized labor grew in a number of cities, especially after 1820, until it was greatly weakened in the economic depression of 1837. National unions emerged in the 1850s. The Civil War gave some temporary assistance to the unionization movement, but the time had not yet come for labor to possess sustained political power. Still, there were important incidents to presage what would come later. Thus, the workingmen of Lowell became politically assertive in 1865, seeking particularly a shorter work week. The Democrats took over their entire legislative slate, and even though only one man from it was elected, the development caused a great stir.

In local politics labor has always been interested in seeking the sympathy, or at least the neutrality, of policemen during labor disputes. Workers of the nineteenth century were strongly oriented toward pushing for consumer amenities for their neighborhoods, perhaps in part because nearly all of them were renters and probably few recognized that they, too, paid local property taxes, if only indirectly as part of their rent.

Liquor Dealers and Vice Lords

Community leaders in nineteenth-century America were generally tolerant of prostitution, gambling, and the consumption of alcoholic beverages, provided that such activities did not generate notoriety or threaten to discourage the growth of the community. Tolerance was especially to be found along the frontier. Protection against police interference was purchased if necessary. But gambling and prostitution were generally illegal, and their political concerns were typically of a negative sort—they did not seek to control city politics, but only to avoid public policies that would interfere with their activities.

The liquor interests assumed a somewhat different position. Most of their activities were legal, but they were dependent upon local government for licenses and had an important stake in enforcement policies. This applied especially to the emotion-charged question of permission for, or tolerance of, Sunday sales. As a result they were always influential in local politics and sometimes, especially when merchants chose not to participate directly, were dominant forces in the local urban political scene.

There were other interest groups, too, for politics in that era was not as simple as it may seem from a later perspective. But in the preindustrial city of America, the merchant and his close allies were the political and economic elite.

Closing Note

Because it demonstrates much that was characteristic of the period, it is worth recounting A. Theodore Brown's picture of Kansas City:

> Between 1838 and 1868, a group of ten to twenty men really made the town's decisions. As the community developed, more and more its long range interests were seen to parallel their own, and private interests (if in conflict) were even put aside. They subscribed jointly to establish a newspaper and sold it shortly to Robert Van Horn, a newcomer. The business men were so grateful that they refused his money.[3]

In the following years the most characteristic aspect of early Kansas City, its unquenchable thirst for growth—investment, building, population—came to be almost completely personified in this one man. Together, he and the leadership group surmounted the issues raised by "bleeding Kansas"; rivalries with Leavenworth, Lawrence, and St. Joseph, riots; their own deeply felt divisions and loss of population; and the question of slavery and secession. Most of them felt "law and order" to be of greater importance even than secession. Striking efforts were made to attract railroads, and the voters as a whole gave support to these. Public improvements were also undertaken. Perhaps the decisive victory took place when the Burlington Railroad chose to build its river bridge at Kansas City rather than Leavenworth. The former city was better organized, its hinterland in Kansas was booming, the railroad's representatives were given the opportunity to buy city land, and Van Horn was in Congress, where he could help both city and railroad. The bridge brought the city the cattle trade. By 1870 there were seven railroad connections, and the city's future was assured.

Although every city was unique, a great many of them simply played variations on this theme.

Notes

1. George R. Stewart, *Committee of Vigilance* (New York, 1964).
2. Charles Howard Shinn, *Mining Camps: A Study in American Frontier Government* (New York, 1884).
3. A. Theodore Brown, *Frontier Community* (Columbia, Mo., 1963).

Chapter 9

GOVERNING BODIES

ALTHOUGH THE FORMS of early American urban government reflected some Dutch, French, and Spanish influence, the primary model was local government in England, and the early charters reflected the common practice in that country. Thus, the council was more than just a gathering of respected citizens who made basic policy; it was also an agency that performed administrative and judicial functions. Indeed, there was no tradition of separation of powers. Vestiges of an aristocratic tradition were manifested in two ways. One was in the use of the "close" corporation, in which either members of the council and other officers were appointed by the governor, or the council itself filled vacancies as they occurred after the original appointments. Annapolis, Charleston (probably), Norfolk, and Philadelphia were so organized. The close corporation ran counter to the spirit of the Revolutionary period, and the form was eliminated after the war, beginning in 1787 with Norfolk. The other practice borrowed from a more highly class-structured England was that of distinguishing between aldermen and common councilmen. The former were generally somewhat older, well-established members of the community who literally fitted their title of aldermen, that is, the elders of the community. Usually there were two to four times as many common councilmen as aldermen, and they lacked the judicial responsibilities that the aldermen possessed. But this was not a time of true bicameral councils. There was one legislative body, usually called the common council, which consisted of the aldermen, the councilmen, the mayor (who presided), and the recorder, an officer who also acted as a judge and the city attorney. Each had one vote. The aldermen and councilmen were elected for one year, while the mayor and recorder were appointed, usually by the governor, either for a particular term or indefinitely. The aldermen were usually chosen from the councilmen.

There were some exceptions to this general pattern, but the diversity of local government in America did not really develop until after the beginning of the nineteenth century. Once begun, however, it continued throughout the period of the great growth of American cities. As the American political style emerged, two definite councilmanic patterns developed. In the older cities of the East there was something of a reaction against the class orientation and at the same time, with the growth of urban population, an increasing demand for better representation. Out of this came the bicameral council, with the upper house representing, roughly, broader community interests, and the lower house representing matters of more parochial concern. Logically extended from this was the election of the lower house and sometimes both houses on a ward basis, replacing the earlier custom of at-large election that had been almost universal, although both Albany and New York had elections by wards in the eighteenth century. The use of ward elections made possible much larger councils than those of the eighteenth century, which had typically consisted of from twelve to twenty-five members. There was, however, resistance to such change away from the traditional. Boston voters in 1854 were not alone in rejecting a proposal to elect by wards. (In the same election the remainder of a new charter was accepted 9,166 to 990. The fact that voters were not excited about the change is indicated by the low turnout, for some 13,000 ballots had been cast in the previous election.)

The second development took place among the newly founded cities of the South and Midwest, and later the Far West. Here, with typically very small populations at the time of incorporation, small, unicameral councils were the general rule, and this pattern, rather than that of bicameralism, always was the more common one for the nation as a whole. The unicameral councils did, however, copy one characteristic from those of the Northeast in that the members were nearly always elected by wards.

These patterns were merely over-all trends. There were many exceptions, and, because many cities west of the Appalachians were founded by people who had migrated from the Northeast, there was a good deal of mixing of the two forms. In an area where the small council was the rule, an occasional large council could be found, and vice versa.

Bicameralism

In 1787 the Virginia legislature declared that the close corporation of Norfolk was "impolitic and unconstitutional" and made provision for the popular election of the common council. This has been cited as the first bicameral council,[1] but evidence would seem to indicate that the new structure provided by the legislature was that of a typical eighteenth-century American city. The governor continued to appoint aldermen to fill vacancies, as had been the case under the close corporation; he did so only upon recommendation of the remaining aldermen, indicating that the old process of co-optation was continued. The councilmen were elected for three-year terms. The mayor was chosen by the aldermen. But it appears that the aldermen and councilmen did not meet separately, for the legislative charter specified: "The sole and exclusive right of passing by-laws and taxing the freeholders and inhabitants of the said borough, together with the appropriation of all monies belonging to the same is hereby vested in the Common Council." This was the eighteenth-century use of the term common council, meaning the aldermen and councilmen combined, rather than the later usage in which the term referred to the lower house. Certainly, the prestigeful aldermen were not excluded from the process of adopting ordinances and appropriating monies.

Philadelphia in 1796 appears to have been the first city to adopt bicameralism. The city had suffered considerably during the War for Independence and had been occupied successively by armies on both sides of the conflict, with the result that the old close corporation had deteriorated badly as an instrument of local self-government. So Philadelphia was given a new city charter in 1789, and the close corporation was ended. In its preamble, the new charter noted that "the administration of government within the city of Philadelphia is, in its present form, inadequate to the suppression of vice and immorality, to the advancement of the public health and order, and to the promotion of trade, industry, and happiness." The new charter was, however, quite in keeping with the common eighteenth-century pattern. It provided for fifteen aldermen to be elected for seven-year terms and thirty common councilmen with three-year terms. But they, together with the mayor and recorder, constituted the council. This charter was amended in 1796 to provide for what was unquestionably a bicameral system. It provided for an upper house to consist of twelve members who would serve three-year terms, with one-third of the membership to be elected annually. The lower house was to consist of twenty persons elected for one-year terms. The existing city council was opposed to this change, but neither its members nor the Philadelphians who had petitioned for the change was given a hearing by the state legislature.

In Philadelphia and elsewhere, especially in Pennsylvania, the upper house came to be known as the "select council" and the lower house as the "common council," a term that previously had referred to the aldermen, councilmen, mayor, and recorder acting together. Elsewhere, and more typically, the upper house, always the less numerous, came to be known as the board of aldermen and the lower house the common council. In some cases other terms were used.

The following year Baltimore, an intense rival of Philadelphia for commercial supremacy, also moved to the bicameral chamber. Two members were elected to the lower house from each of eight wards, while an electoral college arrangement chose the upper house and the mayor. Typically, the mayor presided over the upper house, while the common council would elect its own presiding officer, usually called the president. It became the usual practice to choose many administrative officers at a joint session of the two councils over which the mayor presided. Increasingly, the mayor was also given veto power. (See Chapter 10.)

Obviously, the bicameral plan was an imitation of the structure of Congress in the United States Constitution, which had gone into effect in 1789, and also of the state legislatures, some of which had been unicameral in colonial times but for the most part had shifted to bicameralism. The checks-and-balances system, with the two houses representing two different perspectives of city politics, fitted into the Madisonian idea of limited government, and the large lower house elected by wards enhanced the popular role and fitted in nicely with the views of Jefferson and Jackson.

In 1806 the governor and judges of the Michigan Territory, acting as the legislature, granted a charter for Detroit that provided for a bicameral council. But this charter did not abandon the tradition of small councils. It provided for one house to consist of three members to be elected annually by ballot in September and the second chamber of equal size to be elected each March. The council was given authority to increase its size at a later time. Considerable controversy arose over this charter when it was discovered that the mayor, who was to be appointed by the governor, had an absolute veto power. Since his term was for only one year, it meant in effect that Detroit had only such powers of local government as the governor was willing to tolerate. In the political squabble that followed, the city was in effect disestablished by the territorial legislature in 1810. This was the end of Detroit's experiment with bicameralism, for when the territorial legislature, spurred on by Governor Lewis Cass, who was favorably disposed toward local government, granted another charter in 1815, the return was essentially to the town (i.e., village) government charter of 1802, which provided for a council consisting of five trustees elected at large.

Other cities began to adopt the new bicameral system. The Pittsburgh charter of 1816 followed that of Philadelphia. Although at least as early as 1784 Bostonians had talked about incorporating their town, it was not actually done until 1822, and bicameralism was included in the plan. This action spurred imitations in many other communities of Massachusetts and the rest of New England. It is likely that bicameralism had a particular attraction in New England because a parallel could be drawn between the common council and the annual town meeting, and between the board of aldermen and the selectmen. In this sense the Boston city plan presaged the representative town meeting that developed in the twentieth century. At the time of incorporation Boston had a population of about 40,000. The council was to consist of a board of eight aldermen elected at large and a common council of forty-eight members, four from each ward. Voting was initially concurrent by the two bodies. At first the specialized administrative committees were drawn only from the mayor and aldermen, but eventually members of the council participated jointly in such committees. Other New England cities followed, such as Bangor in 1834, with a council of seven and twenty-one, respectively, Cambridge in 1846, and Augusta in 1850.

The justification for the system was outlined by the incoming mayor of New Bedford, Massachusetts, when that city adopted the plan in 1847, a generation after Boston:

> A city government with two council boards, each having the power to negative the proceedings of the other, and consisting of a limited number of persons in whom the electors have reposed confidence, affords the surest guarantee that important measures will receive mature deliberation and be satisfactorily administered, while it secures greater accountability in the expenditure of the public money.

New Bedford at that time had a population of about 15,000, and its whaling industry was at its height. The charter provided for ward meetings at which members of the common council were chosen. It was standard for the councilmen to be chosen by voice vote or show of hands, but the aldermen, elected at large, were chosen by ballot. This was the provision in the Providence charter of 1832. However, eleven years later the procedures were changed to call for the selection of councilmen by ballot as well. It seems likely that, as the conflict level rose in American cities, people became increasingly reluctant to vote in public.

Bicameralism also spread west of the Alleghenies, but it was never very popular in the Midwest. The largest city to adopt it was St. Louis, where the upper chamber was known as the House of Delegates. The plan, adopted in 1839, was abandoned twenty years later when a council was established consisting of two members from each of ten wards. It was later re-established. Cincinnati in 1827 and Cleveland in 1836 both provided for aldermen as well as trustees, but the form was essentially that of the eighteenth century, for the two groups met together as a unicameral body.

Adoption by the nation's largest city, New York, in 1830 was important for the bicameral movement, and a few other cities followed suit in that geographical area. This included New Brunswick, New Jersey, in 1838.

The first charter for San Francisco in 1850 provided for bicameralism. In 1854 the second popular charter of Philadelphia reaffirmed a commitment to it, and Wheeling adopted it in 1863. Milwaukee in 1858 introduced bicameralism and the mayor's veto as reform measures, reflecting the American faith in checks and balances as deterrents to an endemic corruption that was affecting the city. By the time of the Civil War, however, the movement had largely run its course, although some of the larger cities continued to be attracted to bicameralism into the 1890s.

Experiments with the Commission Plan

There was some experimentation with variants of the colonial style of city government in addition to the move to the simple common council. When Alexandria, Virginia, was incorporated as a town in 1779, the charter provided simply that the freeholders and housekeepers of the town could vote for twelve men. The winners served as a unicameral council, but they also divided their own number up into the offices of mayor, recorder, and four aldermen. The remaining six served as the common council. The Richmond charter of three years later was identical.

Some cities tried out what was later to be known as the commission plan. Perhaps the earliest example was that of Nachitoches, Louisiana. When it was incorporated in 1819, the charter provided for five trustees to be elected. From their own number, they chose a president, secretary (clerk), treasurer, assessor, overseer of highways, and tax collector. (Obviously, someone had to hold more than one job.) Collectively they acted as the legislative body. The Sacramento charter, in effect between 1863 and 1893, provided for a three-member board of trustees elected at large. They chose one of themselves to be mayor. This officer was in charge of the police department and had general supervisory powers over administration. A second trustee was in charge of streets and public works, while the third served as superintendent of the water department. Collectively they acted as the council, with the mayor presiding. A similar arrangement was established for New Orleans by the "carpetbagger" legislature in 1870. Until 1882 the voters elected at large a mayor and seven administrators. Each had charge of a department, with the mayor having general administrative responsibility. Collectively, they acted as the council with the mayor presiding, although he had no vote except in case of a tie. There were other cases of the use of the commission plan prior to the famous Galveston Charter of 1901, but it was not deliberately worked out as a new type of government. Rather, it was a development consistent with the colonial practice of giving aldermen and sometimes the entire council administrative responsibilities.[2] (There appear to be no precedents during this period for the council-manager plan, except for the common usage of the city clerk as a kind of general administrator and factotum, often re-elected for years and decades on end.)

Unicameralism

When Chicago was incorporated as a city in 1837 and Springfield, Illinois, in 1840, both special-act charters were based on the pattern of the town (that is, village) government. The president and four trustees became the mayor and four aldermen. (At that time Chicago had a population of only 4,170.) In 1837, when the Texas Republic incorporated a number of towns, including Houston and San Antonio, the charters provided for a mayor and eight aldermen.

Columbia, South Carolina, was incorporated in 1805 with a unicameral council called the board of wardens. This term, along with "trustees," was quite common in the South and on the frontier, although later there was a tendency to borrow the old, prestigeful term "aldermen." Other terms were used, too. When the North Carolina legislature incorporated Nashville in 1784, it provided for a unicameral board of commissioners to be appointed by the legislature. The term "commissioners" appears to have stemmed from the fact that the members of the first board were assigned the administrative tasks of laying out the town, plotting it, and selling the lots. The term was continued when the commissioners were made elective in 1802. In 1806 Nashville was incorporated as a city, and the governing body was renamed the council. Cities that were incorporated by the Florida territory, including St. Augustine (1821), Tallahassee (1825), Pensacola (1826), and Key West (1832) all had small councils of from five to nine members. At first they were appointed by the territorial governor, but they were later made elective. After statehood Florida continued this practice, and the General Charter Act of 1869 provided for cities to have a mayor and from five to nine aldermen.

The pattern of the small unicameral council, usually but not always elected by wards, became very common in the South, the Midwest, and the Far West. Atlanta was incorporated as a village in 1844 with five commissioners. Omaha was incorporated in 1857 with nine aldermen, and the following year the number was reduced to six. Until 1864 all Nebraska cities were incorporated by special acts of the legislature; typically they provided for a city council to consist of the mayor and three aldermen. When Portland, Oregon, was incorporated in 1851, it was given a council of nine members. Cheyenne, which had been founded by the Union Pacific Railroad in 1867, was incorporated as a city by the legislature of the Dakota Territory early the following year, and a small unicameral council was provided for. When the Wyoming Territory was established the following year, the new territorial legislature granted another charter to Cheyenne providing for a board of trustees to consist of the mayor, elected at large, and four other members, elected by wards.

Unicameralism was also to be found in some of the cities of the East, including even New England. It was especially common in New Jersey, New York, and the smaller cities of Pennsylvania. In 1832 citizens at a town meeting in Newark called for the division of the town into wards with separate meetings, because there was no longer a hall large enough to hold the annual meeting. This was done, and when Newark was incorporated as a city four years later the four wards were continued with one alderman to be elected from each. The mayor was to be elected at large and also serve on the council. Burlington, Vermont, was incorporated in 1864 with a unicameral legislature.

The Mayor and the Council

The colonial charters typically provided that the mayor should be a voting member of the council, and this pattern prevailed well into the nineteenth century. The separation of powers doctrine had not applied in English local government; even after being adopted by the national and state governments in this country, it was slow to be applied to American municipalities. There were some early indications of a different trend, but they were probably not recognized for a long time. The New Orleans charter of 1805, for example, provided that the mayor should preside over the council, but the first mayor acting under that charter chose not to do so, and his precedent was followed by his successors. The fourth (1857) charter of the city of Detroit removed the mayor from the council, as did the Camden charter of 1850. The independent election of the mayor, which soon became standard after 1822, together with the more and more common provision granting him a veto power, increasingly made it clear that the mayor should not serve on the council, because the trend was away from a miniature parliamentary system and toward the presidential system, with its separation of powers and checks and balances.

Term of Office

Almost everywhere the term of office for councilmen was one year, but there were some exceptions. The Philadelphia pattern of longer terms appears to have been a transitional development between the earlier system of a close corporation, in which councilmen served for life, and popular government. There were also other exceptions, as in the New Orleans charter of 1812, which provided for two-year terms. But the one-year term indicated to everyone interested that service on

the council was considered a community responsibility and duty, not a
steppingstone to a higher political career. Until well after the Civil War
it remained the ordinary term of service for members of the local governing body.

Those Who Served

The men who served on councils, at least until the post–Civil War
years, did not do so because they considered themselves or were considered by their fellow citizens to be politicians. In the East many of them
were high-status individuals who served out of a sense of obligation,
and this motivation continued to predominate in other parts of the
country as cities moved beyond their earliest period of development. In
new communities along the frontier councilmen were often developers
and land speculators. Everywhere, the Main Street merchant was the
dominant figure. In Springfield, Massachusetts; Poughkeepsie, New
York; and elsewhere, a minority of artisans and laborers were usually
returned from certain wards, but these men often showed due deference
to the merchants. In Springfield the working-class representatives made
up 32 per cent of the council in the 1850s. This had declined to 7 per
cent in the 1870s. In some instances, of course, councilmen were individuals on the way toward success as professional politicians, although
this was not the reason that they were elected to office initially. Andrew
Johnson, a tailor later to become the seventeenth President, was elected
an alderman in Greenville, Tennessee, at the age of twenty-one in 1829
and became mayor the following year. Along the frontier, as was to be
expected, members of the council tended to be younger than were those
in the established cities of the East.

Southern cities were fairly similar in their choice of council structures,
if not of councilmen. Richmond's were men of integrity, and so also
were those of most other cities. Memphis and New Orleans were tainted
with spoils and corruption. Natchez was in the hands of the middle
class; the gentry and the wealthy showed little interest, with the majority not even bothering to vote. The ports of Norfolk, Charleston, and
Savannah were served well by their councils.

Service on the council was definitely viewed as a citizen's obligation,
and the one-year term made it easier to accept membership, because it
offered at least a hope that the individual would not have to act for very
long. Even so there were some problems in getting reluctant citizens to
take on the task. In Augusta, Georgia, by a provision of 1798, individuals
were fined if they refused to serve on the council. And even though
service on the council was not considered a political activity and individuals did not usually run for office on the basis of any particular pledge
of voting position, voter retribution did occur occasionally in response
to particularly emotional and dramatic councilmanic decisions. In 1851

the councilmen of Boston paid the political price of their failure to find a way out of what was probably a hopeless dilemma. They refused the use of Faneuil Hall for a meeting of Abolitionists, who were considered radicals, and then, apparently in an effort to show neutrality, also refused to allow it to be used for a reception for Daniel Webster, a conservative. These decisions did not offset one another, but rather managed to alienate both radicals and conservatives, and many councilmen were defeated in the next election.

Vacancies

During this period councilmanic vacancies were uncommon because of the shortness of the term. But this brevity also made it logical to permit the council to fill vacancies by co-optation. This practice had been known in some of the close corporations of the colonial period. Furthermore, because service on the council was viewed primarily as a community responsibility for civic leaders, this arrangement seemed logical, convenient, and inexpensive. It was carried on throughout the period and is still used in many parts of the nation today.

It was assumed that council members would serve without pay or expense allowances, and this was overwhelmingly the case. There were exceptions, however. Although the councilmen of Providence received no pay in 1833, the aldermen received $100 each per year. In 1853 this amount was doubled, and each councilman was given $100 per year. This compared with $800 for the city solicitor and $1,500 for the mayor.

Conflict of Interest

The problem of conflict of interest arose early and was perhaps made more tempting because of the lack of salary. Furthermore, as the nineteenth century progressed, members of the legislative body became less and less likely to be members of the most affluent merchant and professional groups. The usual provision was to prohibit members of the council from holding any paid administrative office, such as overseer of the poor or city attorney. This did not, however, prevent merchant members from doing business with the city or lawyers from providing professional services.

In many cases the councils, either under pressure or out of a sense of civic obligation, placed themselves under greater restrictions. Sometimes this was done by the legislature through charter provisions. For example, in 1804 Savannah, Georgia, adopted an ordinance that prohibited members of the council from being interested in any contract, office, or appointment in the city. This provision remained in force throughout the remainder of the century.

The reputation of the council was jealously guarded by its members most of the time. Except in some frontier cities where bribery was not uncommon and in a few where the beginnings of the great political machines were beginning to develop, councilmen cherished the image of themselves as civic leaders and boosters. In 1803 the Savannah council censured one of its members for publishing an anonymous letter reflecting on the council for allowing theatrical performances on Saturday evenings, an issue of some importance at that time. The alderman was condemned for reflecting on the "dignity and responsibility" of the council, and he resigned. In that same city in 1809 an alderman was convicted of bribery in connection with the illegal importation of slaves from the West Indies, but this was probably an isolated incident.

Despite a concern for the appearance of rectitude, the boondoggle and the concern for personal profit from public office appeared early. In Schenectady (which had been incorporated as a borough in 1765, but as a city only in 1798), there were complaints as early as 1801 that the aldermen appointed

> . . . each other committees of one on building bridges, contracting for the sending home of paupers, inspecting elections, and doing anything that came in their way. They were always very particular in paying themselves and the items of "necessary expenses" are frequent. "Necessary expenses" then, it is more than likely, covered many of the good things of this world which aldermen find pleasant in the performance of public duty. Every extra service meant extra pay. An alderman at a fire could put his friends to work and the council paid for the labor. . . . For instance, in June, 1803, "John Corl and three other persons," were paid two dollars "for services at the fire at Mrs. Taylor's" and the same John Corl and "six other persons" [the writer may be implying that they were fictitious] were paid $4.38 each at another fire. The mayor got 75¢ for every deed he signed, and he signed a great many. If he took part in looking through the city account books he got ten dollars, as did each of the councilmen on the committee with him. Councilmen used to appoint themselves appraisers and pay themselves well for the work. Here and there are entries of a couple of dollars apiece to various councilmen for "extra services," three dollars to the clerk of the board on the same account. Besides, the councilmen appointed each other to build bridges, repair highways, and do all sorts of public work. The appropriation was made directly to the councilmen.[3]

Obviously, even though the councilman of the period was typically a solid burgher, he was also not above picking up a few public dollars. And obviously the public was already suspicious of profiteering public servants, whose dollars may have been honestly come by but were not necessarily believed to be honestly earned. Where corruption occurred, especially in the larger cities, its center was usually in the council. An alderman or councillor already could retain his seat by due attention to the interests of his ward and its voters. The voters were not greatly

shocked if the same men were suspected of graft in connection with
contracts or other special interests affecting the city as a whole.

The Institutional Power Struggle

As the forms of government moved away from the colonial pattern,
and as the separation of powers doctrine was increasingly accepted at
the local level, power struggles between the mayor and the council could
be expected and did, in fact, occur. As early as 1804 the Savannah council forced the mayor to give up exclusive authority to appoint trustees
of the exchange and to substitute election by the council. In Philadelphia after 1839 and in many other cities, the mayor gradually lost administrative powers to the council and, beginning in the 1850s, to independent boards and commissions. The new Chicago charter of 1863
worked to weaken the mayor's powers and strengthen those of the council. Some powers of appointment, however, were returned to him in
1867. On the other hand, the separation of powers doctrine gave the
mayor a new weapon of his own, that of the veto (see Chapter 10).

Council Procedures

Council procedures were based on tradition and were much the same
as they are today. The major development in the first half of the nineteenth century was the change from initial consideration of items by
the council as a whole to the use of the committee system. This was
made necessary by the growth in the size of councils and the increase
in their agenda, and was, of course, already a familiar procedure in the
state legislatures. Some problems also occurred because of the lack of
a separation of powers system in many cities. Thus, in 1819 the Savannah, Georgia, council provided that no committee could enter into a
contract involving more than $100 without laying the question before
the entire council. The committee in this case was being treated as a
plural department head and not as a legislative subdivision.

In 1863 the president of the Providence common council recommended that every important matter of business should be referred to a
standing or special committee before final action by the council. (Special committees were not new—they dated from the colonial period.)
For the most part this procedure was followed. It worked to distribute
the load of the council, but almost immediately there were comments to
the effect that too much reliance was placed upon committee judgment
rather than that of the entire council, and there was considerable confusion about financial responsibility within the council. The following
year the mayor, who had been a councilman before the committee system was put into effect, complained that the council had fallen under

clique domination and that there was a good deal of logrolling. He attempted to resist the tendency of the committees to seek detailed administrative control over the functions for which they were responsible.

Bicameralism caused some problems in procedures. Under the Boston charter of 1822 common councillors were jealous of the administrative powers of the aldermen and were concerned that the members of the upper house were in a stronger position to dominate policy because of their greater experience with day-to-day operations. Finally, in 1835, the aldermen agreed to a joint committee system that reduced suspicion and permitted the councillors to benefit from the greater detailed knowledge of the aldermen.

Throughout American history there has been a conflict between the desire of the council to proceed confidentially on some of its matters and the desire of citizens and newspapermen to know everything possible about governmental decision-making. Legislators are often suspected of wishing to maintain secrecy because they are involved in something of doubtful legality and possible personal profit, but it is also true that communication and successful probing to the roots of a problem may be more difficult when conducted in public. A letter to the mayor and aldermen of Nashville in 1823 suggested greater publicity for their proceedings, and the writer added:

> Therefore, Gentlemen, do now unveil; put off the mantle of obscurity which has heretofore concealed all your doings, and exhibit all to the view of the public. Then the people will be satisfied with what is done, and then perhaps you will do more. . . . Perhaps some of you could then inform us why we have no fire companies, why some streets are improved to the exclusion of others, why some most abandoned characters are suffered to go at large and insult the better portion of our citizens with their gross immoralities; why gambling houses and tippling-shops, and all other nuisances are permitted to exist without restraint; why some of our public springs are allowed to become unfit for use for want of attention to them; why the Negroes overrun the town on Sundays.[4]

The letter was probably from a newspaperman. Whether he was more interested in a "right to know" or in the possibility of furthering newspaper sales through the publication of "inside dope" cannot be known. In any case, the aldermen felt the sting of the letter and a few days later published the minutes of the meeting that was held just prior to the receipt of the letter. These minutes showed activity in an effort to organize fire companies, the engaging of a policeman for Sunday duty, and the appointment of committees on schools, public springs, improvement of streets, and fire companies, as well as the appointment of an inspector for the waterworks under construction. Perhaps the letter was solicited, although this seems unlikely. It is more probable that the council held an adjourned session of the meeting after receipt of the letter, as it seems unlikely that the council would by sheer coincidence deal with so many of the complaints mentioned in the letter at a single and most timely meeting.

The Powers of Councils

The powers of the council were broad, despite the increasingly narrow interpretation of powers taken by the courts under Dillon's Rule (see Chapter 2). In general, the council was responsible for the enactment of ordinances relative to public matters and responsibilities as delegated by state law and also for items designed for the comfort and convenience of citizens (such as public utilities and, in many states, parks and water supply). Executive powers usually rested in the mayor and the aldermen or, in unicameral cities, in the mayor and council. The appointive powers that did not rest with the mayor belonged to the council, and in bicameral cities positions were often filled at a joint session of the two houses. In addition members of the council, particularly aldermen in a bicameral body, sometimes had judicial powers and the council also had important, though gradually declining, powers over public education.

Sometimes the powers of the council were restricted, as when the state took over control of the police of some cities (see Chapter 3) and after the rise of the independent boards and commissions to head particular functions. There were other exceptions, too: The sidewalk commissioners of Providence enjoyed some independent powers granted by the legislature until 1841, and some statutory powers were granted to the surveyor of highways until an even later date. But in general, within the limits of state law, the council was the legislative body.

The appointive powers of the council were broad. The board of aldermen or the entire council chose the mayor if he was not elected. The appointive powers of the bicameral council in Reading, Pennsylvania, in the charter of 1847 are typical. Acting jointly, the two houses selected the solicitor, street regulator, street commissioners, market commissioners, high constable, scavenger, and the president and clerk of the council. (The mayor, treasurer, and three auditors were elected, as were four aldermen who, in Pennsylvania, quite commonly had only the powers of municipal judges.) The council also commonly had removal powers. Thus, under an 1856 charter provision in Wheeling (then in Virginia), the council could by a two-thirds vote remove from office the city clerk, treasurer, or any alderman, municipal judge, or councilman. This was true even though these officers were selected for one-year terms.

Sometimes the appointive powers of the council were increased in an effort to improve administration. Thus, the Boston council was empowered in 1864 to appoint the overseers of the poor. This was not a premature move toward the short ballot, a development that was still more than a generation away, but rather was designed to discourage profiteering in public welfare. Previously the overseers had been elected by wards and often were grocers or coal dealers seeking to use the job in order to increase their own business volume. Even in the case of those officers appointed by the mayor, it was usual for the council or one of its chambers to have to approve the appointment before it could go into effect.

Councilmanic Administrative Duties

In a day before professional administration had developed, it was quite common to assign administrative duties to councilmen. This was especially true of the aldermen both under the colonial form and in bicameral cities later on. Members of the lower house were not usually given administrative duties, although there were some exceptions. Thus we find in Savannah around the beginning of the nineteenth century the aldermen at work. They took turns patrolling the streets on Sundays, together with the marshal and one or more constables. And on other days,

> Attended by the clerk of the market and the marshal, an alderman would visit the several bakeries and shops, weigh and examine the bread. Loaves not complying with the requirement [of the assize of bread] were seized and distributed among the poor and the offenders brought before Council and fined, generally four and eight.

The Providence charter of 1832 vested executive power in the mayor and aldermen, who were elected at large in a bicameral council. These powers were sharply distinguished from the ordinance or policy-making powers, which belonged to the council as a whole. The Cambridge, Massachusetts, charter of 1846 provided for a bicameral council. The mayor and aldermen were established as a board to sit together and serve as the executive. This was simply a continuation of the earlier use of the selectmen. They controlled the police, licensing, elections, fire protection, and a few other activities.

With the councils dividing themselves into committees on a functional basis and each committee feeling itself responsible for administering its particular function, certain developments followed naturally. As cities grew—Chicago and Richmond will serve as examples—departmental organization of the full-time city employees followed the committee division of labor. Patronage sometimes became a committee prerogative. Committee recommendations on policy normally prevailed in the council as a whole. The situation gravitated rather naturally to turning such departments over to boards.

The Development of Boards and Commissions

In the Boston charter of 1854 the board of aldermen in the bicameral system was increased in membership from eight to twelve and was given all executive powers of the corporation which had formerly been vested in the mayor and aldermen. Although this had the effect of increasing the powers of the upper chamber, it took place about the time that a new trend was setting in relative to the administrative responsibilities of the council. As the cities grew in the years before the appearance of a professional bureaucracy, increasing efforts were made by legislators, mayors, and members of the council to find more adequate means of providing administrative leadership for the city departments. The councilmen, serving with little or no pay, found the responsibilities increasingly burdensome and the possibilities for corruption more tempting. The result was that in the 1850s and particularly in the 1860s many administrative responsibilities that had belonged to the council or the aldermen were transferred to boards and commissions, which had varying degrees of independence from the council. These boards (an early tenuous distinction between them and temporary "commissions" soon disappeared) served as the collective administrative agency head. They were usually constituted of leading members of the community who served on a part-time basis, the same kinds of people who a generation earlier had dominated the councils. As a result of this development, urban administration became increasingly decentralized and remained so until the trend toward the concentration of executive leadership in the mayor evolved in the 1880s and 1890s. Decentralization was a logical extension of the basic tenets of Jacksonian democracy, even though it came along a generation after the first wave of that populistic movement.

The first and most nearly universal of these boards was the one to control public education. Most of the boards also were given their own financial powers, a pattern often followed in the case of other such organizations. The use of boards spread until they were commonly used in connection with most of the important and expensive functions of city government, including streets, water works, police, fire protection, parks, and libraries.

One of the earliest uses of the board system appeared in Detroit in 1854, and the system there was greatly expanded with the adoption of a new charter three years later. Between 1861 and 1867 many departments of the city of Chicago were placed under administrative boards. Some of them were at first elective, but the mayor gained the power to appoint several of them under an act of 1867.

In New York City the council lost its direct administrative oversight with the charter of 1830. Boards and individual administrators were established, but the council appointed these officials and so had opportunities to remain involved in details of administration and especially of patronage. In 1849, however, these positions were made elective. This practice was in turn replaced in 1857 by mayoral appointment with councilmanic approval, except that the corporation counsel and comptroller remained elective.*

The council was not always cut off completely from a voice in the departments administered by boards, but its powers were sharply reduced. Thus, when a board of water commissioners was created in Providence in 1866, the membership was to be selected by the council for three-year terms. But the board was given virtually complete control over the water-supply system and members could not be removed except for cause and then only by a two-thirds vote of the council. (Their assigned task was to construct the first water-supply system for the city. It was not uncommon at this time to create a special temporary commission to construct a building or a water system.)

The controls over educational policy were among the first the council lost. Even in the first charter of Boston in 1822 the council did not have full control over education. Instead, a school committee was created consisting of the mayor, eight aldermen, and one person elected from each ward. In 1835 an almost complete break was made between education and other functions of local government. The school committee was reconstituted to consist of the mayor, the president of the common council, and two persons elected from each ward. Comments at the time indicated that the aldermen were too busy to serve on this separate governing body, but they were also being subjected to criticisms from the members of the common council who were jealous of their greater powers. (The school committee at that time controlled only the grammar schools. The high schools, or primary schools as they were called, were controlled between 1818 and 1854 by a self-perpetuating committee.) The transfer of powers to an independent board of education probably took place with more reluctance in New England than elsewhere, but everywhere it was gradual and inexorable during this period. For example, control over public education in Springfield, Illinois, was not transferred from the city council to a board of education until 1869, and even then the nine members of the board were chosen by the council. In some communities and states boards of education were never made elective, and various ways were devised for their appointment.

The use of boards and commissions spread even in New England, where Jacksonian precepts were weakest and this approach to government seemed alien to the town government tradition. Thus, control of

---

* On the reasons for the 1957 changes, see above, pp. 52–53.

Boston streets was transferred in 1870 from the council to a board of street commissioners, which had a membership of three persons popularly elected. The use of the board was later extended to other departments in that city. And elsewhere in the country the practice continued to expand for more than a generation after it first appeared in Detroit, and it has left a strong impression upon the pattern of city government up to the present time.[5]

At times the transfer of powers to a specialized board was (as in the Milwaukee Board of Public Works of 1859) designed to remedy the extravagant and corrupt administration of the council. Like so many "reforms," it brought some initial improvement, but the scattered responsibility eventually caused the city to retrogress.

Judicial Duties

In colonial cities not only were the mayor and recorder justices of the peace and judicial officers, but so were the aldermen. This practice was generally continued when bicameral councils were developed, thus giving the aldermen legislative, executive, and judicial duties. There were variations. In an occasional city, such as New Haven, the aldermen were almost wholly judicial officials. In a few others, especially in New England, where they were regarded as replacing the selectmen, they and not the councillors administered the functions. The Providence charter of 1831 is an example. However, there the council chose the officials.

With rare exceptions, councillors in unicameral cities did not have judicial responsibilities. Perhaps this was because of the development of the Jacksonian tendency to elect judges and thus to create an office of municipal judge, under one title or another, separate from the council. But the term alderman was so strongly perceived as belonging to a municipal justice that in Pennsylvania and Virginia the term was continued in use for the municipal judge. Few of the aldermen were trained in the law, but at that time in history that was not considered necessary. The assumption was that these men, typically older than the average age in the community and typically members of the community elite, would apply the predominant values of the community to the relatively minor crimes and small civil claims that came before their courts.

Generally, though by no means universally, the aldermen had been deprived of their judicial powers and responsibilities prior to the time of the Civil War. Their powers were not usually taken away by a single legislative act but were in most cases gradually transferred to some type of municipal court. The change took place at different rates and irregularly in different parts of the country. Thus, the aldermen of New Brunswick, New Jersey, lost their judicial powers in 1838, while their colleagues in Trenton, not far away, had theirs reaffirmed in the previous year. In New Haven the divestiture took place in 1842, and a recorder's court was established. This was a common pattern.

Ex Officio *Duties*

Various members of the council were given *ex officio* responsibilities, holding membership on some board because of the position held on the council. The president of the common council was particularly likely to serve in such a position, for example, as a member of the school board or the park board. Chairmen of council committees also quite often had such responsibilities. Thus, the chairman of the council committee on public libraries or water supply might serve, *ex officio*, as a member of the library or water board. The board of health, along with the board of education, an early example of the board system of administration, often contained *ex officio* members. Thus, the board of health of Augusta, Georgia, in 1843 consisted of the mayor and four councilmen (all of whom served without pay). An Iowa statute of 1866 decreed that the mayor and council of each city should constitute the health authority for the community.

Although government in the first seventy years of the nineteenth century was simple, at least by comparison with a century later, the councils had a great deal of work to do. Members could understand more easily than can their counterparts in today's complex, technological world the problems confronting them, but their tasks were nevertheless complicated. Thus, the New Orleans council in the two years beginning in 1815 enacted ordinances dealing with, among other things, street paving, the carting of firewood, port charges, fees for the use of public halls, compensation for houses torn down during fire-fighting, the regulation of gambling, providing aid to the library society, controls over the public morality such as the prohibiting of river bathing during daylight hours, the prohibition of wooden houses within the city limits, the prohibition of any interference with natural drainage, the regulation of the hiring of slaves by nonowners, the establishment of a system of house numbering, the annual establishment of the price of bread, the licensing and regulation of theaters, the rules for the censorship and conditions for performance of theatrical plays, fire regulations, and the letting of contracts to collect taxes from gambling proceeds.

During the first century after American independence, city councils moved from a situation in which they were made up of the leadership of the city collectively to one in which there was an increasing emphasis upon the separation of powers; from one under which the council was dominant in all phases of municipal policy-making to one in which it was of relatively less importance, having to share the spotlight with various boards and commissions, the mayor, and a number of independent elective officers. But the council was never without importance in shaping the development of the community, and it was never without an impressive work load.

Districts and Wards as Government Units

Because of the contemporary interest in devolving municipal functions upon smaller units with a measure of district or neighborhood control, the experience of some of the growing cities of our first century has some relevance. It is not reassuring.

For a while there was no clearly thought-out role of the ward in city government. Was it merely a convenient unit for local representation in the electoral process, or did it have administrative functions? Whatever may have been the charter provisions, in many of the larger cities the individual aldermen or councillors during the first century of the United States acquired certain roles in the allocation of city employment, the distribution of outdoor relief, the granting of favors and immunities tied in with the police, and the modern role of legislators generally—serving as an informal ombudsman for constituents. In Chicago under the 1837 charter public improvements were to be distributed according to the assessed valuation of each ward.

More formally, certain cities like Milwaukee and Pittsburgh set up their schools on a ward basis and gave the local legislators or school board members formal powers over their ward schools.

In Milwaukee, where there were several councillors to a ward, these constituted a formal authority over the streets and certain other improvements in the ward. Not even the council as a whole could override such expenditures for many years. Until 1852 each ward remained a corporation and could decide which functions it would support. This system proved both extravagant and corrupt and was superseded in 1869 by an appointed Board of Public Works.

New Orleans also furnished an interesting case study. In 1830 it was divided into three municipal corporations along fairly logical regional or district lines. Only minor powers were granted the city as a whole. Each of the three had an elected council and a recorder (police court judge). These councils made and enforced laws and carried out public works for their respective districts. The mayor (elected at large) presided over a General Council made up of the three councils. It could fix wharfage rates, impose certain taxes and licenses, and enact police regulations of a general nature. Its permission was necessary for any of the three councils to sell real estate valued at over $2,000.

In 1850 a majority of the voters supported this *status quo*, but in 1851 the Whigs swept the city on a platform calling for consolidation, which the state granted in 1852. Only the third district (the polyglot municipality) had voted against it. The consolidation was a victory for the merchants and other stable elements.

Notes

1. See J. Woldrige, *History of Nashville* (Nashville, 1890).
2. See Ernest S. Griffith, A *History of American City Government 1870–1900: The Conspicuous Failure* (New York, 1974), pp. 236–37.
3. Quoted in Schenectady County Teachers' Association, *History of the City and County of Schenectady* (Schenectady, 1887).
4. Quoted in J. H. Thomas, *Old Days in Nashville* (Nashville, 1897).
5. See Griffith, *op. cit.* Chap. 7.

Chapter 10

EXECUTIVE OFFICERS

THE STRUCTURE FOR AMERICAN municipal administration evolved from the English pattern introduced during colonial times. In the colonial form the mayor was appointed for a one-year term, usually by the governor. Although the mayor was the nominal head of the municipal corporation, his powers were not extensive. He was a member of the common council over which he presided. He was a justice of the peace but had no particular executive powers, although sometimes the council would assign him certain special duties, such as that of tax collector or overseer of the poor, for which he received an emolument. There was no restriction on holding more than one office at a time, and these administrative duties were assumed independently of the office of mayor. This was the pattern in the majority of the cities. There were some cities, three of them close corporations, in which the council chose the mayor.[1] Rarely was the mayor directly elected. During this period the mayor and aldermen possessed important judicial functions.

After the War for Independence, when governors were generally in disrepute, mayors were ordinarily made elective by the common council, although this development was gradual, and it was not accompanied by any increase in the powers of the mayor. It was overwhelmingly required or expected that the mayor would be chosen from among the aldermen. A little later the emerging idea of separation of powers gradually caused a move away from this notion. Thus, in 1806 the Georgetown, District of Columbia, charter was amended to eliminate this restriction upon the common council.

Sometimes experiments were conducted that were not successful and were not imitated. For example, the mayor and other officers in Paterson, New Jersey (1791), were selected by the state legislature and served at its pleasure. In Natchez (1779) voters chose a panel of three, from among whom the Spanish governor selected the *alcalde*. This plan was dropped after transfer to American control. The 1797 Baltimore charter,* deliberately imitating the national government plan, called for the

---

* Enacted by the Laws of Maryland, 1796, Ch. 68, but effective the next year.

voters to choose an electoral college, two members from each of eight wards. This collegial body then chose the mayor.

Some city charters were slow to be amended. The power of the common council to elect was not granted to Washington, D.C. until 1812 or Mobile until 1819. And this power was not conferred upon the councils of New York until a new state constitution was adopted in 1821. Previous to that, mayors had been appointed by the governor, with the consent of his council of appointment.

The Popularly Elected Mayor

The beginnings of the idea of an elected mayor can be found in the Colonial period.[2] It reappeared in the charter granted to New Haven in 1784, which provided for election of the mayor by such persons as were then eligible to vote but also established an indefinite term of office. The mayor served at the pleasure of the state legislature, which thus had an absolute veto over the local selection. But what happened as a result of this provision is testimony to the essential political impotence of mayors in the early days of the nation. During the forty-two years this provision was in effect, New Haven had only four mayors, and two of them died in office. In 1826 the provision was changed to provide for an annually elected mayor.

The always populistic frontier provides the first instance of a regularly elected mayor. The first Nashville Charter of 1806 called for annual election. The mayor in this case was simply another councilman, all of whose colleagues were elected at large. His only distinction from the other six members of the council was that he presided over the body. This experiment did not last long: In 1811 the charter was changed to provide for seven aldermen, with these to select one of their own as mayor.

Although New Orleans apparently began to elect its mayor in 1812 and Annapolis in 1819, the movement toward an elected mayor began in earnest in 1822, a few years ahead of the developments leading toward Jacksonian democracy. In that year the mayor of St. Louis was made popularly elective, and so was the mayor of Boston in the first charter granted to that city. The Boston charter provided for a bicameral council; the mayor presided over the board of aldermen, while the lower house elected its own president.

Andrew Jackson first ran for the Presidency in 1824, and from that time on his populistic ideas had an important effect upon urban government. The mayor was made elective by the Detroit charter of 1824 and a recognition was given to the separation of powers idea when he was, for the first time, established as a city official but not a member of the council. (This idea, however, had earlier precedents. Under the Baltimore charter of 1796 and an amendment to the Philadelphia charter in the same year, the office of mayor was established separately from the council, even though the mayor was not popularly elected.)

Provision for the election of the mayor now spread rapidly to Mobile (1826), Cincinnati (1827), Georgetown (1830), Baltimore (1833), and New York (1834). In New York a constitutional amendment was necessary, since the 1821 state constitution had empowered the common council to elect the mayor, and this was passed in part because of the strong support given by Governor DeWitt Clinton. Other cities adopted the principle both in the older areas of the East and along the frontier. Thus the mayor became elective in Cleveland (1836), Philadelphia (1839), and in Rochester and Albany (1840). Smaller cities were sometimes somewhat slower to adopt the plan, perhaps because of the lesser importance of urban politics in those cities. Not until 1849 did Manchester, New Hampshire, make the mayor elective, nor until the following year did Augusta, Maine. However, many cities had elective mayors from the time of the adoption of their first city charters. This was true, for example, of Columbus, Ohio (1834), Newark (1836), and Chicago (1837).

Another factor, apart from Jacksonian influence, accounted for the election of numerous officials in the early days of many cities, especially in the Midwest, West, and South. These cities tended to incorporate when their population was quite small. At this stage, almost everyone knew everyone else. Whether by consensus of the ruling merchant group, at city or ward meetings, or by party instruments, it was quite easy to justify the popular election of numerous officials—for the neighbors knew each other. As the population grew, either such a multiplication became an instrument of a party machine or a new and simplified charter eventually shifted such officials to an appointive basis.

The 1831 city charter of Providence made the mayor elective but restricted the voting to "freeman." In 1853 those eligible to vote for the mayor were increased to include all property and registry voters. This gave the mayor a much more broadly based franchise than was allowed the council. It laid the groundwork for a cleavage between a liberal mayor and a conservative council that lasted for many decades.

Election of the mayor became nearly but never quite universal in the United States. Even in the 1970s the council still elected some mayors, particularly in cities under the council-manager system. Similarly, the separation of powers concept never was totally applied. In many small cities in the 1970s, and in a few larger ones, the mayor continued to perform the traditional function of presiding over the council. In numerous council-manager cities and commission-plan cities, he continues to have voting power, as he does even in some mayor-council cities.

The Title of the Chief Executive Office

The mayor was not always known by that title. In cities founded by the Spanish the executive, who represented the governor, was known as the *alcalde*. He had broad administrative authority and ruled most of the time without a council. Although basic policy was made by the Spanish governor and not locally, the *alcalde* was a man of awesome power. As an early American in California, Charles Howard Shinn, noted: "One and the same person was often supreme judge, clerk of court, town-constable, sheriff, recorder, treasurer, justice of the peace, land-officer, government-agent in land deliveries, superintendent of roads, town board of health, board of school trustees, arbitrator in petty disputes, general advisory board for young and old, and even, near the coast, judge in admiralty to pronounce upon marine cases!"

Perhaps because this tradition was so different from the Anglo-American, when the Spanish and Mexican areas were taken into the United States, the form of government was ordinarily changed promptly to that of the English tradition and the *alcalde* became the mayor. In many areas, particularly in the South, the mayor was often known as the *intendant*, a term borrowed from the French. The *intendants* of France were local administrative officers representing the Crown and later the Ministry of the Interior. Under American law they assumed the conventional powers of the mayor but, unlike the *alcalde*, the title of *intendant* was sometimes continued for some time. Thus, in Augusta, Georgia, it was not changed to mayor until 1818. (The term *intendant* was used in some cities that were never under French control.) In some municipalities, particularly in Virginia, the term chief burgess was also used.

Incorporated villages ordinarily had the weak-mayor-council form. The presiding officer of the council was usually known as the president of the village but was sometimes also called mayor, as in Ohio villages after 1847. In villages, even up to the 1970s, the separation of powers principle never became important, and the mayor or president remained essentially a legislative and judicial officer rather than an executive.

The Status of the Mayor

With the coming of local selection of the mayor, and particularly after his popular election, the office gained in visibility and probably also in status. Until the coming of professional municipal politicians and the beginnings of the big-city machines in the 1850s and 1860s, the mayor was typically a leading figure of the community, often a merchant or attorney. Sometimes he was an individual with a very pronounced interest in politics who moved up into state and national political affairs, but more commonly he was likely to be an individual who did not view himself as a politician and never sought elective office beyond the community. Often, too, he was a notch below the most prestigious and wealthiest men in town, though there were some exceptions. Because the mayor ordinarily took the office out of a sense of civic obligation, in quite a few cities it became common for him to serve only a single one-year term and not to seek re-election. But again, in other cities the mayors became community father figures, serving until death or disability.

In his 1823 inaugural address, Mayor Josiah Quincy of Boston implied the prominent position he proposed to take. He made himself chairman of all council committees. First, he gave his attention to improving sanitary conditions of the city—street cleaning and garbage collection. The powers of the old Board of Health had been vested by the charter in the council, which had set up three committees. When these stood in the way of the mayor's reforms, he swept them away. He then began to establish a new market, which was conceived of on such a grand scale that considerable opposition was engendered. He reformed the police and fire departments and indoor poor relief by separating the honest poor from rogues and the lazy, and juveniles from older persons. By the end of his sixth term he had earned the opposition of the older firemen and of those whose private interests had suffered in the reorganization of the market and of the penal institutions, as well as those who objected to his enforcement of the vice and liquor laws. Furthermore, his activities were directly responsible for a $637,000 increase in the city debt (although he had also led a drive to reduce the tax rate from an average of $8.15 under the old town government to $7.27). The city grew rapidly during his tenure, reaching a population of 61,392 in the 1830 census.

By 1829, Quincy had to pay the price often exacted from an active mayor with a positive action program. He failed to receive a majority on the first two ballots and withdrew from the election. His successor, Harrison Otis, served two terms and tried to carry on Quincy's policies, but by 1831 the middle class of Boston took part in a taxpayer revolt against the magnificent plans of the mayors, and Wells was elected to the office. He served for two years, during which time he sought to consolidate and retrench. Innovation had temporarily come to an end in the mayor's office.

A mayor who served only one year, of course, had little opportunity to imitate Quincy. Thus, between 1834 and 1850 not a single mayor of Columbus, Ohio, was re-elected. But the first mayor of Providence after its incorporation in 1832 was re-elected each year until he died in 1840. His successor served continuously from 1841 through 1852.

The Men Who Served

The early mayors of Newark were always among those who had already achieved much recognition in the community, and they were looked upon as representative of the best and highest expression of citizenship as it was then understood. The city was dominated by the Whig party, and all mayors were members of that party from the time of incorporation in 1836 until the first Democratic mayor, Moses Bigelow, was elected in 1857. The first mayor of Newark was Theodore Frelinghuysen. He was a former United States Senator and was later a candidate for the Vice Presidency with Henry Clay. He was a member of a distinguished family and served as president of two colleges.

The first mayor of Utica was General Joseph Kirkland, who took office in 1832. He was succeeded the following year by Henry Seymour, whose son Horatio was later also mayor and then the Democratic candidate for President in 1868. The early mayors of Utica were described as "dignified and courtly in manner, perfect gentlemen of the old school, men of clear, cool heads, of unquestioned integrity, and who properly magnified their office and faithfully discharged its duties." In their day, "The righteous flourished like the palm tree and corruption stood afar off."[3]

In Worcester, Massachusetts, the first mayor, elected in 1848, was Levi Lincoln, who had served nine years as Governor of Massachusetts, a Judge of the state Supreme Judicial Court, and a member of both houses of the state legislature. In Mobile, Alabama, only thirteen mayors served in the period between 1826 and 1859. Although the term was only one year, the average service was about two years and eight months. Obviously, some men found that the office of mayor offered important prospects for community service or a chance to gain more public recognition than might be possible in their routine daily jobs. In Richmond, for example, Joseph Mayo was re-elected every year after 1853 until the Civil War years.

The laboring classes had candidates for mayor from a fairly early period, but they were seldom successful. In ordinary times the working man was not usually disposed to vote for another of his class but tended to prefer to go along with the Main Street merchants or one of the factions led by a middle-class person. One of the first working-class successes was that of Mayor Monroe of New Orleans, who was first elected in 1859 by the Native American Party. He had at one time been a stevedore.

Some outstanding men served as mayor, and some who were politically ambitious sought the office. But by and large the man who held the job was a solid member of the community, not a dramatically different or brilliant personality. Occasionally but not often they showed imagination or an innovative bent. But they did demonstrate a potential for leadership that later was to encourage reformers to vest in the office a great deal of administrative power.

While most historians have been inclined to give the title to Josiah Quincy, Richard Wade has called William Lane of St. Louis "the most able urban statesman of the period." He was re-elected five times. Other mayors notable for their leadership were John Wentworth of Chicago, Robert Van Horn of Kansas City (an outstanding newspaper publisher), and Gerard Stith of New Orleans.

Much of the time the mayor was elected without opposition, and there were seldom more than two candidates, but in hotly contested elections problems could develop. The primary election had not yet been invented, and there was a general feeling that the mayor should enjoy the support of a majority of the voters. Although elections were partisan in character, they were by no means restricted to the national parties. Local parties were not uncommon. Multiple candidacies created a problem occasionally that was rarely an issue at the state or national levels, where the two-party system prevailed and nominations were closely controlled by caucus and convention. The usual solution was to require run-off elections if no one received a majority, but unlike the common nonpartisan election of the twentieth century no one was eliminated from each successive ballot, and a series of elections would have to be held before a winner could be determined. This was the arrangement provided for in the first Boston charter of 1822, but no run-off election was required in that city until 1829, when three ballots were required.

There was a great deal of interest in Augusta, Maine, when the mayor was first made elective in 1850. There were three candidates and no winner until the third election. Gradually some changes were made in the charters after experience revealed the clumsiness and impracticality of the original voting system. Thus, after a number of years in which it was necessary to have from two to five elections annually, the Manchester, New Hampshire, charter was amended in 1849 to provide for election by simple plurality. The same method was adopted in Boston and Philadelphia in 1854. The Nashua, New Hampshire, charter of 1853 retained the majority requirement for the first ballot but reduced it to a plurality for the second. Simple plurality gradually became the common practice.

The Mayor as Executive

Until the reforms of the late nineteenth century most mayors had relatively few administrative powers. Those that he did have were unstable in many cities, with both additions and subtractions taking place. Similarly, although he generally held on to his judicial powers, there was some movement away from the mayor's court as cities grew in size. It was only in the matter of legislative powers that the mayor's office substantially increased in strength during this time.

Appointment powers were typically vested in the council and remained there throughout this period, for the most part. It was only around the time of the Civil War that any change in this pattern began to emerge. Chicago gave the mayor the power in 1857 to appoint the comptroller and some other administrative officers. He was also given the veto at that time. Until 1869 the mayor presided at council meetings—a responsibility later restored. These and other steps laid the groundwork for the distinguished mayoralty of Carter Harrison in the 1880s.[4] The Baltimore charter of 1797 allowed the mayor to make appointments without the consent of the upper chamber, as would have been logical given the charter's inspiration by the U.S. Constitution, but he could only choose from a slate submitted to him by the council.

Because the mayor presided over the council and had a vote in the typical city, however, he was able to influence but not control appointments to nonelective offices. According to the 1855 charter of St. Anthony, Minnesota (later incorporated into Minneapolis), the mayor, who presided over the council and had a vote, participated in the selection of the treasurer, assessor, attorney, collector of taxes, printer, and city clerk.

In the 1850s, as the emphasis upon separation of powers advanced, the mayor picked up some additional appointive powers. In 1857 the Baltimore mayor was given power to appoint the comptroller for a two-year term, with the approval of the common council. The next year, when a paid fire department was created for the city, an unsalaried board of five commissioners was established to head it, and members of the board were appointed by the mayor.

Prior to 1867 the Detroit fire department was operated under the control of a committee of the common council, but an act passed that year by the legislature established a fire commission to consist of four members appointed by the mayor with the approval of the common council. In 1846 the Iowa legislature authorized the mayor of the small city of Farmington to fill all vacancies other than those on the board of aldermen. This was a rare grant of power and appears not to have spread to other Iowa cities, where the usual practice of authorizing the council to fill vacancies continued.

Removal power was similarly left with the common council. The mayor generally had no such executive powers. Even in those cases where he appointed members of a board or commission, he was not permitted to remove the members. On the other hand there were some indications of an emerging recognition of the mayor as more than just the presiding officer of the council. Thus, the 1850 city charter for Grand Rapids, Michigan, listed the mayor as "chief executive officer," even though he was not given the powers that would make it possible for him to act in this capacity. However, the charter provided that the mayor, recorder, and aldermen could remove at pleasure any of the officers they appointed and fill all vacancies in appointed offices. They could also remove the elected marshal, recorder, and clerk under certain conditions and appoint someone to fill the vacancy for the unexpired term.

The idea that the problems of administrative inefficiency and the high cost of government might be ameliorated by the concentration of executive leadership in the office of mayor was put forth, however, even before the Civil War. In Utica in 1855 a meeting of taxpayers protesting the high cost of government resulted in the appointment of a study commission, which recommended an increase in the appointive powers of the mayor. However, until a much later period, extension of executive powers was generally suspect in the United States and generally took place out of a sense of necessity rather than of desirability. A revised charter proposed in New Bedford, Massachusetts, in 1867 was defeated by a vote of 381 to 61, with the principal objection relating to the office of mayor, namely, the unpopular proposals to increase the powers of the mayor and to increase his salary.

It was primarily in the area of law enforcement that the mayor had some executive and administrative powers. In the original charters of Cincinnati (1827) and Columbus (1834), the mayor was made head of law enforcement. The same was true in Louisville in 1851. In Grand Rapids (1850), the mayor was made head of police and for many years thereafter was active as the actual chief of police. A more common arrangement was that of St. Anthony, Minnesota, which established a police department by ordinance in 1858. It was placed under the mayor's direction, but the council (which included the mayor) appointed a marshal who was actually in charge of the department. The council also determined how many policemen should serve under the marshal.

The Davenport, Iowa, charter of 1851 established the mayor as "chief executive officer" but gave him few powers beyond the right and duty to report to the council or to initiate proceedings against public officers who violated the law. The mayor was not given direct control over the police department, which was headed by an elected marshal. If the marshal died, resigned, or was removed, the vacancy was to be filled by the council. It was not until 1888 that the mayor assumed control of the police department and the power to appoint and remove policemen at his pleasure. This was a fairly typical pattern of development.

Occasionally a mayor attempted to extend his duty to protect the peace of the city to power over the state militia. In 1857, during the time ·of tension, intimidation, and riots instigated by the Know-Nothings, the Baltimore mayor and the governor got into a dispute over whether the governor had the right to use militia within the city in the event of election disturbances. The mayor wanted to keep the governor and the militia out of the city and said in his communication: "As Mayor of the City of Baltimore, I hold my commission directly from the people, and am accountable to them for the manner in which I discharge my trust. . . . I can recognize 'subordination' to no other power within the sphere of my duty." The governor replied that his power came from the state constitution, the mayor's only from legislation. The governor then proposed to proceed with his plan but was dissuaded by a promise and proclamation by the mayor and by some citizens who were fearful that the police might clash with the militia. The governor reluctantly gave in (his own job was at stake in the election), but the mayor failed to deliver on his promise. Through intimidation at the polls the Know-Nothings were able to triumph both in Baltimore and in the gubernatorial election.

The mayor was seldom responsible for the fire departments, which were run by the council or a council committee until the board and commission pattern began to develop in the 1850s. Even so, in times of community emergency or disaster the mayor was expected to be on hand, if for no other than symbolic reasons. Thus the Albany, New York, council in 1809 passed the following resolution: "Resolved that it be the duty of the Mayor, Recorder, Aldermen, and Assistants at all fires to appear with a white sash across the right shoulder as a badge of distinction."

Ex Officio *Powers*

The mayor often had administrative powers that resulted from the fact that he was a member of a council committee engaged in administration of various functions. Sometimes, following the pattern of Josiah Quincy, he appointed himself chairman of the committees and gained considerable executive power as a result. Once in a while such a position was his by charter. Later, with the rise of the boards and commissions, it was common for the mayor to serve on such bodies and sometimes to preside over them. In the original Boston charter of 1822 the school committee was to consist of the mayor, eight aldermen, and one person elected from each ward. This pattern was changed in 1835, but the mayor remained on the school committee, where he was joined by the president of the common council and two persons elected from each ward. (The aldermen had complained that they were too busy, and the common councilmen had demonstrated jealousy over the special executive powers of the upper house.) In Detroit the mayor was made an *ex officio* school inspector in 1842 (the inspectors served collectively as the board of education) and was given additional such powers with the adoption of boards and commissions for administration in the 1850s. In Salem in 1842 the mayor and aldermen, together with one councilman from each ward, served as overseers of the poor.

When a regular police force was established in Detroit in 1861, it was headed by a police commission consisting of the mayor and two other members appointed by the council. The mayor was shortly to lose this power, however. A serious anti-Negro riot in 1863 caused merchants and legislators to be dissatisfied with the police force, and under the Metropolitan Police Act of 1865 the police were placed under the control of four commissioners appointed by the governor, with Senate confirmation. This pattern of control continued in force for thirty-five years. When the Detroit House of Correction was opened in 1861, it operated under a board consisting of the mayor and three superintendents appointed by the common council.

Changing Powers

As the nineteenth century progressed, the mayor was increasingly referred to as the chief executive officer, apparently paralleling the language common in state constitutions, and he was often given a mandate to act in this capacity but without the necessary power. This was true, for example, of the New York charter of 1830 and the Davenport, Iowa, charter of 1851. After 1839 the mayor of Philadelphia gradually lost executive powers to the council. This may have been a result in part of dissatisfaction with that city's government that came about because of a plague of riots and lesser disturbances from the 1830s until the beginning of the Civil War.

The power of the mayor of Boston was sharply curtailed by the charter of 1854. The board of aldermen was given all of the executive powers formerly vested in the mayor and aldermen jointly, and the mayor was deprived of his vote on the board of aldermen. He continued, however, to preside over the board. The school committee was greatly expanded, thus reducing the mayor's influence upon it, and he lost his chairmanship of the councilmanic committees. In return for these losses, he was given a qualified veto power, particularly over appropriations. Various committees of the board of aldermen administered the city departments and acted as administrative commissions. Separation of powers had been recognized, but not the principle of executive leadership. In 1861 control over the St. Louis police passed from the mayor to the governor, and the same happened in Detroit in 1865. City government was being restructured, but the day of the mayor as leader had not yet come.

Powers and Duties

The list of powers and duties of the mayor varied through time and by location, but in most cities it fitted into a definite pattern. Perhaps typical is the special-act charter granted to Davenport, Iowa, in 1851. It provided that the mayor should preside over meetings of the city council and should vote in case of a tie (earlier, the mayor would have been given a vote in all cases). He could call a special meeting of the council. He was to "at all times be active and vigilant in enforcing the laws and ordinances for the government of the city," although he was not given the powers to carry this out except by prosecution and by communicating to the aldermen his recommendation for "all such measures as in his opinion, may tend to the improvement of the finances, the police, the health, security, comfort and ornament of the city." He was made a justice of the peace and "as such shall be a conservator of the peace in the said city."[5] He was given exclusive jurisdiction in all cases arising under the ordinances of the city and concurrent jurisdiction with the other justices of the peace in all cases within the county over which they had jurisdiction by state law. And that was the extent of the mayor's powers in a typical city at mid-century.

There were variations in the pattern, of course. The mayor of New Orleans received appointing powers earlier than most others. Under the charter of 1805 the mayor and recorder were appointed by the governor, and the mayor, in turn, appointed the administrative officers. These included the weighers, constables, scavengers, and wharfingers. He was the licensing official for taverns, boardinghouses, and carriages for hire. He was a justice of the peace and was "to be informed of the intent of every order from the council ordering the disposal of any money or public property." In a new charter of 1852 the mayor was also given control over the police force, including appointment and removal of police officers subject to the approval of the board of aldermen.

When Rochester, New York, received its first village charter in 1817, the president was given the power to enforce the bylaws, to call special meetings of the board of trustees, to receive complaints and reports, and to appoint firemen with the approval of the trustees. The 1834 charter of Bangor, Maine, designated the mayor as "chief executive magistrate" and enjoined him to be "vigilant and active in causing the laws and regulations of the city to be executed and enforced, to exercise a general supervision over the conduct of all subordinate officers and to cause the violations of law or neglect of duty to be punished"—a typical exhortation, also typically without any of the necessary powers needed to carry it out. He was authorized to call special meetings of the common council and to preside over the upper house and over joint sessions of the two houses. He could vote only in case of tie.

One other characteristic of the mayor's office that presaged the later expansion of his administrative powers was the tendency to assign to him many tasks in addition to that of being the chief executive officer. In the smaller communities of the day many jobs needed to be done, but few of them involved full-time work. Although many of the mayors did not want administrative tasks, some were willing to accept them. Thus, in 1850 the mayor of Atlanta was also the chief of police, the police court judge, the street superintendent, and the general utility man, or "troubleshooter." By the New Orleans charter of 1852 the mayor had power to grant licenses.

Legislative Powers

The legislative powers of the mayor were probably his most important. He presided over the council or the upper house of it. He normally either had a vote in all cases or could break a tie. Often he appointed the council committees, and sometimes he served as the chairman of one or even all of them. Josiah Quincy of Boston, who made himself chairman of all major council committees, brought himself much criticism from a generation that still harbored the critical attitude toward the executive that characterized the years of the War for Independence: "He prepares all reports. He permits nothing done but by his own agency. He does not sit solemn and dignified in his chair, and leave general superintendence to others; but he is everywhere and about everything—in the street, at the docks, among the common sewers—no place but what is vexed by his presence."

Sometimes the legislative powers were provided for in the charter, but others were authorized only by ordinance. The St. Anthony, Minnesota, charter of 1855, for example, left the matter to the council, which authorized the mayor, as presiding officer, to appoint members of the standing committees through which most municipal business would have to move. The committees included those on claims and accounts, ways and means, streets, health, fire protection, markets, taxes, printing, and licenses—a typical committee pattern. The office of mayor gained in public visibility after it was made elective, and this added to the mayor's influence by supporting him in the roles of policy developer and community consensus builder. As presiding officer and as an influence upon the committees, he was able to influence the pattern of growth and change in American cities during this period of rapid development of municipal services.

The one area in which the mayor definitely gained power throughout

the nineteenth century was in the use of the veto. No veto had existed
in the colonial cities. The first one was provided for in the trailblazing
Baltimore charter of 1797, strongly influenced by the United States
Constitution, which had gone into effect a few years earlier and had
been written in nearby Philadelphia. The Baltimore mayoral veto could
be overridden by a two-thirds vote in both council chambers. As this
power was added in other cities, various formulas were adopted for the
overriding of the veto. This new recognition of the checks-and-balances
doctrine did not spread rapidly and was confined for the most part to
the largest cities. In many cities, however, the mayor as presiding officer
was expected to sign ordinances and resolutions, as is usually the case
with the presiding officer in legislative bodies. Of course, such a signa-
ture was originally intended only as a certification that the house had,
indeed, given its approval. It seems likely that some cases of the adoption of the veto power resulted when it was necessary to clarify what
was to be done in the event that the mayor—imitating the governor or
president—should refuse to sign.

The New Orleans charter of 1805 provided for a power of veto, but
here the situation was somewhat different from the theory used in Baltimore. Louisiana was still a territory, and the mayor was appointed by
the territorial governor. His veto power may have been as much a reflection of his role as representative of the governor, that is, as "prefect,"
as it was an imitation of the federal system. After all, New Orleans had
a government inherited from its Spanish and French days. Indeed, this
power was lost when the city was divided into three municipalities. It
was not regained until the consolidation charter of 1852. (The Detroit
charter of 1806 provided for a veto, but it, too, seemed to follow the
prefect concept.)

Others of the larger cities began to adopt the veto. The mayor of New
York received a weak version of it in 1830, involving principally financial matters. The Boston and Philadelphia charters of 1854 also provided for a limited veto, as did that of Pittsburgh in 1867. But in the
more typical small cities of America the veto power was slow to be offered. The mayors of Iowa, for example, were not given the veto until
1897.

Judicial Powers

The judicial powers of the mayors had existed in colonial times and
had not entirely disappeared even in the 1970s. Throughout the nineteenth century, they remained fairly constant powers of the mayor,
probably because they did not require much of his time and, if he were
to be replaced in the job, it would quite certainly be by another person

untrained in the law. The idea in the nineteenth century, as in the previous century, was that the justice of the peace should apply the prevailing standards of what was right and wrong with a rule-of-thumb justice that did not particularly require any formal legal knowledge. So the mayor, as a father figure dispensing "common sense" justice, presided over a tribunal that was variously called the mayor's court, the police court, or the justice of the peace court. (In the Spanish and Mexican areas that came into the United States, the *alcalde* served as a judge.)

Occasionally, though not often, there were signs of dissatisfaction with the mayor's court. It was given extensive powers in Natchez in 1803, and these were extended two years later, but the arbitrary use of judicial power by the mayor led to a public protest meeting. A satisfactory solution was eventually worked out.

Under the Detroit charter of 1824 the mayor's court was established to consist of the mayor, the recorder, and two aldermen. As happened in many other cities the mayor or other presiding judge would levy a fine or sentence, but the convicted person could appeal to the council and was often able to secure a remission of the fine or be released from the city jail, for most of the offenses coming before the mayor's court were relatively minor and of the sort that might become charges against many another citizen, citizens of the kind who elected members of the council.

The Detroit charter was amended in 1832 to allow the council to employ convicted persons to work on the streets. This changed the interest of the council in the matter of prisoners and ended the wholesale releasing of them, but the new approach was not satisfactory because of the large number of prisoners who escaped. So persons sentenced from the mayor's court tended to sit out their terms in jail doing nothing—until 1839, when the council authorized the street commissioner to employ jail inmates upon the streets, giving them customary wages for their work, the earnings to be applied to the payment of fines and costs.

In 1850 a police court was established to supplement the mayor's court. It was given the powers normally possessed by justices of the peace. Finally, in 1857 the mayor's court was abolished and replaced by the recorder's court. The same thing happened in New Haven in 1842. Similar mayor's courts were established elsewhere in the nation and continued to operate until the population of the city and the demands upon the mayor's time became too great for the practice to be continued. The judicial functions of the mayor were then typically stripped away and transferred either to justices of the peace or to professional lawyer-judges. Thus, the trend toward separation of powers at the local level continued.

Ceremonial Functions

Throughout American history the mayor has had important ceremonial functions to perform. He has always been recognized as the symbolic head of the city and, as such, has greeted visiting dignitaries or presided at ceremonies opening new water systems or paved streets. It has been the least-changing part of the job.

Prerequisites and Perquisites

Once the mayor became elective, rules were commonly established for determining eligibility for the office. These varied from one community to another, but typically they required that the candidate be a citizen of the United States and a qualified voter in the community. In addition, there was often a minimum age requirement, although this was commonly twenty-one after about 1830. There were also residence requirements, including a certain amount of time spent living in the city—this was often only one year—and a common rule that the mayor vacate his office if he moved outside of the city. For the most part, these were not important restrictions.

In most cases the mayor could not expect to do much more than be repaid for his direct expenses, although in the larger cities there was some trend fairly early toward paying the mayor for the work done on behalf of the city. Under colonial practice mayors received fees for their work as judicial officers and some payment for certain other activities, but they did not receive a salary. Shortly after independence, however, this English practice changed. In 1790 in Savannah, Georgia, although the mayor received no salary, the city treasurer and clerk each were paid 45 pounds plus fees, the marshal 30 pounds plus fees, the scavenger 15 pounds plus fees, and the clerk of the market, fees. (At this time, insignia of office were established to be worn at fires and other important or dramatic situations. The marshal was given a white staff, six and one-half feet long and one inch in diameter, the scavenger a black staff, seven feet long and two inches in diameter.) The first payment for the mayor beyond fees and emoluments was provided for in the Baltimore charter of 1797. A small salary was provided for, as was also the case in the 1822 Boston charter. By 1815 Baltimore was beginning to pay its public officials in accordance with their contribution of time and effort on behalf of the city. In that year the mayor received a salary of $2,500 annually, the register $1,400, the clerk $2,400, the port wardens $1,600, and the superintendent of streets and pumps, $960. In contrast, prior to 1812 the mayor of Washington received no salary.

Gradually the idea that the mayor should receive at least a small amount of pay in return for his time and effort came to be widely accepted. In 1825 the mayor of Albany was given a salary of $400 annually. This compared favorably with others who were expected to spend most or all of their working day on the job. The superintendent of the almshouse received $400, the overseer of the poor $200, the constables $400, the clerk of the common council $150, the police justice $450, the city physician $550, and the part-time bell-ringers, $40.

The mayor of Providence received a salary of $1,000 in 1833 and $1,500 twenty years later. It may possibly be an indication of the rising importance and status of the mayor that the clerk of the market received the same pay, $200, throughout the same period.

Because many of the mayors were relatively prosperous merchants or professional men, they did not always see fit to accept the salary offered them. From their point of view they were gentry, not local government employees. Thus in the 1830s the mayors of Utica (incorporated in 1832) gave their $250 annual salary to the city dispensary. And in 1859 the mayor of Worcester, Massachusetts, gave his $1,000 salary for school prizes.

The annual salaries varied considerably but in general moved upward: in New Bedford, Massachusetts, in 1847 it was $800; in Springfield, Massachusetts, 1852, $400; in Mobile, 1840, $1,000; and the New Orleans charter of 1852 provided that the mayor was to receive not less than $4,000 annually, a considerable sum for the times and an indication that the mayor of that city, who had from the beginning had more executive responsibility than in the typical city, was expected to spend much of his working day at this public job. In the typical case, however, the mayor received only fees and certain special allowances. The full-time officers and employees of the city were paid on an annual basis and at a rate that was probably no higher and often less than the pay they might receive for reasonably similar work in private endeavors. Furthermore, at that time they had no kind of tenure in office, although from the time that the clerk and treasurer became elective their offices were typically almost certain to extend for a lifetime or as long as the individual wished to remain in the position, for there was seldom much competition for the well-known incumbent.

The Mayoral Term

Colonial mayors, with the exception of those in close corporations and a very few others, had served a one-year term. In some cities the mayor was not eligible for immediate re-election, and in others it was customary for him to serve but one year. Nevertheless, there was something of a trend toward longer terms quite early after independence, and this trend expanded very gradually throughout the nineteenth century. Nevertheless, until the mayor came to be recognized as an administrative and executive leader late in the nineteenth century, the annual term remained the characteristic pattern.

Outside of the close corporations, the Baltimore charter of 1797 once again served to lead the way. It provided for a two-year term for mayor. The 1801 charter for New Brunswick, New Jersey, gave a five-year term to both the mayor and the recorder, but these officers were appointed by the governor with legislative approval. The first elective mayor to serve for more than one year appears to have been that of Cincinnati, where a two-year term was established in 1834, seven years after the office of mayor was made elective. A term of office longer than two years was most unusual, although there were a few cases. The mayor of Philadelphia was given a three-year term in 1854, and so was his counterpart in Wilmington, Delaware, in 1869, when the term was extended from one year and the mayor was also made eligible for re-election.

Other Executive Officers

The lesser executive officers of the city were, typically, appointed by the governor during colonial times. Later they came to be selected by the council, usually with the mayor participating. With the coming of Jacksonian democracy in the 1820s, there was an increasingly strong tendency to elect these officers. The Detroit Charter of 1824 provided for many of them to be elected. This was a pattern slow to be adopted elsewhere, but Jacksonian democracy eventually won out. Then, with the emergence of the boards and commissions to replace the council committees in the 1850s and after, these boards also tended to be made elective. As this happened, other department heads, particularly the chief of police, were also made elective. This was the general pattern, though there were many exceptions and variations.

New Yorkers, even in colonial times, elected constables, assessors, and collectors in each ward. This was unusual, as was the fact that there were some elective boards in Philadelphia, a close corporation, at that time.

The officers who later were frequently elected were the clerk, treasurer, auditor, assessor, overseer of the poor, the superintendent of public works, the school inspectors, the superintendent of streets or public works, the tax collector, and, later on, the comptroller, the public health officer, and the chief of police. In addition, there were the older offices of marshal, constable, and recorder. Some of these, particularly the assessor, tax collector, school inspector, and overseer of the poor, were often elected by wards.

The tasks of most of these local officials are self-evident. Perhaps it

should be mentioned, however, that the school inspectors were the predecessors of school board members. They often served as lay superintendents in the days before educational administration had become a profession. The constables were old English peace officers who usually
operated in rural areas and in villages. It was common, when a city
was incorporated or at least when it grew to considerable size, to establish the office of marshal, who was commonly elected and served in fact
as the chief of police. When this latter term became commonplace toward the middle of the nineteenth century, the office often remained
elective.

In colonial times the recorder was usually appointed by the governor
but sometimes selected by the common council. His was the one office
that usually had tenure only at the pleasure of the appointing official or
body. His primary job was what would today be called that of city attorney or corporation counsel, the chief law officer of the municipality. In
colonial times he also served as a voting member of the common council, and he was also a justice of the peace, for in those days no conflict of
interest was seen between the office of city attorney and municipal
judge. After the War for Independence the recorder continued to be a
member of the council for a while, but with the coming to dominance
of the separation of powers theory the office was gradually eliminated
and replaced by the separate positions of city attorney and municipal
court judge, as in Buffalo in 1854. The "recorder's courts" that are still
to be found in some parts of the United States are legal descendants of
this old office.

The city clerk, sometimes called the "common clerk," kept the records of the common council as well as of the municipal court. Apparently the practice of long service by a single individual in this office,
even though the term might be for only one year, emerged early. New
York, for example, had a single clerk serving continuously from 1692
until he died in 1739.

The recorder, together with the clerk and treasurer, were often made
elective at the same time as was the mayor or very shortly thereafter.
But the pattern varied considerably. In Natchez in 1803, although the
governor appointed the mayor, recorder, and marshal, the treasurer, assessor, and tax collector were elected, and the practice of election did
not necessarily develop faster in the South and Midwest than it did in
the East. The common council of Columbus, Ohio, still chose the officers other than mayor in 1834. The recorder was still selected by the
bicameral council in Mobile in 1840, and the officers of St. Anthony,
Minnesota, other than the mayor, were still appointive in 1855. Most
boards and commissions were appointed prior to the 1850s, although
some exceptions went back to colonial times. Often, when some service

was not satisfactorily operated, the Jacksonian solution was to provide for election. Thus, Cincinnati in 1846 established a three-member board of trustees for the water department.

Election of department heads became common, particularly after the City of New York adopted this pattern in 1849. Examples are numerous: Reading, Pennsylvania, in 1847 elected the treasurer and three auditors annually. Omaha (1857) elected the recorder, treasurer, assessor, and marshal. Jacksonville (1859) elected the marshal, treasurer, and clerk. The St. Paul charter of 1868 provided for the election of eight executive officers.

Summary

During the first century after American independence, the municipal executive underwent enormous changes. In addition to the emergence of the application of the separation of powers doctrine, executive responsibilities tended to be transferred from council committees to relatively independent boards and commissions. Individual department heads that had been named by the governor or his appointee, the mayor, came first to be named by the common council and later by the voters themselves through direct election. Others of them, including many of the various boards, were named by the mayor, usually with the consent of the council. The mayor, who was primarily a legislative leader and court justice during colonial times, lost some of his powers, especially within the council, but gained others stemming from the separation of powers approach, in particular the veto and independence from both the state governor or legislature and the council by development of the practice of direct election.

The mayor, at first commonly the local spokesman for the governor, became more a truly local official immediately after the War for Independence, when the common council was given power to choose him and other major local executive officers. He, and they, gained further independence when they were made elective, first the mayor and then the others. The Jacksonian ideology that became dominant in the 1820s and continued to shape local government policy until after the Civil War, called for bringing municipal administration "closer to the people." The argument for this was nicely demonstrated in New York, where a municipal charter convention was held in 1846. It recommended that the voters should directly elect the department heads, because election by the council had led to the "banishment of the true exercise of decorum and political virtue from our legislative halls, and had created in the city government an unsteady, ill-directed, and changeable course of policy." The new city charter, granted three years later, provided for the direct election of many department heads.

The new form of city government was only a modification of the traditional, affected particularly by the separation of powers doctrine and the Jacksonian ideology. It remained a weak-mayor-council form (as measured by executive authority or administrative responsibility), and the mayor and council were both weaker than when the period began. The principal result of the pattern of change was a decentralization of executive authority and a general deconcentration of power. No doubt many voters thought the government was now closer to them and more subject to their control, particularly if one considered that during this same time the council moved from the typical pattern of election at large to one that was somewhat larger in membership and with at least one chamber elected by wards. However, the new weak-mayor system, with a long ballot on which were to be found candidates for one or two houses of the common council, many executive officers in addition to the mayor, and candidates for membership on various boards and commissions, resulted in increasing confusion concerning the pattern of decision-making and of responsibility for the actions of government as urban areas grew in population. The resulting chaos in the nation's largest city has already been described.* Yet one writer in complaining about dishonesty seemed to have been much more concerned with inefficiency and lack of service:

> We could afford to pay even more than the four or five millions of dollars now annually expended, and the unknown additional millions exacted in the form of fees, assessments, bribes, etc., if we could have an efficient government for the money.[6]

The executive function had changed greatly, but it was not yet the modern operation that such protesters sought. Many more significant changes were to take place in the following half-century, changes that would basically affect the mayor, council, administrative leadership, and bureaucracy.

Notes

1. George F. Robeson, *The Government of Special Charter Cities in Iowa* (Iowa City, 1923).
2. Ernest S. Griffith, *History of American City Government: The Colonial Period* (New York, 1938), p. 172.
3. William L. Stone, *History of New York City* (New York, 1872).
4. Ernest S. Griffith, *History of American City Government 1870–1900: The Conspicuous Failure* (New York, 1974), pp. 102-4.
5. Robeson, *op. cit*
6. Stone, *op cit.*

* See above, page 52.

Chapter 11

MUNICIPAL FINANCE

THE PERIOD IMMEDIATELY after independence was marked by the continued gradual divergence of American from British practices in local finance. Although the pattern of expenditures did not immediately change much, as the nineteenth century progressed there was a great increase in the scope and complexity of local expenditures. Administratively, this period preceded the advent of the executive budget and financial policy development, and administration largely followed the pattern of that for substantive policy, with the shift away from council committees toward boards and commissions. The one administrative office that in the process came into importance was that of the comptroller, but the common council committees on taxation (often called "ways and means") and on appropriations became the most powerful element of the councils after the committee system emerged. (See Chapter 8.) Until the development of the executive budget around the time of World War I, the process remained highly decentralized, with different personnel and committees responsible for finding receipts adequate to meet the expenditures that were planned for by others.

Typically, revenues and expenditures were provided for in separate councilmanic acts, and the only comprehensive overview of the process came with final councilmanic action upon the recommendations of its committees. In the case of bicameral councils, no such overview took place at all. Not surprisingly, cities occasionally found themselves deeply in debt and or even faced with bankruptcy. The administrative process did not seem strange or particularly inefficient at the time, because the same one was being used by state and national legislative bodies. The problems arising, together with the fact that the impact of local taxes is more difficult to hide than is that for higher levels of government, probably were in part responsible for the spread of the mayor's veto, particularly the item veto on appropriations, and the virtual universality of the referendum on bond issues pledging the public faith and credit and taxes beyond a certain level. Both of these mechanisms developed prior to 1870.

The Origins of Property Taxation

Sam Bass Warner, Jr., and others have called attention to the profound effect on the cities of fee simple land tenure, as against the semi-feudal landlord system that prevailed in Britain at the time of colonization. There were and are landlords in America. For example, the Dutch began the patroon system in New Netherlands, and it survived for a long time under the English in rural New York. The plantation system based on slavery was characteristic of the rural South—as it was also of the West Indies—during the entire period up to the Civil War. For decades thereafter, the sharecropper and the tenant farmer still were characteristic of plantation organization.

But in the cities of the entire nation, fee simple land tenure, even in those times and places in which home owners were in a minority, became the established pattern. This was the major factor in developing a local taxation system based upon ownership rather than income.

As Warner has also pointed out, it went hand in hand with the developer and the American emphasis on "privatism," in turn reinforced by the dynamics of private enterprise in commerce, manufacturing, transportation, and utilities. The assumptions of "privatism" were partly negative—anti-expenditure. But the assumptions of "privatism" were also consonant with those of "boosterism," urban rivalry, and growth, which made for a civic cooperation in which it was assumed that each and every one—especially the merchants—would prosper. Public improvements, public health, and law and order especially flourished as objectives in this atmosphere. Along with these came the infusion of another, richer ideal from the Jeffersonian strand, that of public responsibility for education, which eventually outdistanced all other city functions in expenditure.

From Business Revenues to Taxation

Colonial America raised many of its funds through some practices that were modifications of privileges and practices going back to the middle ages. In medieval times there were few actual taxes, with most monies coming from feudal dues or rents and special privileges of one kind or another. Taxes were still not the primary source of revenue in the eighteenth century. The cities made a good deal of profit from the sale of land, but they also had various trading privileges, rents, business activities (including some monopolies), the operation of municipal docks, ferries, and markets, and the right to require citizens to perform various kinds of public works and services, particularly work on streets and highways. Various kinds of licenses, then as now, were also a significant source of income.

Taxes were levied only for special purposes as needed. But shortly after independence the regular annual levy for the general fund became increasingly common. Thus, in the last decade of the eighteenth century special taxes remained frequent in Providence, although the annual levy became increasingly customary. During that decade, significantly, the budget increased from $6,000 to $16,000 annually.

Gradually cities moved away from the practice of raising most of their revenue needs from municipal activities and toward the modern practice of all governments of raising funds primarily through taxation. Long before 1870, citizens had come to expect municipal functions paid for on a cost-of-service basis to operate without a profit. A municipal gas plant or water supply system was eventually expected to provide its services at the lowest possible cost. The result, necessarily, was an increase in taxes as municipal services expanded. But the process was gradual.

The General Property Tax

A tax designed to raise revenue for a local government jurisdiction must have several characteristics. First, it must be levied against something that is relatively unmovable, something permanently located within the community. It must also be capable of raising adequate funds—relatively large amounts as in the case of the backbone of the local tax system. It must be one that is considered by residents of the community to be reasonably equitable, so that the load placed upon it will be borne by the local taxpayers with willingness. Finally, it must be a tax that is practical to administer and one that has the appearance, at least, of fairness in its administration.

The general property tax developed in early America as the levy that most clearly fitted these requirements. Most property, particularly valuable property, is difficult to move from its site. Such a tax is potentially capable of raising large amounts of money and, since it is levied against either something approximating total wealth or the income from such wealth, it was generally viewed as equitable, or at least potentially so. And with the tax valuation determined by one's neighbors, presumably people aware of values in the area and individuals trusted there, administration was both feasible and equitable in the early years of the nation.

In colonial America the basis for evaluation was not uniform. However, the total value of property rather than its annual rental value seemed to be the most equitable basis upon which to establish taxpaying ability. Therefore, in contrast to England, where the rental value developed as the base for local taxation, total property wealth became the American standard.[1]

The general property tax came to consist of taxes upon real property and personal property. The former consisted of land and the reasonably permanent structures built upon it. Although there were various interpretations of its meaning in the various states, everything that was not so classified was personal property. This, in turn, was divided into tangible and intangible property. The former consisted of livestock, furniture, and a variety of other things, even including musical instruments, in most cases. Intangible personal property consisted of such symbols of wealth as stock, bonds, and bank deposits. It was, obviously, the most difficult type of property to capture for tax purposes and rarely raised much revenue. Personal property, in general, never generated much tax revenue except for the tangible assets of business and industry, particularly stock inventories.

Although it was not recognized at the time the property tax was becoming a basis for local revenue raising. In the twentieth century it is particularly a burden upon the lowest income groups, because they spend a disproportionate amount of their income upon housing, and it tends to be a relatively light burden upon the highest income categories. This is, however, the case only in the relatively short run. If one takes into consideration the benefits that result in expenditures from such income, particularly considering its use for educational purposes, the tax is probably basically progressive in its effect.[2] Although this was not fully realized in the early nineteenth century, when public educational systems were being developed, the strong objections to the use of property taxation irrespective of the number of children enrolled in public schools certainly indicates that there was an intuitive recognition of this type of redistribution of wealth. On the other hand, it has been recognized from the earliest times that the tax tends to be distributed unevenly among individual taxpayers, however equitable it may be for particular classes through time.

Because the tax was developed during an overwhelmingly rural period in American history, it seems unlikely that the effect of the tax upon urban life, particularly upon urban housing, was recognized until long after it had become a firmly established American institution. In fact, however, the tax appears always to have served particularly as a consumer levy that has a disproportionately heavy effect upon consumer expenditures for housing. Yet, despite the disadvantages often attributed to the tax and its unfavorable effect upon the visual appearance of the American metropolis, no serious objections were raised to the taxing system—although there were many to particular and specific levies—until after the publication of a pamphlet called *Our Land and Land Pol-*

icy in 1871 and a more complete statement in a book called *Progress and Poverty* in 1879 by Henry George. George advocated a "single tax," that is, a tax on the site-value of land. He had been particularly influenced by his observations concerning the increase in land site values in the San Francisco area during one of its periods of rapid growth (in the 1860s). He had noted that many persons, through either accident or acute study, had purchased land just before it was subdivided and developed. They had profited enormously without any additional effort on their part, through the "unearned increment" of value added to the land by the fact that it was located in an important position at an appropriate time.[3] The theory developed by George has remained attractive ever since he first published it and has also aroused much controversy over its validity and probable effect.[4]

From Income to Property

Until 1819 Connecticut followed the practice of using the probable net revenue as the tax base rather than the "fair market value" that later became commonplace:

> Those pursuing any trade or profession were assessed on an estimate of their annual gains. Real estate was rated, not according to its value, but in proportion to the annual income, which on the average it was deemed likely to produce. Lands as distinguished from buildings were put in the list at a fixed rate for each kind, prescribed by statute. The best meadow land went in at $2.50 an acre . . . not because this was deemed to be the value of the land, but because it was thought to represent the average income it would produce. Houses and other buildings were likewise listed at fixed sums, determined by their size, material, number of fireplaces, etc., but all described by the statute itself, and beyond the control of the assessors. Under such a system there was little opportunity for evading taxation. The acreage of each farm, the general character of each lot and the dimensions, use, etc., of each building were readily ascertained, and the law then fixed the rate of assessment.[5]

The general property tax first appeared in New England and in general spread southward, with the most Southern states the last to adopt it. As it was adopted, the legislatures at first authorized it on the basis of special acts, which specified the municipality, the maximum rate, and the property that could be taxed. They even determined valuation by statute. In the early 1820s in Ohio a horse had to be assessed at $40, a cow at $8. Only gradually did the tax become general and the rate uniform for all property.

New Hampshire abandoned income as the base and substituted value, but not until 1833 did the legislature stop assigning values to each class of property and call for assessment of all property at its full and true value. Virginia did not adopt this rule until 1850, while the first Illinois constitution of 1818 called for uniformity, although it was not achieved until many years later.

During the twenty years preceding the Civil War, the pressures for uniformity and away from classification were greatest. Many states adopted constitutional rules requiring uniformity (which later were to prove a straitjacket as interest in classification as a means of achieving greater revenue was revived). There appears, however, to be great disparity between constitutional and statutory provisions—and local practices in the administration of the tax often seemed to be based more on local custom than on statute. Thus "constant experimentation was the order of every legislative session prior to the Civil War, with the statutory requirements and the administrative practices conforming rather loosely to the constitutional requirements."[6]

One of the major problems was the assessment level. As early as the 1820s there was pressure from state legislatures for assessors to evaluate at full market value. The reason was that the local assessment was also used for county and state tax purposes, hence there was great pressure for competitive underassessment. Massachusetts in 1830 required 100 per cent of value, but this was not effectively enforced. Prior to 1860 Connecticut used assessments of only 3 to 6 per cent of true market value, apparently in part because these figures approximated the annual rental value, which had earlier been the basis for taxation. When Baltimore was reassessed in 1833 and 1834, values were increased by about 1,000 per cent, and tax reform continued to be an important issue in that city until 1841. In Albany, New York, in 1850 assessments were about 65 per cent of market value despite state requirements. This was justified on the grounds that other communities did the same.

After the Civil War an occasional state withdrew from reliance on the property tax, leaving it to local units of government. Competitive underassessment was then somewhat lessened. The greatest difficulty remained in the attempts to assess personal property. The task became nearly hopeless as these "intangibles" grew as a proportion of individual wealth.

Throughout the era, there were complaints that tax procedures were lax. The assessors early became elected officials, often being chosen by ward meetings, with a chief assessor responsible for coordinating their activities. In the area of public finance, friends-and-neighbors politics reigned supreme.

Some Early Experiences

In 1782 special commissioners were created in Baltimore to grade and pave the streets (all at that time were unpaved). Abutting property owners were to pay $1.66⅔ a front foot ($5 per yard) for this. Other sources authorized in order to help pay the cost included a tax on the gross receipts of auctions within the city—a favorite source of revenue in the late eighteenth century—a tax on exhibitors, and an annual lottery, another favorite. For other purposes, Baltimore's municipal income at the end of the eighteenth century was characterized by its inflexibility. Maximum levies permitted by charter and state statute were assessed from the beginning, so receipts could grow only as the city did. The chief revenues during the period were from licenses, auction receipts, special assessments, wharfage receipts and, after these, the property tax.

In 1832 the Baltimore tax rate amounted to nearly five dollars per hundred, a high rate that apparently resulted from the fact that the city had no power to raise any valuations that had been placed on the tax books twenty years earlier by the state. The total valuation of property in the city at that time was only a little less than $4 million. The statutes were finally altered, and a new tax ordinance was adopted in Baltimore in 1834. It resulted in assessments being increased on the average about 1,000 per cent.

The revenue situation in Boston late in the eighteenth century also reflected close state supervision, as this 1782 report indicates:

The estimates made by the assessors of the value of the real and personal estate of the inhabitants appear to be nearly the same, with the estimates made by the general court [the state legislature] on which the town's proportion of the state tax was assessed.

That the income of the real estates deducting repairs amounts to upwards of 9,000 pounds [pounds sterling rather than dollars continued to be used for tax purposes in many cities until about 1800] and the interest on the personal estate including money on hand and at interest, stock in trade, vessels and income by trade and faculty at 6 per cent amounts to nearly 26,000 pounds—from these two sums amounting to about 35,000 pounds they deduct the amount of the poll tax and the remainder is the sum on which the twelfth tax is apportioned. On this sum the assessors calculate how much in the pound will raise the amounts to be assessed; and what it amounts to in the pound every inhabitant is charged with the amount of his particular valuation both of real and personal estate being 8 shillings and eight pence on the state tax, and 4 shillings on the town and county.

In the tax now coming out the income [presumably the proceeds of the tax] of the real estate amounts to 10,926 pounds and the personal to 20,594, and turns out five shillings and 11 pence to the state tax and three shillings and five pence to the town.

But the assessors have no certain rule by which to estimate the personal estate of the most part of the inhabitants as not more than 120 persons have given in lists.[7]

In Albany the largest single source of revenue in 1811 was derived from the sale of land. Indeed, nearly 60 per cent of that year's receipts came from this source. Taxes were far behind in second place and only slightly ahead of rents. The city received income from the operation of a ferry across the Hudson, the renting of hay scales, and the sale of street dirt, oil casks, paving stones, and cemetery lots. It even received $555 in dividends on its turnpike stock.

By 1825 Albany was in some financial difficulty, having allowed its debt to pile up. The council chose to find its way out of the situation in a fashion that was typical of the day: It sold some more land and authorized the running of a lottery. By then, however, the lottery, which had been a favorite of municipalities for more than a generation, was coming under considerable criticism. The city was accused of running a "gambling establishment." The council responded to the criticism by selling the lottery to a private firm, thus raising additional revenue for the city. The debt, which had been as high as $269,000 in 1817, now stood at $255,400. The planned economy resulted in a gradual reduction in the debt and by 1836 it was only $65,000, low enough for the council to reduce the ferry rates, always a popular political move.

Albany represents a good example of the shift to dependence upon the property tax. This resulted from the establishment of new functions. Thus, in the 1840s the cost of policing a growing city was vastly greater than it had been two generations earlier. The demand for street lighting, a safety factor, also greatly added to the burden on the tax. The city spent $6,438 for street lighting in 1843, $9,207 in 1848, and $10,489 in 1850. This was a 63 per cent increase in the space of seven years. Another major and growing burden on the property tax was the need for poor relief, required by the arrival of immigrants at a faster rate than they could be absorbed into the labor force. The Irish potato famine of 1845–47 and the unsuccessful rebellions or political agitations in many European nations in 1848 caused particular problems for the Eastern cities. The outdoor poor relief, that is, welfare payments made to persons not living in the municipal almshouse, increased from $6,294 in 1843, just before the unsettling developments in Europe, to $12,885 in 1850. In addition, in that year the almshouse cost $15,405 to operate.

The Albany general property tax yielded $7,000 in 1811. In 1843, about a generation later, it produced $63,885. Then in the next five years it increased very sharply, to $170,503. Despite this, by May 1, 1848, the city treasury was virtually empty, largely because of the need to repay short-term loans that had been issued in anticipation of the annual property levy. Meanwhile the debt was growing once again as a result of inattention to detail and an unwillingness to levy still more taxes in order to cope with the problem. In 1847 the council seems to have decided that it could not trust itself and recommended to the state legislature adoption of a requirement that all expenses of the city and the deficiencies arising from the nonpayment of assessments for street improvements, together with the amount needed to pay the interest on the debt and to retire at least $10,000 of the principal each year, be required to be raised by taxes annually. This was adopted by the legislature the following year. The law furthermore provided that appropriation bills would require a favorable vote by two-thirds of the total membership of the common council. These stringent requirements pushed the property tax still higher. Within two years the debt was reduced from $752,896 to $541,132, a reduction of about one-third. A part of this was brought about, however, by the state's assumption of some of the Albany debt for the Erie Canal.

The taxing powers of cities were carefully controlled by the states in the older part of America, and Congress did nothing in the frontier territories to encourage any different tradition. Thus, when the United States took over control of Florida in 1821, General Andrew Jackson issued orders establishing a government at St. Augustine, with the mayor and six aldermen, all appointed by the governor, to serve as the city council. The council promptly established a local tax levy that many residents considered exceptionally burdensome. A protest was filed directly with Congress, which very quickly repealed the taxes. When Key West was incorporated by the territorial legislature in 1832, the charter adopted by the legislature restricted real estate taxes to a maximum of one-half of one per cent of market value. The charter also authorized a per capita tax on blacks, both free and slave.

Around mid-century, the property tax had come to be the most important source of income and the yield from the sale of business services had declined considerably. For Chicago between 1848 and 1871, the property tax provided 30 to 40 per cent of its revenue, and loans almost as much. Lancaster, Pennsylvania, in 1865 levied a property tax of $.90 per $100 and had an assessed valuation of $3.5 million. (As is always the case, it is difficult to determine what percentage of actual market value was used by the assessors.) This produced receipts of $31,500, more than one-half of the total budget for the year. Water charges amounted to $11,250, but other receipts, including licenses, fines, forfeitures, and rents in the public market, produced unimportant yields.

Knoxville in 1859 levied $1 per $100, but, as early became the case in the South, an elaborate system of business licenses existed. Thus slave dealers, wholesale and retail merchants, confectioners, and commission merchants were charged $20 plus $.15 on each $100 of capital or inventory in excess of $13,333.33, with a maximum tax of $100. Receiving and forwarding merchants, auctioneers, brokers, hack drivers, theater owners, pool hall operators, and many other businesses and businessmen were taxed at varying rates. In 1844 the Columbus, Georgia, property tax, including a tax on slaves, was $.25 per $100. Among those required to have licenses to do business in Columbus were attorneys, physicians, the operators of factories, and brokers, all at $4 annually. The license fee for a saloon was $25. There was also a $6 head tax on free Negroes, a levy that must not have been enforced or, if it was, was designed to encourage freed slaves to stay out of the city.

Head or poll taxes were levied not just upon free Negroes but commonly upon all free men between certain ages, usually sixteen and sixty-five. Prior to the efforts to enfranchise blacks following the Civil War, the poll tax was not used as a prerequisite for voting. Rather, it was a tax designed to raise funds for the maintenance of streets and roads. Commonly, in lieu of paying the tax, one could devote a certain number of days each year to working with gangs under the control of the street commissioner, engaged in constructing or repairing streets. Thus, in Mobile, Alabama, in the 1820s men either worked on the roads or paid $3 a day for the hiring of a substitute.

In a sense, this was an example of the "subscription" stage of municipal services through which many cities passed. In the very earliest days the night watch was often an obligation of all citizens, just as all were often called upon to join the bucket brigade to fight fires. This latter evolved into the volunteer fire companies. Still later came work on the streets. Then the Main Street merchants often subscribed to the paving costs of their streets. Still later street lighting might similarly be financed by subscription. Garbage and trash collections and sewers were also favorite subjects at similar stages in their development. To this day the special assessment, in a sense the linear successor to the subscription, is the approved method for street paving and improvements in many cities.

Many of the business taxes or licenses so common in the eighteenth and early nineteenth centuries stemmed from the earlier notions of how the city should be run, with the government either performing the function itself or giving a monopolistic franchise to someone else in return for certain payments. As the concept of free competitive enterprise developed, however, there were increasing objections to this type of business tax. Thus, in 1791 there were formal protests from many influential Baltimore citizens against a new auction receipts tax levied on those who were given exclusive privileges to serve as auctioneers. The objection was not to the tax itself—that was a traditional business tax to which everyone was accustomed—but to the exclusive privileges and to the fact that the proceeds went not into a general fund but to the fund of the port wardens for the development of the port of Baltimore. The system was continued, however, and in 1802 the tax was increased to 1 per cent of gross revenues of the auctioneers. In Raleigh the same tax rate and exclusive right existed in 1806. It was not until a generation later that exclusive grants, other than upon "natural" monopolies in the public utilities, disappeared.

Many of the other business taxes of the day have continued to the present time. For example, in 1797 and 1798 Baltimore established license taxes on theaters, billiard tables, market traders, and dogs. (The dog license fees were collected by the City Superintendent of Chimney Sweeps. They remained controversial. Belfast, Maine, adopted one in 1863, after long debate at a city meeting, by a vote of 264 to 95.) In addition to saloons, gambling was often legal. It was not until the 1830s and after that the Puritanic opposition to gambling became dominant in the older cities, and it never became so along the frontier. Thus, in 1779 in Savannah gambling was considered legal if licensed. But the license fee was high, $500 a year per license for the operation of equality or "E.O." tables. The operator of a modern casino in Las Vegas would find it unnerving to learn that the gambling houses of Savannah were required to close at 11 p.m. In 1841 the Toledo council provided that no person should "act as a runner for any hotel, tavern, stage, steamer, or canal boat within the limits of Toledo" unless he was licensed for that purpose. The council also prescribed the type of conduct that was expected of a person so engaged.

Fines were an important though not a dominant source of income throughout the first century of independence. In the 1790s the most frequent offense resulting in a fine in Savannah was the galloping of horses through the streets. As many as twenty persons a day were summoned and fined, but without any apparent deterrent effect. No excuse was accepted completely, although the fine might be lessened under some circumstances, for example, in the case of a physician on a house call. Sailors were frequently fined for being ashore after the call of the ship's bell, and citizens were fined for entertaining them after that time. Owners of slaves were fined whenever the latter did not appear at a time when the owner was responsible for the cleaning of the streets. Like countless communities throughout history, Savannah experienced chronic troubles in collecting fines from some of those found guilty.

Special Funds and Special Assessments

From very early times the practice of "dedicating" various taxes, including portions of the property tax, for specific purposes, was commonplace. Americans have had difficulty relating a specific tax to a specific governmental service at the state and national levels. But at the local level they have definitely wanted to know what they were getting for their money, hence many special funds in addition to the general fund, and dedicated taxes and other resources have been commonplace.

The special assessment became, and has since remained, an important way of financing capital improvements. Sometimes, as for gas street lights in the downtown area, the necessary money would be raised by voluntary contributions from those whose businesses benefited. No formal council action was necessary. In other cases the council would order the installation and assess the costs according to what it considered equitable. Thus, in 1835 Hartford went to the state legislature and received power to order the construction of sewers and to assess the costs on those benefited. The city had previously had few powers over sewers, which were usually privately constructed by interested residents, if at all. In the 1820s Baltimore regularly had a "direct levy" as well as a number of special levies. The latter included the court levy, poor levy, school levy, levy for county expenditures for city purposes, and the internal improvements levy. One purpose may have been to help taxpayers understand what their money was being used for, but the most immediate reason was that state law placed a limitation upon "direct taxation," whereas the special levies were authorized by specific state laws, which allowed them to be imposed upon the aggregate tax base. Once the monies were collected, however, the practice in Baltimore was to place all of them in a general fund, not the usual policy of the day. The practice resulted in a chronic dispute between the city council and the school commissioners, the latter arguing for their right to exclusive control over the school fund and eventually prevailing in the 1830s and 1840s, as the nation accepted the principle of universal education.

Although most cities could from an early time levy against all taxpayers for special purposes, not all cities could at first assign the levy against only the benefited property owners. Thus, Danbury, Connecticut, which became a town in 1702, was not given special assessment powers until 1816, and Hartford not until 1835. Sometimes the special assessment was used to make improvements that would encourage urban growth, always considered "progress" in the nineteenth century. Where such improvements increased the value of particular property, the benefited owners would be assessed. Thus, in 1854 New Orleans proposed a special drainage tax to reclaim swamp lands within the city limits. The special assessment was not used in Boston until 1866.

Lotteries

Taxes are never popular, and Americans have devoted a great deal of energy to making them less painful. One of the most popular alternatives tried in the early nineteenth century was the lottery. It was used most commonly for special projects, of which there was a great variety, as this sampling will indicate: Annapolis sponsored a lottery in 1804 to raise money for street improvements and fire engines, among other things. Baltimore made frequent uses of lotteries through the 1840s. Philadelphia authorized a lottery in 1789 to build a new city hall. Coventry, Rhode Island, ran a lottery in 1804 to build a bridge, as did

Wickford, Rhode Island, the following year. Providence conducted one in 1808 to build an academy (high school). St. Augustine held a lottery in 1834 by special legislative authorization to build a school.

Intergovernmental Payments

A final source of revenue was state and federal aid. These were not particularly common, although they were used to some degree throughout the first century after independence. Federal aid consisted primarily of land grants and the lending of technical specialists to cities, particularly civil engineers, for the United States Military Academy had virtually a monopoly in the supply of such specialists for many decades. They were needed by cities for the construction of streets, highways, harbors, wharves, and bridges, among other projects requiring special skills.[8]

On January 8, 1835, President Andrew Jackson for the first and only time in American history paid off the entire remaining national debt. Congress then provided that the Treasury surplus, after a modest reserve, should be divided among the states in 1837, technically as a loan. Because of the effects of the panic of 1837, not all of the states received their share of these monies, but many that did redistributed some or all to local governments for school purposes. This was a period of rapid expansion of the public school systems under the influence of the ideas of Jacksonian democracy. New York took its surplus revenue loan and established a permanent school fund of $4,014,520, the revenue from which was to be used for a state school-aid program.

State aid was hard to come by in the early nineteenth century, for the state governments had financial problems of their own. It was therefore not unusual for the state to impose additional responsibilities upon city governments with no additional financial aid or even expansion of the local tax base. In the early nineteenth century the many epidemics of various contagious diseases were a common basis for requests for state aid, but these were usually denied. For example, Savannah in 1817 unsuccessfully sought state financial aid to fight a smallpox epidemic. Local governments, particularly the semi-autonomous or completely independent local school boards, were usually more successful in getting monies. And many of the nineteenth-century arguments over state financial aid have continued to occupy political debates. California established a state tax for school aid in 1851. The assistance was granted to parochial as well as to public schools, but after a political battle aid was withdrawn from the former in 1855. (School districts offering at least three months of instruction per year were eligible for the aid.) By 1856 Connecticut furnished 39 per cent of school operating costs, and that year it established a subsidy for school libraries, with the provision that the local school committee pay at least 50 per cent of the costs. By

1864 one-third of the state's districts had qualified for school library aid.

The State of New York gave its local governments a fair amount of aid toward the expense of caring for certain classes of the poor. From 1797 nonsettled immigrants were subsidized by state funds transferred to the locality. State support increased for special groups—the insane, the physically handicapped, and refugees.

In the South little progress was made in the development of public education prior to the Civil War, except in New Orleans. Afterward, state financial aid was used as an inducement for the establishment or re-establishment of the public schools. Florida in 1869, for example, established a generous state aid program.

Tax Limits

Tax and debt limitations were common in early America. Limits generally were established by the legislature, although somewhat later sometimes by constitutional provision. Baltimore, for example, operated under very severe tax limitations prior to 1818, when they were removed. This change was probably brought about in part as a result of the intense rivalry between Baltimore and Philadelphia that had been under way for some decades. The city sought to become more competitive and, toward that end, was also authorized to borrow up to $1 million for improvements. When Rochester was incorporated in 1817, its charter provided by the state allowed it to levy a property tax with a limit of $1,000 total receipts and it provided that each specific new tax could be authorized only by popular referendum.

The rural-controlled state legislatures sometimes sought to protect farm land from excessive property taxation. If such land were to be taxed on the basis of its potential urban use, the levy could be ruinous to a farmer, keeping him from making a profit. This particular problem for the farmer often proved to be a windfall for the land developer, because land held in speculation could often be disguised as farmland, and it was difficult to distinguish between the legitimate farmer who had no wish for his land to become urbanized and the speculator who was waiting for the proper moment to reveal his intentions. It was not uncommon, therefore, for legislatures to write into city charters provisions such as that for Hartford in 1867, in which the city was prohibited from levying a city tax exceeding six-tenths of one mill on the dollar upon any land within the city limits that was being used exclusively for farming purposes. Apparently the activities of the speculator were recognized, for this rule did not apply in cases where the market value of the land exceeded $600 an acre, an extremely high figure for land in that day, well past the point where the land was obviously being bought and sold for speculative purposes anticipating urban use.

Expenditures

The expenditures of the cities were a mirror of their functions. They also illustrated the extent to which capital expenditure was paid for by loans or by taxes. In comparing two or more sample years or cities, one runs into the difficulty of allowing for substantial changes in price levels, growth in population, and differences in the definition of a particular function. Nevertheless, certain data are illuminating.

The same explosion of debts after the Civil War was paralleled by great increases in expenditure. Boston's expenditure in 1821 was $4 per capita; in 1859, $20 per capita; in 1873, $65 per capita, or $18 million. In Chicago 1848–58 government expenditures multiplied twenty-eight times; in 1865–70 the increase was 277 per cent. Between 1848 and 1870 the per capita tax on property increased from $1.10 to $13.50; the per capita debt from $1.01 to $36.01. Some Chicago functional expenditures about 1870 were: sewers, $1,204,000; streets (including cleaning), $1,-000,000; schools (not including construction), $547,000; police, $525,-000; fire, $407,000; lighting, $404,000; health, $80,745; bridges, tunnels, river improvement, $3,309,000. In 1850, except for streets ($40,000), not one of the other items had even reached $7,000.

Providence is another city whose expenditures are quite well documented. In 1800 (population 7,600) its total expenditures except debt operations were $10,400. Care of the needy accounted for $2,800, health for $2,000. None of the other functions, including schools, exceeded $700. No money was spent on parks or lighting. In the years 1830–33 (population 16,800), care of the needy was again first with $11,200 (1830). Streets accounted for $6,500; schools for $5,700; police, $4,200; fire, $3,400; health, $2,900; lighting, $2,000. The total reached $53,900, including interest on debt of $5,900. By 1860 (population 50,666), the total was $406,700—to a considerable extent reflecting growth in the city's population. Schools were now first with $84,000; fire, $51,000; police, $43,400; streets, $41,400; lighting, $28,400; care of needy, $21,500; and $1,000 was spent on parks. Interest had grown to $71,500. By 1870 (population, 68,904), the total had quadrupled to $1,637,700. Streets were first with $394,800; schools, $220,300; police, $131,100; care of needy, $111,300 (but this included $75,000 for construction); lighting, $88,000; fire, $60,000; prisons and prison reform, $50,900; health and sewers, $22,400; finance and general government, $29,200; interest, $106,900. The waterworks were built in 1870.

Municipal Debt

Being in debt was a useful, almost a necessary condition in an expanding frontier economy. Yet, perhaps because so many individual taxpayers and public officials were themselves in debt and apprehensive about it, strenuous efforts were commonly made to avoid municipal debt during the first century after American independence. In any case, debt always meant higher taxes, which were always to be avoided. It was only in a later era that public debt was accepted as proper and possibly an unavoidable urban government condition.

In 1812 Baltimore officials noted with pleasure that there was no local debt of consequence, and three years later that there was none at all. But such a condition could not long endure, of course. In the twenty years following 1835 interest charges in Baltimore mounted to from one-third to one-half of ordinary net outlays. These stemmed from increases in expenditures for schools, police, lighting, and, to a lesser extent, the courts, charities, corrections, and administration.

In the terminology of the day, the most important types of debt were so-called funded and floating debts. Funded debt is represented by bonds or other formal evidences of indebtedness that are expected to continue to be municipal obligations for several years. The floating debt is represented by less substantial evidence but always includes obligations not payable from the current year's revenues. Examples include municipal accounts payable, certificates of indebtedness, unpaid judgments against a city, and outstanding warrants. Then, as now, any such items that were considered payable from the revenues of the current fiscal year were not considered to be debt.

The extent of the debt actually remaining to be raised could not necessarily be determined on the basis of the debt figures. Whenever a debt was funded, it was common to establish a "sinking" fund as part of the plan to retire it. This fund was made up of taxes and service charges received and deposited in some kind of interest-earning account or other instrument that would earn money while awaiting the due date on the bonds or other indication of indebtedness. The gross debt, or total amount owing, minus the amount available in the sinking fund equaled the net debt.

By 1850 the Baltimore floating debt had reached $60,000 owed for street repairs because of the unwillingness of the common council to appropriate for current work. Such delays appear to have been not uncommon and had the effect of increasing the total cost of municipal services, particularly for capital improvements. The funded debt of cities increased at a great rate. Between 1830 and 1844 that of Baltimore increased from $500,000 to $5,500,000, largely as a result of municipal support for internal improvements. But once this competitive desire for "progress" calmed down somewhat, the pattern changed. Between 1844 and 1850 the funded debt of Baltimore remained practically static, and almost all increased expenditures were borne by increases in the general property tax. Prior to the coming of the powerful bosses and machines,

New York attempted to keep its debt at a minimum. In 1835 its funded debt amounted to less than $1 million at a time when the assessed valuation of property was more than $180 million. Expenditures were also relatively low, amounting to less than $2 million per year.

Still, the debt problems of cities began early in the national history. The debt of Providence increased from $26,800 in 1790 to $38,000 six years later. By 1800 the amount had been reduced to $22,000, but it increased again by 1810 to nearly $40,000, mostly as a result of unfunded expenditures for schools, public welfare, and public improvements. But the taxpayers who were attentive to public affairs never felt comfortable with expanding indebtedness. By 1818 the Providence debt had been reduced to $27,500, or about the same as it had been a generation previously.

Many cities were unable to avoid going heavily into debt. The debt of Memphis increased from $8,000 in 1847 to about $1 million in 1860 and to about $4 million by the close of the Civil War. Undoubtedly a substantial bit of this was the result of graft and incompetence. It has been estimated that $43,000 was paid for a wharf, when its actual value was about $17,000.[9] It was customary for public employees to profit illegally from their positions. For example, some officials arranged to buy underfed horses, fatten them at municipal expense, and then sell them at a large profit. During this period the voters also approved more than $1 million for subscriptions to railroad companies, about one-half of which was lost.

Incompetence and dishonesty had emerged in American cities after about 1830, and the waste and thievery that resulted were an indication of what was to come in the following period. This type of activity resulted in the virtual bankruptcy of Mobile in 1843 and of many other cities. Even so, in 1848 Mobile was authorized to subscribe $1,100,000 for railroad construction, to be raised by property taxes over a five-year period.

In 1857 an examination of the situation in Atlanta indicated that the bonded debt consisted of $47,000, including $4,000 for the development of a fairgrounds, $16,000 for a city hall, $20,000 for a gas plant, $3,000 for a bridge—and all for a population of about 10,000 persons. (The gas plant and fairgrounds may have been self-supporting.) More important, however, the city owed $5,000 for its annual payment on a total subscription of $100,000, authorized by the voters in 1858, for stock in the Airline Railroad, which was to connect Atlanta with the large cities of the East. Worcester subscribed in 1869 to 1 per cent of the stock of the Boston, Barre, and Gardner Railroad at a cost of $262,-200. The railroad was opened two years later—and failed to make a profit. Imprudent debt encumbrances were a characteristic of the optimistic age and the competitive desire to run all kinds of risks in the hope of surpassing other cities in the area which were involved in the same kinds of activities. In the case of Atlanta the risk paid off, but for each case where this was so, there must have been many failures, bankruptcies, and defaults on debts. The prevailing view was that such undertakings would be to the long-run profit of all citizens of the community, even though expensive in the short run.

The striking increase in city debts after the Civil War and the inflation that was present may be illustrated by the figures for Providence. Interest, which was $5,900 in 1830, had reached $71,500 in 1860 and $106,900 in 1870. The per capita debt of Chicago was $1.01 in 1844 and $36.01 in 1879. Debts contracted for subsidizing railroads were also major factors. Chicago's total debt in 1858 was $2.5 million, a tenfold increase from two years earlier. Most of this was for contracts and aids to railroads.

The Referendum in Financial Policy-Making

During the early part of the nineteenth century the referendum emerged as a device by which the voters could participate directly in the making of public policy, especially in constitutional and financial matters.

The annual meeting in New England towns had to approve both the annual budget proposed by the selectmen and the tax rate. The town meeting was often continued in communities even after incorporation. Thus, the 1817 village charter for Rochester, New York, provided that the tax levy had to be approved by a vote of the people in open meeting. Until cities became too large for it to be practical, this type of provision remained quite common in New England and New York.

In the early nineteenth century it became commonplace to require a referendum on proposed bond issues and tax levies beyond a certain level. (Later this procedure came to be used also for charter adoption and amendment, franchises, the prohibition of the sale of alcoholic beverages, and eventually a great variety of substantive questions.) The common council of Trenton was forbidden in 1849 to borrow any money except after approval by referendum. Although city governments were sometimes criticized then and in later times for becoming unwisely involved in deep debt for the sake of internal improvements, such decisions were in fact commonly made by the voters, as in the Atlanta case mentioned above. By 1870 the popular referendum had become a major part of fiscal policy-making in American cities. Bond issues, at least those pledging the full faith and credit of the municipal corporation and tax overrides (taxes beyond a certain amount, usually expressed in some form that amounted to a particular percentage of value), required popular approval before they could go into effect.

Financial Administration

Financial administration in cities remained, as at higher levels of government, relatively simple and rather decentralized during the first century after independence. The executive budget was not yet developed, nor was executive leadership for financial policy-making. Some changes did take place, however.

In general, the council developed both taxing and spending policies. At first it did this collectively, but greater decentralization took place in the method after bicameralism became popular and, with the expanding size of councils, the committee system came into general use. In the early days the tax collector and the treasurer (who kept the records of income and outgo and made payments upon warrants from the council) were councilmanic appointees. Later these two were among the first administrative officers to be selected by popular vote, and this resulted in even greater decentralization. However, neither of these officers ever became an important policy-maker. Although Jacksonian ideology strongly supported their election, much of the public probably has always been confused as to the amount of discretionary power they possess. In the early nineteenth century, some cities began to add an additional fiscal officer called the controller (often using the old Norman French spelling, comptroller). This officer was essentially the municipal accountant, thus separating the treasurer who was custodian of funds from the individual responsible for explaining their use. In many cases the controller's office also became elective, and in later years, although not by 1870, it gained in importance by becoming the forerunner of the budget officer, and budgeting was incorporated within the office.

Some efforts were made to coordinate revenues and expenditures, but these were not very common and were often unsuccessful. This frequently resulted in a debt carryover to which the term "floating" was applied. Where the process continued for several years, the total of this debt mounted, and it was often funded.

Boston created a committee on finance in 1813, while it was still a town. The committee consisted of the selectmen, the overseers of the poor, and the members of the board of health. It was authorized to choose a town treasurer and tax collector, the two offices being combined in one person, as was often the case elsewhere, too.

Closing Statement

During the 1789–1870 period the general property tax emerged as the principal means of financing municipal (as well as county and state) government. The characteristic criticisms of the tax emerged, as did the problems involved in its administration. Cities became less dependent upon revenues from operating businesses and more upon tax revenues. Debts increased rapidly in the 1830s and afterward, and the special assessment became an important device for financing capital improvements.

Many states established tax and debt limits for cities, and the referendum became a common requirement before taxes could be raised beyond a specified amount or debts incurred that pledged the full faith and credit of the city. By 1870 a pattern of finance had been established that was still to be dominant more than a century later.

Notes

1. See Ernest S. Griffith, *History of American City Government: The Colonial Period* (New York, 1938), Chap. 12.
2. Dick Netzer, "Property Taxes," *International Encyclopedia of the Social Sciences* (New York, 1968), 15:545–49.
3. Henry George, *Progress and Poverty* (New York, 1879).
4. Netzer, *op. cit.*
5. Special Tax Commission of Connecticut, *Report*, 1887.
6. See Daniel J. Elazar, *The American Partnership* (Chicago, 1962).
7. *Report* of the Record Commissioners, Boston Town Records, 1782. Style has been modernized.
8. Elazar, *op. cit.*
9. See G. M. Capers, *The Biography of a River Town* (Chapel Hill, 1939).

Chapter 12

CONCLUSION:
TRENDS AND CHANGES

In 1770 THE UNITED STATES was a colonial nation that had nothing more in the way of cities than was absolutely necessary for conducting a mercantilist colonial trade system. In 1870 it was on the verge of its headlong rush toward becoming a metropolitan-industrial society. Most cities that developed in the interim were still primarily trading centers and launching points for the trek westward, or for servicing the mining and forestry areas that were so important for the development of the nation. Only in New England and in isolated other cities had industrialization come to be a dominant factor in growth.

In 1770 the thirteen colonies had a population of about 2,150,000 people, 4.2 per cent of it urban (urban, that is, by the generous interpretation of the Census Bureau in later years, when this meant places containing more than 2,500 individuals not engaged in agricultural pursuits). In 1775 only two cities had populations in excess of 20,000—Philadelphia with 28,000 and New York with 23,000. In the following century the national population increased nearly twentyfold, to about 40,000,000. (The Census of 1870 listed 39,818,449 persons, but the Bureau has always had problems with underenumeration.) Of this figure, 25.7 per cent was urban.

In 1870 America still had no cities of over 1 million population, but 10.7 per cent of the people did live in cities of over 100,000. The trend toward concentration of much of the population in relatively few urban centers had already begun. The Census of 1790 identified twenty-four urban places, all of them well under 100,000 population. In 1870 there were 649 urban places under 100,000 and fifteen more above that figure. Thus, nearly 11 per cent of the population lived in only fifteen urban places.

The crises of Europe, particularly the potato famines of Ireland, in the 1840s and the numerous liberal uprisings, generally unsuccessful, of 1848, had spurred immigration into the United States. This was slowed somewhat by the Civil War, but by 1870 the greatest of the waves of the immigration was about to get under way, reaching a peak in 1907. As

218

the decades of the nineteenth century progressed, immigrants showed an increasing tendency to locate in cities, particularly those of the East Coast, if for no other reason than because this minimized their cost of migration.

Between 1820 and 1860 the most numerous non-Anglo-Saxon immigrants came from Germany (1,486,044) and Ireland (967,366). Almost all of the latter and a considerable percentage of the former were Catholic. This added a further complicating factor, culminating in the anti-immigrant, anti-Catholic Know-Nothing movement of the 1850s. The economic anti-immigrant component seems to have been the stronger component, inasmuch as the party in New Orleans included a considerable number of Catholics, most of whom were native-born Creoles.[1]

In the Southwest and in California, many Catholics of Mexican background were incorporated into what became American cities after the Mexican War of 1846–48. By 1870 the beginnings of an ethnic-based politics had already occurred. The working-class immigrants, together with the factors that would be needed for the development of giant industries, had laid the groundwork for the era of the boss and machine.

The early years of the nineteenth century marked one of the greatest changes in the history of political participation. With the coming to dominance of the ideas of Jacksonian democracy, the association between the ownership of property and the right to vote declined. Cities retained a more restrictive suffrage than did state governments for a longer time, but by 1870 participation for all white, adult males was accepted with relatively few exceptions for all elections. Universal white manhood suffrage in the United States occurred about a generation earlier than it did anywhere else in the world. In the short run, this change had relatively little effect on local governments, with the Main Street merchants remaining dominant in the politics of cities and villages. In the long run it was to have very great effect, particularly when Irish-Americans, whose cultural background made them particularly at home in a political environment, began to serve as the political brokers of American cities and to dominate the working-class-oriented urban political machines.

Political organization was changed significantly, though not dramatically, through the 1789–1870 period. It is probable that not many persons recognized at the time what was happening, but the change following the Baltimore Charter of 1797 was definitely in the direction of establishing a pattern of executive leadership with a decline in the overall powers and particularly the administrative powers of the council. After the adoption of the United States Constitution in 1787, there was a gradual shift in the role of the mayor away from the traditional undifferentiated responsibilities he had had under the colonial (British) system. In colonial times he had been primarily a legislator, particularly as the presiding officer over the council, and secondarily a judicial officer, essentially an urban justice of the peace. Only after these responsibilities was he an executive. Gradually the notion of separation of powers, the hallmark of the Federal Constitution, came to be applied to local government. As a result, the mayor was gradually given the veto power and was increasingly separated from the functions of the council, eventually being deprived of any participation in that body in most cities. His judicial functions in the "mayor's court" continued throughout the period but were definitely showing signs of decline as cities grew in size.

The mayor did not develop modern administrative powers over personnel or finance during this period, although some indicators of what was to come could be seen. The mayor's modern powers over administrative matters were delayed because of a transitional phase in which the administrative responsibilities over particular functions by council committees were assumed in the larger cities by semi-autonomous boards and commissions, a movement that gained momentum in the 1850s. The mayor had some control over these, because the growing pattern was for him to appoint their members, usually with the approval of the council. In general, the mayor became more visible to the public, but it was a transitional period during which the office moved toward its modern form but did not quite emerge into maturity.

The council underwent enormous changes during this period. It began as a relatively small body, except in a few instances elected at large and consisting of a single house. It began with relatively simple administrative powers, with much of the detail of work in the hands of the city clerk and persons appointed by the council, often individuals who managed to combine a number of part-time jobs into a full-time occupation. The public official and public servant of the late eighteenth and early nineteenth centuries often wore many hats.

In imitation of the Federal government, cities began in the last decade of the eighteenth century to adopt the bicameral system. There were some precedents for this in colonial times, but primarily the United States Constitution was the factor encouraging such a development. The state government practices also contributed to a trend in the bicameral direction. As cities grew in size and the practicality of the town meeting declined, there was also a development toward the use of wards for the election of councilmen. Again, there were some colonial precedents for such procedure, primarily in Albany and New York, but they seem to have been encouraged primarily by the growth of the size of cities combined with a desire to preserve a sense of access and accountability in the local government representative.

Modern administrative concepts and the use of professional bureaucrats remained matters for the future, but increasing efforts were made to associate knowledgeable public servants with the supervision of particular municipal activities. First, the committee system on city councils made it possible for individual members to specialize in particular functions of government. But because the councilmen were commonly individuals who had full-time jobs in business or the professions, council committees as administrative supervisors became increasingly a burden upon the participants and less practical as an administrative structure. An alternative that emerged early but did not take on definite form until the 1850s was the appointment of boards and commissions. These agencies were expected to be responsible for the day-to-day operations of particular functions and to operate within the policy limits established by the council, but they gradually became increasingly independent and even often had their own sources of financial support. Probably the earliest general use of the specialist was that of a physician or board of physicians in charge of health activities.

The functions of cities throughout the nineteenth century became increasingly complex and expensive. At the end of the colonial period the methods of financing of cities were not far different from those in medieval times. Cities operated many business activities and counted upon the profits from them to finance those functions for which service charges could not be levied. Gradually, however, the responsibilities of the municipal governments became increasingly of a character that could not be handled by special charges or the profits of municipal business activities or from the sale of land. Before the end of the eighteenth century a regular annual tax levy had become routine, and early in the nineteenth century most of the states had moved away from the colonial and British practice of levying local taxes based upon the annual rental value of property and substituted full market value. Special funds remained commonplace, and indeed became more used, but the idea of a general fund to be used for purposes determined by the council was established and was reluctantly accepted by the voters. There was also the emergence of certain other bases for taxation (e.g., certain forms of business), although these never threatened to overshadow the general property tax. In addition, the popular referendum emerged as a requirement for decisions relative to the issuing of bonds involving the commitment of the "full faith and credit" of the municipal corporation and to the levying of property taxes beyond a level established by the state constitution or state law.

The style of politics changed greatly during the 1789–1870 period. The competitive level was low immediately after independence, with the problem often being one of needing to encourage or even to draft citizens to serve in public office. Fines for failure to accept office or attend meetings were sometimes used. Local office was considered largely a matter of civic obligation for which there was no pay, and a burden and responsibility to be passed around among the professional and mercantile leadership.

After the coming of Jacksonian democracy in the 1820s, the style of the political campaign changed considerably, for the common man could now vote. Because there were so many such men and cities were growing in size and complexity, the primary appeal of a campaign shifted from rational discussions about growth and "progress" toward symbolism. Because of these developments, cities were also experiencing more competitive election campaigns. The prototype campaign of the era was that of the Presidential election of 1840, matching William Henry Harrison and John Tyler ("Tippecanoe and Tyler, too") against Martin Van Buren, who had no running mate.[2] The formula for that campaign was so successful that it has not been changed in any essential qualities up to the present time. Although the tactic of manipulating symbols rather than making rational arguments or simply asking for support on the basis that one was a community leader did not develop as rapidly at the local level as it did in state and national politics, the formula of 1840 was suitable for competitive politics in all but the smallest cities and had come into use in urban politics well before 1870.

Political conflict increased greatly during the century after independence. This was a result in part of the increasing heterogeneity of American society and in part of the declining acceptance of the notion that the social and economic elite should also automatically be the political elite. The nation had come to accept what Clyde Kluckhohn was later to call "the cult of the common man."[3] In particular the Irish immigrants refused to accept the traditional notion of the obligation of the higher classes to lead, and, because of their interest in and aptitude for American-style politics, they became brokers within the political system and offered leadership and direction for immigrants of all countries, many of whom had little understanding of the processes of democracy or of the English language.

While intergroup conflict increased, so did political competition. As 1870 approached, the tensions between the Main Street merchants and their professional colleagues, on the one hand, and the leaders of the low-status immigrants, on the other, sharpened. The pattern for the next generation—the boss and machine that secured votes from the working-class immigrant groups in return for social welfare programs paid for by funds, legal and illegal, variously extorted from municipal employees, merchants, and industrialists was emerging. Percentage payments on contracts and special considerations for railroads became increasingly profitable to those in positions of municipal power.

The patterns of extreme political action were also developed during this period. Riots and other violence stemming from direct confrontations became a part of American politics after the coming of Jacksonian democracy.* The lower-status groups, if organized, now had significant political power and hence were seen as threats, a view held particularly by those on the next higher step on the social ladder. The most important clashes were between the Irish immigrants and persons whose ancestors had come to this country some generations earlier and were generally known as "Native Americans" or "Know-Nothings." The discrimination against the Irish Americans in the 1850s and onward was very possibly the greatest this country has ever seen, yet in less than one generation leaders of this ethnic group had become a major political force in America. Some race riots took place between blacks and whites, but this was not commonplace—only about 3 per cent of the urban population was black in 1870. Meanwhile, the summer ghetto riot had become an established event in the American city beginning in the early 1830s,[4] and it was to continue to be a basic aspect of American life from that time onward indefinitely.

Service Levels

Great changes took place in the level and quality of services. At the beginning of the Revolutionary War there were few water systems, and most water was taken from neighborhood wells. Sewage systems were virtually nonexistent, except in the form of privies, cesspools, and open drains. Many urban communities had no paved streets at all, although usually the main ones were cobblestoned. Public health programs were virtually unknown, and so were the causes for the epidemics of communicable diseases that even then were common. Except in parts of New England, education was still considered a private matter. Special programs for the children of paupers were still some years off, and general "free" public education for all was still many decades away. In some places, especially the South, it did not arrive until after the Civil War. The public welfare system was still based upon the Elizabethan Poor Law of 1601. There was no public transportation, and the lighting of homes, businesses, and factories was strictly a do-it-yourself project.

Police protection consisted often of the volunteer night watch and a part-time constable for the daytime. Often men were required to take their turn on the night watch. Uniformed full-time police were unknown. Fire-fighting companies existed, but in nearly all cases they were sponsored by insurance companies and would respond to an alarm only if the home or place of business were insured by that company, or they demanded payment in cash before going to work on the fire. Even if they did attack it, the chances of success were poor, for water supplies often were not available. Conflagrations that would wipe out all or a sizable portion of a town were commonplace.

* See the Appendix for a listing of some riots and other major disturbances in cities.

Changing technology, rising expectations, increasing national wealth, and complications that resulted from the increasing size, complexity, and heterogeneity of cities all contributed to vast changes. By 1870 virtually all modern municipal services had been established, at least at a rudimentary level and were being operated in the large and middle-sized cities by full-time personnel, even though the patronage system was still the basis of personnel administration and, indeed, had not yet reached its heyday. Full-time police and firemen now guarded the larger cities. The police, although often career men in their jobs, had little education and training. But they were badly needed. The firemen still had to cope with the fact that most American urban buildings were made of wood, but they now had water mains and the steam-driven pump. The beautiful matched teams of fire horses and the clanging of the fire bell stoked the imagination of young boys.

This was the gas-lit era, and the fuel occasionally was supplied by the municipality. The most heavily traveled streets were paved, and in the older sections of the city the kidney-jolting cobblestones were starting to be replaced by smoother materials. Along the main streets the horse-drawn streetcar ran, allowing the faster development of the outlying areas and encouraging Americans to continue their preferred pattern of single-family homes. A coal stove and straw spread on the floor helped people to fight off the bitter cold of the Eastern and Midwestern winters. Parks, which had scarcely existed in 1770, were being established in many cities a century later. They were not necessarily located where they were most needed, that is, next to tenement areas to provide open spaces for the poor, but they did exist, and cities competed with one another for the largest and loveliest park, particularly after the completion of New York's Central Park in the 1850s.

By 1870 the idea of free public education was completely accepted. although most Catholics continued to prefer their ethnically oriented parochial schools. Teaching was not yet a profession, however, and most people who appeared in the classroom had little training or even education. Welfare policy in the United States, with its work-oriented ethic, had not changed much by 1870, but there had been a great deal of complaining about excessive welfare costs since the 1840s, and most of the criticism was directed against the foreign-born. Public health programs were by now quite common, especially in port cities. They were usually required by state law but administered and paid for locally. The filth theory of disease still dominated, for the germ theory had not yet been developed. However, the "contagionists" had won out in their dispute with the "anticontagionists," and elaborate policies, centering upon quarantine procedures, were in effect an effort to eliminate the periodic epidemics. The serious pollution of lakes and streams, together with the concern for the need for fire protection, had encouraged the engineering of elaborate water supply systems, some of them private (particularly in the East) but most of them municipally administered.

In the midst of all this activity, of course, one also found rising taxes, climbing city debts, and complaints about both. Efforts, generally unsuccessful, were made to get state grants-in-aid or share taxes or, less commonly, Federal aid. The latter was primarily confined to harbor development. The general property tax, at first in some communities based upon income but later everywhere theoretically upon net worth, remained the backbone of the local tax system. But cities had a variety of income sources, particularly from their own business activities. Local debt was not always well managed by administrators, who were relatively inexperienced, or by councils, which were sometimes better at providing demanded services than in figuring out ways to pay for them. Occasionally state governments (which were themselves often lacking in qualified specialists) had to take over the administration of a bankrupt city government, but for the most part cities managed to make out reasonably well. They did so despite the increasing amount of corruption as the boss and machine system emerged and as the domination of city government gradually was transferred from Main Street merchants and professional men to the leaders of the various working-class ethnic groups, leaders who extracted payments from merchants and industrialists in return for permits, franchises, ordinances, or policies that the city was in a position to grant or withhold.

Closing Statement

As America entered the 1870s, moving along toward its "manifest destiny" to become the wealthiest and most powerful nation in the world, its urban life was entering into a new era. The age of the "robber baron," the financial manipulator, the city boss and machine, and the urban and suburban American was upon us. The American city had nearly completed its tour of duty as essentially the provider of services to rural America. The industrial metropolis, with all of its problems and prospects, lay just ahead. The small city, benignly and benevolently ruled by a respected "power structure," was passing from the scene. But it was to be remembered romantically for a long time. Its idealized image was to become the basis for many a twentieth-century suburb.

Notes

1. Robert C. Reinders, *End of an Era* (New Orleans, 1964), pp. 56–57.
2. For a description, see Charles R. Adrian and Charles Press, *The American Political Process*, 2nd ed. (New York, 1969).
3. Clyde Kluckhohn, *Mirror for Man* (New York, 1949).
4. Alexis de Tocqueville, *Democracy in America*, originally published 1835 and 1840.

APPENDIX:
EXAMPLES OF CIVIL DISTURBANCES IN CITIES, 1800—1870

1806 New York	First notable anti-Irish Catholic incident. Christmas night in front of Catholic church. Fighting, more than rioting.
1812 Baltimore	Assaults upon those opposing the War of 1812
1826 New Bedford	"Ark" riots. Mob stormed and burned brothels.
1828 Philadelphia	First race riot. WASPs against blacks, mainly. Not much damage. Irish took pains to deny any large involvement.
1831 Philadelphia	"Fifth Street" riot. A Protestant-Catholic conflict.
1832 Philadelphia	Election riots involving Clay-Jackson bitterness.
1834 New York	Election riots. First year of popular election for mayor. Polls open three days. Martial law because of wandering mobs. Some ballots destroyed in Whig wards.
1834 Philadelphia	Election riot. Democrats vs. Whigs. One killed, 15 or more wounded. Arson—six buildings burned; firemen driven off by mob.
1834 Philadelphia	Race riot. Provoked by rumors. Militia called out, but size of riot small. Some injuries.
1835 Charlestown	Anti-Irish riot. Convent sacked and burned. Teenagers heavily involved.
1835 Baltimore	Rioting following the closing of several banks.
1835 New York	Riot when Catholics broke up an anti-Catholic meeting. Despite tension, first major religious disturbance in the city since 1806.
1835 Washington	Anti-emancipation and anti-Negro riot. Ended without significant damage.
1837 Boston	"Broad Street" riot. Unclear who started it, but began when WASP engine company encountered an Irish funeral party. Some 15,000 participated; homes of Irish sacked; injuries.
1838 Philadelphia	Anti-Abolitionist riot. Abolitionists' Pennsylvania Hall destroyed by fire. Mayor, police, firemen defied.
1842 Philadelphia	Race riot, transformed into anti-Irish riot. Militia called out. Some property damage.
1842 New York	Election riots. City council's activities suspended for two months.
1843 Philadelphia	"Nanny goat market" riot. Sheriff's posse vs. striking Irish weavers. Mob of weavers drove off posse and attacked the sheriff.
1844 Philadelphia	"Kensington" riot. Native Americans vs. Irish. Fighting, arson, and other property damage. Militia called out.

1844 Philadelphia	"Southwark" riot. Same pattern as above.
1844 Syracuse	"Coffee house" riot. Drunken gang from Salina attacked Syracusans. Militia called out. Little serious damage. Investigating committee placed blame on too many places selling liquor—more than eighty in the village.
1848 Baltimore	Riot involving attack on tavern; reasons unknown.
1849 Philadelphia	Race riot. Three killed, many injured, arson, other property damage. Militia called out.
1849 New York	Irish youths attack theater where English actor was performing. Police fired on crowd that refused to disperse; 25 killed.
1853 New Orleans	Election rioting.
1855 Cincinnati	Riot after rumor that Germans proposed to prevent voting for the mayoralty candidate of the Know-Nothing party.
1855 Louisville	"Bloody Monday" riot, precipitated by Know-Nothings. Great damage in Irish district. Looting, arson, at least twenty deaths.
1855 New Orleans	Widespread election violence. Know-Nothings seized and burned ballot boxes in two precincts.
1856 Baltimore	Election rioting and intimidation by Know-Nothings.
1856 New Bedford	Rioting mob tore down and burned a brothel.
1860 Boston	Anti-Abolitionist riot. City declined to protect Abolitionist meeting in Faneuil Hall.
1860 Syracuse	"Social evil" riots to avenge shooting of a man in a house of prostitution. Reform effort lost momentum with coming of Civil War.
1861 Cincinnati	Street riots in slums as police withdrew with approach of Confederate troops. Martial law declared.
1863 Brooklyn	Antidraft riots. Arson; firemen attacked while fighting fire.
1863 New York	Irish anti-draft riots. Arson, looting, murder. Troops called in. At least seventy-four killed. Irish and other foreign born, hostile to compulsory military service and to blacks. About three-fourths of participants less than twenty years of age.
1863 Detroit	Race riot. Two killed; more than a dozen seriously injured; thirty-five homes of blacks burned; other property damage; pillaging. Many blacks took refuge in Canada. Troops restored order.
1866 New Orleans	Race riot. Federal troops called in. Thirty-four blacks and four whites killed; more than 200 injured.

INDEX

Alcalde, 177, 180
  as local government executive, 46–47
Annexation policies, 104–5
Assessor, 194
  election of, 23
Assize of bread, 75

Bankers and politics, 149–50
Blacks:
  as fire fighters, 93
  in nineteenth-century cities, 22–23
  public education of, 79–80
  suffrage for, 110, 112–13
  in Washington after Civil War, 45
"Blue" laws, 90–91, 102–4
Boards and commissions, 184, 194
  development of, 123, 171–73
Brown, A. Theodore, quoted, 155

Callow, Alexander, on Boss Tweed, 92
Campaigns, political, issues in, 120–26
Charters, municipal:
  general act, 35
  referendums on, 139
  revision of, in New York City, 52–53
  special act, 34
Cities:
  basis for early growth of, 12–13
  founding dates of, 10–18
  governmental services of, 223–25
  images of, 3–6
  origins of names of, 12–13
  summary of governmental trends in, 218–25

City councils (*see* Legislatures, city)
City-county consolidation:
  in Philadelphia, 88
  in San Francisco, 46–47
Civil disturbance:
  in New Orleans election of 1857, 125
  (*see also* Riots, urban)
Civil War, effect of, on cities, 42–45
Clay, Henry, "American system" of, 5–6
Clemens, Samuel L., on cities, 5
Clerk, city, 194–95
Close corporation, 30
Collector of revenue, 194
Commission plan of government, early examples of, 161
Commissions (*see* Boards and commissions)
Constable, 23, 194–95
Consumer protection, municipal, 74–75
Cooley, Thomas N., on local self-government, 40–41
Corps of Engineers, U.S. Army, 63
Crime, organized, early traces of, 90

Debt, municipal, 212–15
Dillon, John F., quoted, 39
Dillon's rule, 29, 39
District of Columbia, urban government in, 31–32

Education, public:
  early advocates of, 76–78
  established, 78
  financing, 78–80

Education, public (*cont.*):
  policy-making, 80–81
  racial segregation in, 79–80
  at secondary level, 81
Elazar, Daniel, 63
  on intergovernmental relations, 50
Elections, municipal, 107–8
  corruption in, 121–22
Emerson, Ralph Waldo, on cities, 4
Ethnic groups:
  in nineteenth-century cities, 21–23
  voting of, 123
Expenditures, municipal, 212

Financial administration, municipal, 216
  (*see also* Assessor)
Fire companies:
  development of, 93–96
  as political organizations, 132–33
  state requirement of pay for, 55–56
Franchises, street-railway, 99–100

Gas, illuminating, 62, 96–97
George, Henry, on taxes, 201–2
Grants-in-aid, 210–11
Griscom, John H., report on public health, 67–68
Grodzins, Morton, on intergovernmental relations, 50

Hamilton, Alexander:
  on cities, 5–6
  on city planning, 147
Health, municipal boards of:
  early experiences with, 69
  membership of, 174
  state control over, 54
Home rule, municipal, 40–42
Horsecars, 99–100
Housing ordinances, 62
  New York tenement act of 1867, 55

Illegal occupations (*see* "Vice" as urban problem)

Immigrants in politics, 152–53, 218–19
Industrial Revolution, effect of, on cities, 6–8
Industrialists and politics, 148
Inherent right of local self-government, theory of, 40–41
Interest groups, municipal, 141–55
  compared to modern groups, 141–42
Intergovernmental relations, 50–64
  in early California, 46–48
  federal-municipal relationships, 63
  and imposition of state will, 53–57
  interlocal, 62–63
  and local requests to add functions, 60–62
  and mayors and state militia, 185–86
  revenue payments in, 210–11
  and state removal of local officials, 57–58
  and substitute administration of police, 58–60
  in West, 48

Jackson, Andrew:
  on bureaucracy, 137
  and urban life, 6
Jails, 89
Jefferson, Thomas:
  on cities, 3–4
  on city planning, 147
  and New York City politics, 135
Journalists and politics, 150
Judicial powers:
  of executive and legislative branches, 173–74
  of mayor, 190–91
Juvenile delinquency, 89–90

"Know Nothings" (*see* Native American party)

Labor, organized, in politics, 153–54
Lamplighters, 33
Land developers in politics, 145–46

Latta, Alexander B., 94
Legal status of cities, 29–48
  and Dillon's rule, 29, 39
  and doctrine of state supremacy,
      31–34
  and early incorporations, 30–31
  and legislative supremacy rule,
      29–30
  and municipal home rule, 41–42
  and Spanish and Mexican tradi-
      tions, 45–46
  special legislation on, 34–39
      prohibition of, 37
Legislators, city:
  perquisites of, 166–67
  social backgrounds of, 118, 164–
      65
  terms of office of, 163–64
Legislatures, city:
  administrative powers of, 170
  bicameral, 157–61
  changes in, in nineteenth cen-
      tury, 220–21
  and conflicts of interest, 165–67
  ex officio functions of, 174–75
  filling vacancies in, 165
  judicial powers of, 173–74
  patterns of organization of, 156–
      57
  powers of, principal, 25, 169–70
  procedural rules of, 167–69
  and separation of powers doc-
      trine, 167
  unicameral, 162–63
L'Enfant, Pierre, 5
Libraries, public, 75–76
Liquor as civic problem, 90–91
    (see also "Vice" as urban prob-
      lem)
Liquor dealers in politics, 154–55
Liquor laws, municipal enforce-
      ment of, 103–4
"Loco Foco" party, 129, 131
Lotteries, public, 103, 205, 209–10

Machines, political:
  basis of support of, 136
  early corruption in, 133–34
  extent of corruption in, 136–37
  factors supporting, 91
  and patronage, 137–38
  police involvement in, 91–92

  "Tweed Ring," 91–92
  as welfare agencies, 153
McQuillin, Eugene, 39
Mann, Horace, and schools, 77
Mayors:
  changing powers of, 187
  chosen by electoral college, 33
  election of, 178–79
  ex officio powers of, 186–87
  executive powers of, 183–89, 220
  judicial powers of, 190–91
  legislative powers of, 163, 189–
      90
  methods of selecting, 177–80
  other titles for, 46–47, 177, 180
  perquisites of, 192–93
  powers of colonial, 177
  removal of, 184–85
  and separation of powers doc-
      trine, 167
  social backgrounds of, 118–19,
      182–83
  terms of office of, 193–94
  turnover rates of, 119–20
Merchants in politics, 142–45
Migration patterns, influence of,
      on city development, 11–15
Mining camps, local government
      in, 47–48
Missions, Spanish, as future city
      sites, 16
Municipal bonds, issuance of, 149–
      50
Municipal employees, 150–51

Native American party, 119, 122–
      25, 131
Neighborhood government, 123,
      175–76

Olmsted, Frederick Law, 101–2
Oregon Trail, 17

Parks:
  authorization for Central Park,
      61
  development of, 93, 101–2
  and parkways, 99
Parties, political:
  local, 130–2
      after Civil War, 43–44

Parties, political (*cont.*):
  national, in local elections, 128–
    30
Patronage, 137–38
Planning, urban, early patterns of,
  146–47
Police:
  chief of, 194
  development of, 85–92
  involvement in politics, 91–92,
    122
  mayor as head of, 185
  state control over, 58–60
Population, urban:
  changes in, 27–28
  in nineteenth century, 19–23
Populism, effects of, on cities, 9–
  10, 139
Ports and harbors, development of,
  100
Poverty (*see* Social welfare)
Presidios, Spanish, 16, 46
Property tax (*see* Revenues)
Public health
  early approach to, 8–9
  early policies regarding, 68–70
  problems concerning, 66–70,
    102
  relationship of water supply to,
    73
Public officials:
  removal of, 57–58
  and types of candidates for of-
    fice, 117–20
Public utilities:
  illuminating gas, 96–97
  regulation of, 57
Pueblos, 16–17

Quincy, Josiah, 88, 117, 181, 189

Railroads in politics, 148–49
Realtors in politics, 145–47
Recorder, city, 195
  as gubernatorial appointee, 24
Referendum:
  and financial policy-making, 215
  history of, 138–40
  on Sunday "blue" laws, 102–3
  use of, 70
Reformers, municipal, early efforts
  of, 151–52

Revenues:
  from business taxes, 204, 206–8
  from head taxes, 207
  from intergovernmental pay-
    ments, 210–11
  nontax sources of, 199–200
  from property taxes, 200–203
  increasing dependence on,
    203–6
  origins of, 199
  from sale of land, 204–5
  and tax limits, 211
  (*see also* Lotteries, public; Spe-
    cial assessments)
Revolutionary War (*see* War for
  Independence)
Riots, urban, 87–88, 111, 125
  list of, 227–28
  Tocqueville on, 24–25

Schools, state authorization of, 61
  (*see also* Education, public)
Sewerage systems, 62, 69, 98
Shinn, Charles H., on mining
  camps, 47–48
Social welfare, 81–84
  political-machine provision of,
    136
Spanish Trail, 17
Special assessments, 60, 98, 208–9
Special legislation, 34–39, 45
State-local relations (*see* Intergovernmental relations)
Street railways, 99–100
Streets:
  development of paving and
    maintenance of, 97–99
  lighting of, 98–99
Suffrage:
  extension of, 109–15
  municipal rules on, 114–15, 179
  property qualifications for, 108–
    12
  removal of religious requirements
    for, 112
  woman, 113–14
  (*see also* Voting)

Tammany Hall, early history of,
  134–35
Tax collector, election of, 23
Taxes (*see* Revenues)

Tenement Act of 1867, New York
    State, 55
Thoreau, Henry David, on cities,
    4–5
Tocqueville, Alexis de:
    attitude of, toward suffrage, 111
    on urban riots, 24–25
Towns, New England, 33, 39–40
Transportation, importance of
    methods of, to city growth, 11
    public, 99–100
Treasurer, city, 194–95
Twain, Mark, on cities, 5
Tweed, William Marcy "Boss,"
    91–92, 135

"Vice" as urban problem, 103–4,
    154–55
    on frontier, 144–45
    as police problem, 90
Vigilantes, 89, 124–25, 145
Voting:
    and development of secret bal-
        lot, 115–16

fraud, 116–17
    (see also Suffrage)

Wade, Richard C., quoted, 26, 62
War for Independence:
    effects of, on cities, 29–30
    influence of, on legal status of
        cities, 33–34
Wards as political units, 175–76
Warner, Sam Bass, Jr.:
    cited, 199
    quoted, 119
Water-supply systems:
    early development of, 70–74
    intercity imitation in building,
        62
    private, 72–73
    state control of, 60–61
Welfare, public (see Social wel-
    fare)
Wilderness Road, 15
Woman suffrage, 113–14
Wood, Fernando, 123–24

Youth gangs, 89–90